The van Roekel Family in America

*The story of Jan van Roekel and
Willemina van Deelen van Roekel*

A Legacy of Life and Love

COMPOSED BY JOHN HERBERT van ROEKEL 2009

The van Roekel Family in America

*Composed and written with love and appreciation
by their grandson, John Herbert van Roekel,
with input from extended family members and friends.*

Copyright © 2009 by John Herbert van Roekel

ISBN-13: 978-0-9841680-0-2
ISBN-10: 0-9841680-0-1
Printed in the United States of America

All rights reserved. No portion of this book may be reproduced or utilized in any form or by any means, electronic or mechanical, including photocopying, without permission in writing from the author. Inquiries should be addressed to:

John Herbert van Roekel, 2425 Highway 9, Black Mountain, NC 28711 USA

Designed and Edited by Nancy E. Williams, The Laurus Company, Denton, Texas USA
TheLaurusCompany.com

Dedication

This book was compiled to honor the legacy of my grandparents, Jan and Willemina (van Deelen) van Roekel. It is dedicated to the spirit of love, adventure, and daring of Jan van Roekel and Willemina van Deelen van Roekel, two wonderful and exciting people, and to all the van Roekels who value the past and the personal values these two vanguards set forth in living their lives. What examples of bravery, creative ingenuity, determination, and caring they possessed! They gave us all an example of amazing courage and tenderness.

Jan and Willemina van Roekel…

…together throughout the years.

Acknowledgements

We give a tremendous word of thanks to **Gijs van Roekel**, a distant relative in Holland, for his many years of research into our family history. (Note: The "ij" in Dutch is our English "y" sound.) His work of putting the family into Family Tree Maker, the following website, and the book, *The Family van Roekels in the Gelderland,* represent a plethora of information that could never have been gathered by us as individuals here in the United States. Gijs is the grandson of Gijsbertus (8-13-1891), Jan's brother closest to his age.

Gijs van Roekel's e-mail address is <g.v.roekel@hccnet.nl>. Gijs would prefer his web page to be used, if possible, rather than his personal e-mail. His website is open for everyone to visit and includes the van Roekel coat of arms, or *wapens*:

> http://www.xs4all.nl/~roekelg/genealogie/ginl.html

To all of you who have supplied information that has enabled us to compile this book, thank you. One day all of the records may be obtained, and they will be available to all of the descendants.

We wish to also express a word of appreciation to the **University of North Carolina Wilson Library** and their "special collection of historical information and clippings file." There are many records by **Hugh MacRae**, **Herman Vogel**, and **Dr. Frederik van Eeden** of the immigration experiment in Eastern North Carolina.

Also, a word of appreciation to the authors of *De Familie van Roekel in de Gelderland* (**E. de Jong**, **L. Overduyn**, **H. J. van Roekel** and **J. van Roekel**).

Finally, much of what we were able to gather in Holland about the families was because of the hospitality of **Wim and Jopie van Hunen Blokker** and **Henni and Amy Buitenhuis**. Wim died a couple of years after our last visit. Jopie now is afflicted with Alzheimer's disease and was placed in a rest home. Their friends, **Jan and Ann van der Zanden**, were truly great friends to them.

Enjoy your reading …

Wim and Jopie van Hunen Blokker

Table of Contents

Dedication	3
Acknowledgements	4
Introduction	10
The van Roekels in Lunteren, Holland	11

THE STORY BEGINS

Jan and Willemina	13
World War I	14
Preparations for Leaving	15
America or Bust	15
The Voyage	16
Arriving in America	16
North Carolina	16
The North Carolina Farm Colonies	17
The Forming of the North Carolina Colonies	19
Dr. Frederik van Eeden	19
Hugh MacRae	22
Other significant people	23
Structure of the Units in the Co-operative Company of America	24-25
Correspondence	26-30
The Selling of the Idea	31
"Own a Home in North Carolina: Image and Reality in Ethnic European Colonies" by W. Frank Ainsley	31
"They Said He Was Crazy" by John Marshall Parham	35
"MacRae's Dream Settled Area" (Wilmington Morning Star)	36
"The Proposed Co-operative Company of America" by William J. Hoggson	37
The Castle Hayne(s) Colony / Surnames of Dutch Immigrants in Castle Hayne(s)	41
The Van Eeden Colony / Surnames of Dutch Immigrants in Van Eeden	42
Life in America: Jan and Willemina build their lives in the new country	45
Jan and Willemina Leave North Carolina	45
Life Back in North Carolina	46
The Founding of Van Roekel Florist	47
The Legacy	49
Willowdale Cemetery, Goldsboro, North Carolina	50
Jan van Roekel: History of the Man and the Name	55
The Name "van Roekel"	57
The Hamlet of Roekel	58
More historical information in "The van Roekel Family in the Gelderland"	59
The oldest van Roekels	59
Van Roekels in Wageningen	59
Van Roekel Heraldry / Coat of Arms or Wapen (weapon)	60-61

Table of Contents Continued

Willemina Hendrika van Deelen van Roekel: History of the Lady and the Name 63
    The Name van Deelen 63
    The van Deelens as Royalty 64
    Hoenderloo: Hometown of Willemina van Deelen 64
    The Hoge Veluwe 65
    Van Deelen Heraldry 66
    The van Deelen Coat of Arms 67-68

Our Trips to Holland: Meeting Relatives and Learning More 73
Second Visit to the Fatherland in 1999 77

GENEALOGY: ANCESTORS

Ancestors of Jan van Roekel (1885) and Willemina van Deelen van Roekel 79
    Details of Each Ancestor of Jan van Roekel (1885) 80
    Family of Origin of Jan van Roekel (1885) 82
    Ancestors of Willemina van Deelen 83
    Family of Origin of Willemina van Deelen 84

GENEALOGY: DESCENDANTS

Condensed Presentation of Descendants of Jan and Willemina van Roekel 85
Descendants of Jan van Roekel (1885) and Willemina van Deelen van Roekel 87
    (I)   William Robert van Roekel 87
    (II)   Hendrick John van Roekel, Sr. 89
    (III) Otiena Hendrika van Roekel 96
    (IV) John William van Roekel 102

DIRECTORY: Van Roekel Descendants • Contacts in Holland 104

APPENDIX 105
    Index 105
    Other Resources on the Internet 105
    Frederik van Eeden and His Perspective 106
    Genealogy of Siblings of Jan van Roekel (1885) 107
    Ancestors of Jan van Roekel (1885) 111
    The Story of Jan de Bakker, the First Dutch Martyr 135
    Ancestors of Willemina van Deelen 141
    Hand-wrtten family history of of the van Deelens 142
    Letter from Kaye Mason to Willem van Roekel (Hendricus' grandson) 144
    Descendants of Tonis Gijsbertsen 145
    Five-page letter from Willemina van Roekel to her family in Holland 150-151
    Ship's Manifest, Alien Immigration, Ellis Island, New York 152-153
    Letter regarding Jan van Roekel's military service with the Yellow Riders 154-155
    Official map (plots) of the Van Eeden Colony, Pender County, N.C. 156-157
    Where is Van Eeden, N.C.? 158-159
    Herman W.D.M. Vogels 160
    Van Eeden-Kolonie in N. Carolina USA, by Dr. Frederik van Eeden 161

Table of Contents Continued

FIGURES

Figure 1.	The home of Jan van Roekel (1836) in Lunteren	12
Figure 2.	Newspaper advertisement Van Eeden Colony in North Carollina, USA	14
Figure 3.	The S.S. Noordam	15
Figure 4.	"The Welcome Center" at Van Eeden	16
Figure 5.	The Six MacRae Colonies (map)	18
Figure 6.	Max Wolf and David Loeb in Van Eeden II	21
Figure 7.	Structural Chart of the Co-operative Corporation of America	24
Figure 8.	Board of Directors Structure, Co-operative Corporation of America	25
Figure 9.	Department Structure, Co-operative Corporation of America	25
Figure 10.	Letter from W. J. Hoggson to Hugh MacRae (aboard ship)	26
Figure 11.	Retyped letter from the Acting Secretary	27
Figure 12.	Sample immigrant sales contract - Parts a and b	28-29
Figure 13.	Memorandum of Agreement to form Colony	30
Figure 14.	A promotional brochure (Own A Home in North Carolina)	31
Figure 15.	Early South ethnic dwelling	32
Figure 16.	Italians clearing land in St. Helena	32
Figure 17.	A three-room L-shaped cottage	33
Figure 18.	A company house in St. Helena	34
Figure 19.	A St. Helena house after landscaping and painting	34
Figure 20.	Dedication of St. Joseph's Catholic Church in St. Helena	36
Figure 21.	Winter lettuce under cloth	38
Figure 22.	An alfalfa field	38
Figure 23.	Italians in the berry fields	38
Figure 24.	Typical farm at St. Helena	39
Figure 25.	Disappearing early South ethnic dwelling	40
Figure 26.	Van Eeden house	43
Figure 27.	Van Eeden tracts with houses	43
Figure 28.	Van Eeden today	44
Figure 29.	Brogden Middle School, Dudley, North Carolina	46
Figure 30.	First location of Van Roekel Florist	47
Figure 31.	Earlene Culbreth van Roekel, John William's wife	47
Figure 32.	"Say It With Flowers" logo	47
Figure 33.	Second location of Van Roekel Florist	48
Figure 34.	Van Roekel Florist as it is today	48
Figure 35.	The van Roekel home in Dudley, North Carolina	49
Figure 36.	Entry gate into Willowdale Cemetery, Goldsboro, North Carolina	50
Figure 37.	Grave stones of Jan and Willemina van Roekel	50
Figure 38.	Grave stone of Jan van Roekel	50
Figure 39:	Grave stone of Willemina van Deelen van Roekel	50
Figure 40:	Grave market of Otiena van Roekel Bradbury	50
Figure 41:	Grave marker of Otiena's second husband, James Thomas Bradbury	50
Figure 42:	Death Certificates for Willemina and Jan van Roekel	51
Figure 43:	Letter from Willemina to her family in Holland	52
Figure 44:	Postcard of the TSS Statendam	52
Figure 45:	Statue of Gele Rijder in Arnham, Holland	55
Figure 46:	Photocopy from De Onderofficier (The NCO)	56
Figure 47:	Photocopy of Jan van Roekel registration in the Yellow Riders	57
Figure 48:	Roekel community in Holland near Otterlo in 1900, by Houten	58

Table of Contents Continued

Figure 49:	Artist rendition of van Roekel Coat of Arms	60
Figure 50:	The van Roekel crest found in the Posthumous section	61
Figure 51:	A wapen of unknown origin provided by man from Groningen	61
Figure 52:	Site of birthplace of Willemina in the Hoge Veluwe	64
Figure 53:	Heldring Church in Hoenderloo and Reverend Otto Gerhard Heldring	65
Figure 54:	House like van Deelens in Hoge Veluwe	65
Figure 55:	The van Deelen family home in Hoenderloo where Willemina lived	65
Figure 56:	Artist rendition of the van Deelen Coat of Arms	66
Figure 57:	Oldest coat of arms dated 1687, from Crumseler family	67
Figure 58:	Coat of arms dated 1586 belonging to Herman van Deelen	67
Figure 59:	Shield awarded to Baronnen van Deelen in 1881 by the High Court	67
Figure 60:	Image on coffee table at Willem van Deelen's home in Apeldoorn	68
Figure 61:	Map of Holland, Amsterdam to Apeldorn, Gelderland	70
Figure 62:	Map of The Gelderland province of the Netherlands	71
Figure 63:	Business card from Jopie van Hunen Blokker	73
Figure 64:	Het Handwerkhuis in Apeldoorn	73
Figure 65:	Gijs Bos family by barn that was home of Jan (1836)	76
Figure 66:	Gijs Bos family home in 1976	76

PHOTOGRAPHS—NAMED

Jan and Willemina van Roekel: The Early Years and The Latter Years	3
Wim and Jopie van Hunen Blokker	4
John Herbert van Roekel and family	10
Jan van Roekel (1836) and Otina van Roekel	11
Depiction of Yellow Riders in ceremonial dress	13
Dr. Frederik van Eeden	20
Herman Vogel family	22
Dr. Alvin Johnson	24
Hugh MacRae	35
Dr. Frederik van Eeden	37
Jan and Willemina with son, William Robert	53
Jan and Willemina at home in Dudley, North Carolina	53
Jan van Roekel (1885) in his Yellow Riders uniform	54
Willemina Hendrika van Deelen van Roekel, age 21	62
Willemina and her sister Ger (Grace)	64
Willem van deelen and Rijke Essenstam van Deelen, Willemina's parents	69
Willemina's family	69
John Herbert van Roekel and his family	72
Jopie and Wim van Hunen Blokker	74
Rijke, Ger, and Johanna	74
Willem and Jacoba	74
Judy van Roekel with the Henni Buitenhuis family	75
Ger and Bertran Buitenhuis	75
Hendricus and Klaasje Roseboom	75
Gijs Bos family	77
Jan and Willemina celebrated their 50th Anniversary!	78
Jan and Willemina with their four children	86
Jan and Willemina with three of their children and the four spouses	86

Table of Contents Continued

PHOTOGRAPHS—GENEALOGY SECTION

William, Elizabeth, and John Herbert van Roekel	87
William Robert and Elizabeth Howard van Roekel	87
John Herbert family	88
Jennifer van Roekel family	88
Amanda van Roekel	88
Hendrick John and Hazel Ruth Davis van Roekel	89
Hendrick (Henry) John van Roekel, Sr., U.S. Army	90
Descendants of Hendrick John van Roekel, Sr. (Henry)	91
Hendrick John (Butch) van Roekel, Jr.	92
Hendrick John (Butch) van Roekel, Jr. with wife, Margaret Rose Redman	92
Hendrick John (Butch) van Roekel, Jr. with wife and daughter, Kimberly Ann	92
Kimberly Ann van Roekel with husband, Timothy Burkett, and son, Zachery Ryan	92
Richard Phillip van Roekel, Sr. family	93
Richard van Roekel, Sr.	93
Cynthia "Jean" Royal van Roekel, Richard's wife	93
Richard Phillip van Roekel, II family	94
Richard van Roekel, II	94
Cynthia Ashley van Roekel Small with children	94
Ashley van Roekel, younger years	94
James Leroy van Roekel and wife, Jean Lilley van Roekel	95
Teresa Ruth van Roekel Godwin family	95
Otiena Hendrika van Roekel Bradbury	96
Descendants of Otiena Hendrika van Roekel Hill Bradbury	98
Katherine (Kaye) Fredricka Hill Mason	99
Descendants of Katherine Hill Mason	99
Thomas Elmer Hill, Jr. family	100
William Robert Hill family	101
Susan Hill	101
John (Johnnie) William van Roekel	102
Earlene Culbreth van Roekel, Johnnie's first wife	102
John (Johnnie) William van Roekel family	103

PHOTOGRAPHS—APPENDIX

Hendricus van Roekel (04-12-1879)	108
Jan de Bakker – Johannes Pistorius Woerdensis (Painting)	135

Introduction

My name is John Herbert van Roekel. I am a grandson of Jan and Willemina van Deelen van Roekel. (*Jan* means *John* in the Dutch language and is pronounced "Yon.")

I grew up around my grandparents in eastern North Carolina when they were in their later years, and I have very fond and loving memories of them. It has been my desire to honor their memory and the legacy they left our family by compiling the story of their life. This book is the fulfillment of that desire, following untold hours of research, letter writing, and two trips to Holland, our Fatherland. I will share later in this book about the events of those trips and the family members and friends we met.

It has been a labor of love to record as much about our family history as possible for our future generations. As Joel 1:2 instructs, "Tell it to your children, and let your children tell it to their children, and their children to the next generation."

My deep appreciation goes to Judy, Jennifer, and Amanda for their patience and support during the many hours I was away from them while working on this project.

I have listed other people on the Acknowledgements page who gave significantly to this endeavor. My thanks to them.

It is my sincere hope that I have not inadvertently or ignorantly infringed on any copyrights in the vast amount of material that has been collected and included here. This book is produced for our family and anyone else who has an interest in the genealogy of the van Roekel family. I have included credits where possible.

There are many people named "Jan" in the van

John Herbert van Roekel with wife, Judy Evelyn Taylor van Roekel and their daughters, Jennifer Deelen van Roekel Strickland and Amanda Carole van Roekel (seated). They live in Western North Carolina.

Roekel family line. To prevent confusion, I have annotated them by their birth year rather than their lineage only, e.g., "Jan (1836)" instead of "Jan (father)." Since this book is in English, I have used the U.S. standard of month/day/year for annotating numeric dates, instead of the European method of day/month/year, except where noted.

It is my prayer that your life will be enriched by getting to know my amazing grandparents.

Jan van Roekel (12-25-1836) and his second wife, Otina van Hunen van Roekel.

This photo is a snapshot of a framed photograph owned by John William van Roekel in Goldsboro, North Carolina. The bright spot is a reflection on the glass from the flash on our camera.

The van Roekels in Lunteren, Holland

My great-grandfather, Jan van Roekel, was born on Christmas Day, December 25, 1836. He was a farmer, married twice, and had 17 children. He died October 22, 1907.

He moved his family from Bennekom to Lunteren in the mid-1850s. It has been assumed that he built the home that is now a barn with the wrought iron numbers "1812" on its face (see photo on page 12). The home was remodeled and some time later was converted to a barn with the thatched roof.

Although the wrought iron numbers show "1812," we were told by Gijs Bos, the current owner, that the "l" in front of the "2" in "1812" is actually a "7" with a portion of the number broken off. It should read "1872," the year a remodel of the home was done. It was actually built 50 years earlier in 1822. It is possible that a previous owner built the house, and Jan (1836) bought it for a home in the mid-1850s when he moved to Lunteren. The property is now owned by E. G. "Gijs" Bos, son of A. J. Bos, my grandfather's friend.

One of Jan's (1836) sons was my grandfather, Jan van Roekel, born to Jan's second wife, Otina van Hunen van Roekel, on August 24, 1885.

Jan (1885) was 22 years old when his father passed away. He was serving his required military duties in the Yellow Riders, an elite division of the Dutch military. It was considered an honor to serve in this select division. Jan was assigned to the 4th Regiment in Arnhem. (You can read more about Jan's life with the Yellow Riders later in the book.)

Arnhem, where Jan was assigned, was and still is the county seat. The van Deelen family lived in Hoenderloo but often shopped in Arnhem. It was four years after his father's death when Jan, then 26, met 24-year-old Willemina van Deelen. After a fun and furious courtship, they were married two weeks later on September 9, 1911.

At the time of their marriage, I'm sure they never imagined that within the next year they would suffer the loss of a child that was stillborn and soon thereafter be on a ship moving to America. Their adventure together began just under three years before World War I came to Europe.

Figure 1. The Lunteren home of Jan van Roekel (1836), purchased in the mid-1850s. It is the birthplace of his son, Jan van Roekel (1885). The building was first constructed as a home in 1822. The wrought iron numbers on the front of the building are supposed to be 1872, but the arm of the "7" was broken off at some point making it appear to be 1812. The home was presumably remodeled in 1872. Still later, it was remodeled to be a barn. The original thatched roof has been replaced with steel. The property is now owned by E.G. "Gijs" Bos, son of A.J. Bos who was Jan's friend. You can see more photos of the building as well as the Bos family on pages 76 and 77.

Photo courtesy of E.G. Bos

The Story Begins

Jan van Roekel meets Willemina van Deelen

One can only imagine the kind of day it must have been in Arnhem that fateful day in late August 1911.

It was probably warm, about 75 degrees, with a breeze moving gently throughout the town square. The local musicians would have been playing the auto-play (like a self-playing piano) on the music box. There was probably a feeling in the air that fall was just around the corner.

Jan van Roekel, a handsome soldier dressed in his Gele Rijder uniform, was probably jesting as usual with some of his fellow soldiers when an attractive woman across the square catches his eye. She was most likely accompanied by one or more of her sisters, or perhaps she was simply having a "girls day out" to observe the lads at the Arnhem barracks of the Yellow Riders. I feel quite sure, having known her, that she may have been doing just that! The barracks were right there at the square and convenient for observing all the "candidates." We will never know for sure.

It was a true honor to be a member of the select group of men chosen to protect the motherland. Being assigned to the 4th Regiment in Arnhem was also conveniently close to his home in Lunteren.

I can imagine Jan, a 26-year-old man, tapping one of his friends on the shoulder and musingly saying, "I'm going to marry that woman." To be sure, Willemina was a striking woman of her day, full of laughter and enthusiasm.

To our knowledge, Jan had never layed eyes on Willemina before, even though their homes were only a few miles apart. Two weeks later, after a whirlwind romance, they were married. It was September 9, 1911.

At age 24, it was time for Willemina to settle

Yellow Riders in ceremonial dress.

down and begin her family. We can only guess the uproar at the van Deelen house about this torrid romance that culminated with marriage in just 14 days. I feel sure her brothers and sisters had many comments on the subject, especially since Jan was of such meager means and the son of a peasant farmer from Lunteren. Uproar or not, the romance and the wedding was moving forward. We have been told that the van Deelen family would have preferred Willemina to marry higher up the social order.

According to the immigration documents from Ellis Island, Jan and Willemina lived with Jan's mother, Otina, in Arnhem. (See immigration documents from Ellis Island in the Appendix, pages 152-153.) Jan's father had passed away on October 22, 1907, and we can suppose that Jan had found his mother a place to live near him in Arnhem. It is possible that he was living with her instead of at the barracks. Jan, being the creative man that he was, may have rented the family farm to his dad's friend, A.J. Bos, in order to provide a living for his mother. At any rate, it would have been very convenient for

Jan to continue his military duties in Arnhem and be there with his new wife and mother.

World War I

War was in the air, and Jan had two more years of service to the Queen. His discharge was not due to take effect until July 13, 1913.

Jan was a man of action. This characteristic would serve him well for the next 40 years. One will never know, but this intuitive and ingenious, take-action man may have assessed the threat of danger to his family and himself from foreign enemies and decided that other opportunities were out there if only one would look. Ironically, he would not have been targeted because Holland declared itself neutral and never activated its military.

One day, while reading the paper, Jan came across an article by Dr. Frederik van Eeden (see Figure 2 below). It was an advertisement for Dutch farmers to relocate to a colony in eastern North Carolina, USA.

The promise of land and the opportunity to escape his pending peasant farmer role was just too good to pass up. "Who knows," he may have reasoned, "we may become fabulously wealthy and retire back to the homeland someday." He most assuredly did not want to be a peasant farmer as was his dad.

The news article shown below was sponsored by either the Carolina Trucking Development Company or by Dr. Frederik Van Eeden. They were working together to create opportunities for many different European ethnic groups. These groups included Italians, Poles, Catholics, Dutch, and Jews as well. They were planning as many as seven colonies in eastern North Carolina. Since Dr. van Eeden already had a community started in northern Holland, named Walden, we feel confident that Jan contacted him about being one of the thirty Dutch farmers to join this exciting venture. It is possible that Dr. van Eeden may have sent Jan a copy of the book he had written, *Van Eeden Kolonie,* about the Van Eeden Colony in America, as well. This book can be found at the University of North Carolina Library at Chapel Hill, and a

Figure 2. The advertisement above (English version shown on right) was probably found in a newspaper by Jan van Roekel in 1910 or 1911. Information was sent to him by Dr. Frederik van Eeden, The Van Eeden Colony in N.C., USA.

Van Eeden Colony in North Carolina, USA

The Carolina Trucking Development Company has land ready for thirty farmers, between Watha and Burgaw, N.C. It is suitable for intensive farming by experienced growers, under the following conditions:

One can get a farm of 10 acres (4 hectares) with a house (to try out) for a rent of $26, with option to buy at $50.00/acre with easy payment conditions. The house will be sold at cost.

In case the colonist wants to build his own home, he can get the land for free of rent for five years, with the option to buy at $50.00/acre (1 dollar = 2.45 guildens). As soon as 40 families have settled, the settlement will get a school and church.

Those who want to participate in Dr. van Eeden's Productive Company can get an option for 5 years and then bring the land into the company, as soon as it is established. The locality is absolutely healthy, with good drinking water. The soil is sandy loam with a base of clay, excellently fertile. You can grow: cotton, sweet potatoes, peanuts, corn, all vegetables, lettuce, cabbage, flowers, fruit trees, and also grapes. The climate is as in Italy, open soil all winter. There is plenty of rain, with cool sea breezes in the summer. You may get free advice from the superintendent (We think he is referring to Herman Vogel). The Van Eeden site is serviced by the Atlantic Coast Line Railroad, with excellent connections with New York, Philadelphia, and other large cities. The nearby city of Wilmington can also be reached by sea from New York (Clyde Line). Several Dutch families have already settled there. Information can be found through Mr. Herman Vogels in Castle Hayne, N.C., or with Dr. Frederik van Eeden, Walden-Bussum in the province of North Holland in the Netherlands, and at the Carolina Trucking Development Company in Wilmington, N.C. USA.

translated version can be found in the Appendix on page 161.

The war finally came to Europe in June 1914. I guess one could say, "the rest is history."

Preparations for Leaving

Jan and Willemina were to leave for America in the late spring of 1912. Much had to be prepared. Many good-byes had to be said. Preparations for the trip of a lifetime were underway. To complicate matters, Willemina gave birth to a stillborn child on April 3, 1912, in Arnhem. This was Record #165 in the Hall of Records in Arnhem for year 1912.

It is a mystery how Jan convinced the Yellow Riders to allow him to leave the country and still be assigned to the barracks in Arnhem. We will never know what he said or how they decided to allow him to spend his last year of active (or passive) duty here in America, but they did allow him to go. It is suspected that the reason he was detained at the Ellis Island hotel an extra day was to allow time for the authorities to confirm that he was not Absent Without Leave (AWOL) from the military.

Leaving for America was a life altering decision. Willemina and Jan would see their families in Holland but one more time, when they returned in 1931 following the death of Jan's mother to sell the farm that had belonged to his father (Jan 1836) to A.J. Bos. His mother had passed away, and there was no reason not to sell it to his friend.

We do find it odd, though, why Jan (1885) was responsible for doing this. There were 16 other siblings, and most of them were older than Jan. Generally, the Dutch method of inheritance was that the eldest son who stayed at the home place to care for the aging parents received all of the estate. Jan was not the eldest, and he certainly could not take care of his mother while in America; that is, unless he had made the arrangements for her care in advance. Was it because he had taken care of his mother's support before he left Holland? We, again, will never know the actual answer; we can only speculate that was the reason. Could it be that the Bos family was renting the farm from Jan, and the rent money was going to support his mom in Arnhem? I believe that was the case. Thus, he was taking care of her and had the responsibility of settling her estate.

America or Bust

The packing was done, the good-byes were completed, the tears had flowed, and their hearts were pounding. Money was in their pockets, although we have no idea where it came from.

The S.S. Noordam (see Figure 3 below) awaited them at the port in Rotterdam. Little did Willemina know that she was already pregnant with her second child. William Robert van Roekel was

Figure 3. The S.S. Noordam, the ship that carried Jan and Willemina to America.

born in America on January 10, 1913, just a couple of miles from Van Eeden in Watha, North Carolina.

The Voyage

The weather was reported to have been horrid during the ocean voyage. Storms prevailed, and to complicate the sadness and fear of leaving the homeland, they were to sail through the floating debris of the infamous Titanic that had sunk on April 15, just three weeks earlier. What a difficult time it must have been. And what a difficult time to begin a new life in America. We do not know for sure how long the journey took, but it was most likely five to seven days at sea.

Only those who have sailed into New York harbor can know how it feels to sail by the Statue of Liberty for the first time. For the Dutch immigrants, it must have been even more special, since the original name of New York was New Amsterdam, and it was settled by a Dutchman named Peter Stuyvesant.

Arriving in New York

Jan and Willemina sailed past the Statue of Liberty on May 7, 1912. They had met other Dutch settlers who were moving to America during their voyage. Many of them went to the Midwest—Michigan and Iowa areas. Their new acquaintances became lifelong friends with whom they would meet again.

Surprises were the hallmark of their adventure. After completing the immigration process, Jan and Willemina were escorted to the Castle Garden Hotel for the night. Unlike many of the friends they had made, they were detained until the following day. Tired and weary, they left Ellis Island and headed to the train station to begin their 30-hour journey to eastern North Carolina. (A copy of the immigration papers is included in the Appendix on pages 152-153).

Figure 4. "The Welcome Center" at Van Eeden. Source: Manfred and Ann Loch Collection: North Carolina Collection, University of North Carolina Library at Chapel Hill.

North Carolina

The train finally arrived in Watha, North Carolina, a small community north of Van Eeden. It was sundown when they arrived and, to their dismay, no one was there to meet them. Herman Vogel, their sponsor, was nowhere to be seen, nor was anyone else he could have designated. They had stepped off the train into a seemingly desolate new world, and darkness was ensuing. I can imagine their thoughts, disappointment, and fear. (See their "train station" in Figure 4 above.)

An interesting diversion was about to unfold before their eyes that brought the short distraction they needed. Forests and glades in Eastern North Carolina are ablaze with fireflies—lightning bugs—in the early spring of the year. These interesting insects do not exist in Holland. Willemina was certain the sky was sparking and trying to catch on fire. Jan, being the brave soul that he was, had to reassure her that there was nothing to fear. I'm sure he went out and caught a few of the insects to show her. Eventually, someone came and escorted them to a place of rest. We are not sure where they spent their first night in their new homeland. They may have been escorted to Castle Haynes, even though their new home would be in Van Eeden.

I can't resist sharing a little paradox. For those of you who have never visited Holland, one truly could think of it as a little "Eden." It could be said that our ancestors came "from Eden" to Van Eeden, which means "from Eden." Just a fun pun.

The North Carolina Farm Colonies

Herman Vogel is identified in the immigration documents as the sponsor for Jan's and Willemina's legal immigration.

We know, of course, that Hugh MacRae, Dr. Frederik van Eeden, and Herman Vogel were working together to make this venture happen. Frederik van Eeden, William Hoggson, et al, formed the Co-operative Company of America to foster the building of Van Eeden. Hugh MacRae formed the Carolina Trucking Development Company to facilitate the development of the six colonies.

The initial Van Eeden experiment failed quite quickly—within a year or so—but in 1939, Hugh MacRae sold 100 acres of Van Eeden to the Alvin Corporation. The Alvin Corporation was owned by Dr. Alvin Johnson, a first generation Dutch Jew from New York. Van Eeden's second existence served with the neighboring community of Penderlea as a sanctuary for Dutch Jews seeking asylum in America against the events unfolding in Germany and Europe. Please refer to Susan Taylor Block's book, *Van Eeden*.

Little has been acknowledged about the excellent contribution of these fine men to save some of the elite in Holland by bringing them to America under the pretense that they were to be farmers. Few people know that Franklin D. Roosevelt and Hugh MacRae were on speaking terms, and even that Roosevelt helped pave the way for some of the Jewish immigrants to get here.

The six communities were as follows: St. Helena, Artesia, Van Eeden, Castle Haynes, New Berlin, and Marathon. What a legacy these men have, and so few know of it. Hugh MacRae purchased 40,000 acres to start this mammoth project. (See map on page 18.)

None of the colonies ever really became established except Castle Hayne(s), and it was developed earlier during the Civil War era.

The best we can understand from the advertisement in the Dutch newspaper, the agreement by the Carolina Trucking Company was that for the immigrants who came and agreed to either rent or purchase the land and stay for a period of time, it is assumed that the developers (Carolina Trucking Co. and/or the Co-operative Company of America) would drain the fertile swampland, provide temporary housing, and eventually churches and schools. In exchange, the farmers were to work the land, and some of their crops would be trucked to markets outside of the area. After three to five years, the 10 acres the family was tending and the house would become theirs, and they could build their own homes. There was also an option to purchase the 10 acres up front; the family could then build their own home as they saw fit. (See Figures 26 and 27 on page 43 for the types of homes that were built at Van Eeden.)

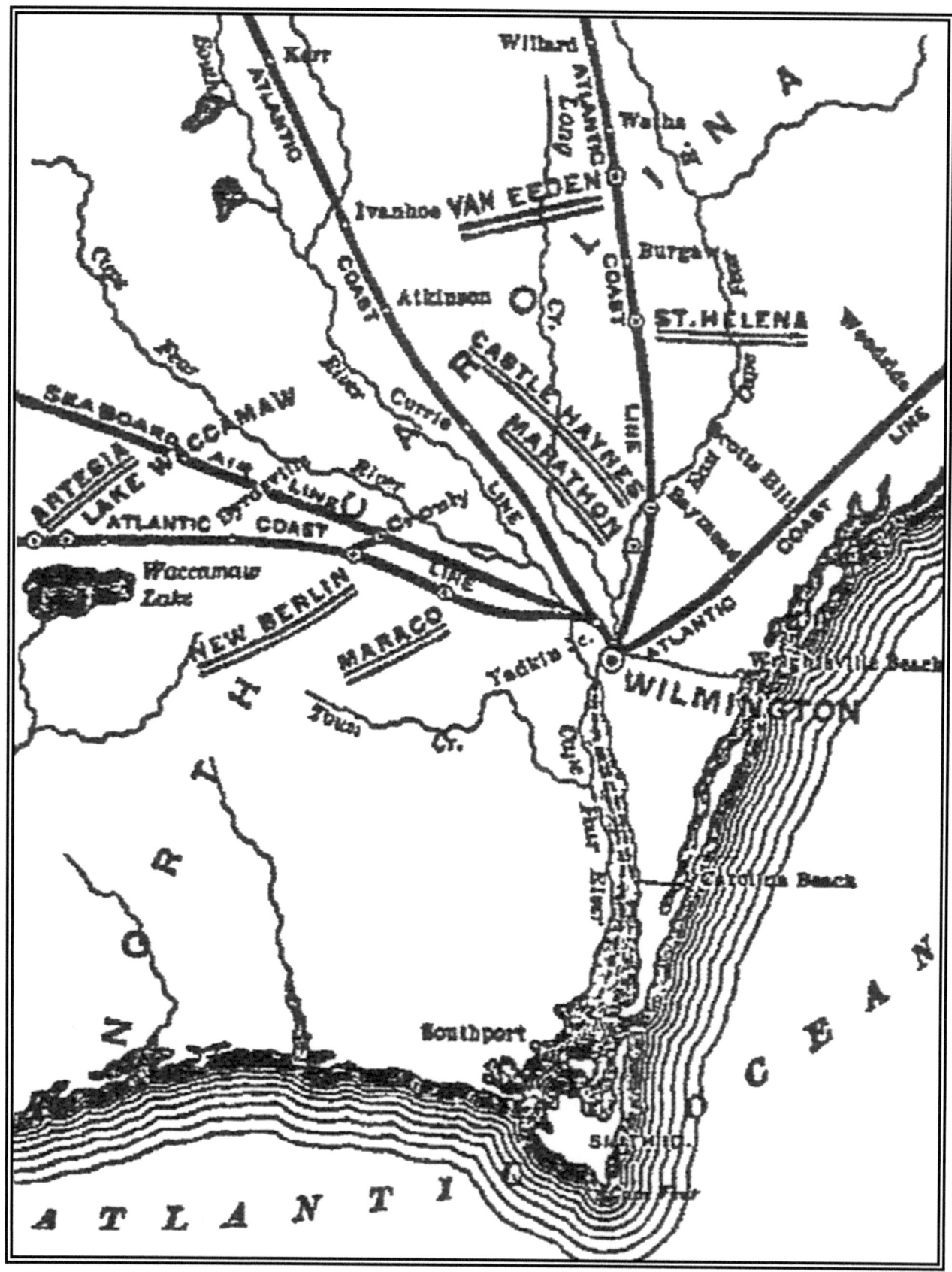

Figure 5: The Six MacRae Colonies and their proximity to the rail lines. Source: Hugh MacRae II Collection, Wilmington, N.C.

The Forming of the North Carolina Colonies

A look at the men who formed the North Carolina colonies and contributed significantly to the van Roekel family history.

At the beginning of the 20th century, the civilized world was moving into an era of industrial, intellectual, political, and social change. Blended with these changes was a sense of grandiose idealism. The knowledge explosion and pioneering new value systems were influencing much of this change.

People around the world were looking for opportunities to escape the Old World entrapments and feudalism and to adopt new ideas and philosophies. The desire for social change motivated millions to uproot themselves from their native land to move to America, a land they thought would provide freedom and opportunities to fulfill their dreams. Many leaders of our United States today are offspring of those peasants who dared to dream of how things could be different if only they had a chance to escape their roots and seize opportunities to work and excel.

Russia embraced a different kind of change. The Marxist-Leninist Bolshevik revolution brought the aristocratic Czarist world to its knees and gave the rule of government to the people in the form of Communism. "All for one and one for all" was the prevailing value system, a communal ownership where no one was better than the next. What seemed a revolutionary idea tragically brought disaster to millions and dragged the world into a vicious roller coaster of competition for power and influence that ultimately could have destroyed mankind with a nuclear holocaust. China followed Russia's lead and adopted a harsh, rigid form of Communism that inflicted bondage onto its people for more than 80 years.

There arose a different revolution in the United States. Here it was an era of unionism. The powerful American Federation of Labor and the Congress for Industrial Organization (AFL-CIO) merged and brought greater opportunity to prosper to the common man in the more urbanized metropolitan areas. The unions supported the concept of more power to the workers than the owners through a form of democracy. The movement was to empower the masses and, thus, redistribute the wealth of the "company" so that the worker got his fair share. Then the worker was able to feed his family well and improve the lot of his heirs by having more income to pass down.

Dr. Frederik van Eeden

There were those in Holland who were revolutionary thinkers as well. They were persons with idealistic utopian values who truly believed that everyone who would work should be able to prosper, and "communal" property was one way to accomplish that ideal.

One of those social reformers, **Dr. Frederik van Eeden**, was a young doctor who was a dreamer, poet, and writer. He was later called the Tolstoy of Holland.

(If you travel to Holland, be sure to visit the museum about him in Amsterdam.) He was also a person of action, brilliant in every way, and able to move people with his rhetoric. In 1959, the *New England Quarterly* clarified his life and goals in an article titled "Walden Goes Wandering, the Transit of Good Intentions." (See Appendix for links to this article, along with a link to the biography of Dr. van Eeden written by Dr. J. Glenn Friesen, and a book by Dr. van Eeden in which he describes the unique experiment, *Van Eeden Kolonie*.)

Dr. Frederik van Eeden (1860-1932)

Dr. van Eeden was profoundly influenced by Thoreau and his book, *Walden*. He also read Bolton Hall's work, *Three Acres and Liberty*. He started a "Walden" community in Holland in 1903. Dr. van Eeden made several trips to America and met many wealthy philanthropic capitalists, such as **Upton Sinclaire**, **William J. Hoggson**, and **Hugh MacRae**. MacRae was a wealthy business entrepreneur from the Wilmington, North Carolina, area who also shared some of the idealism of van Eeden. Hugh MacRae had many business associates, and he wanted to prove that there was a need for immigrants to come and help revive the agriculture of the South. He purchased thousands of acres of land and envisioned the Carolina Trucking and Development Company as a "vehicle" to make the dream of forming these colonies come true.

MacRae, Dr. van Eeden, and their associates set forth a wave of 20th century colonization in eastern North Carolina by establishing seven communities that embodied some of van Eeden's idealistic, "friendly" Communist concepts and marrying them with his own ideas of agricultural capitalism. An interesting marriage it was.

The seven communities were: the already established Castle Hayne(s), Van Eeden, Artesia, New Berlin, Marathon, St. Helena, and Maraco. Maraco is rarely, if ever, actually mentioned in discussions of the colonies. (See map on page 18 for their locations).

In the first effort to establish Van Eeden (1910-1915 period), Dr. van Eeden wanted to prove that friendly communistic ideals could be helpful to liberate hardworking, intelligent, poor families who just needed land to grow their crops and not to be slaves of titles and ownership.

In 1939 under the ownership of **Alvin Johnson** and the Alvin Corporation, Van Eeden's second existence served with the neighboring community of Penderlea as a refuge area for European Jews seeking asylum from the ravages of World War II. **President F. D. Roosevelt** was quietly involved with aiding in this rescue effort. (See Figure 6 on page 21.)

In 1949 the Van Eeden land was sold by the Alvin Corporation to **John Wilkins** to start a dairy, and as far as we know, it is still owned by the Wilkins family.

In preparation for the initial settlement in the 1910 period, Dr. van Eeden made presentations in Carnegie Hall, The Astor Hotel, and San Francisco. (See links to these in the Appendix, page 106). He had already experimented with forming a community in Holland as he, MacRae, and Hoggson were proposing in eastern North Carolina. His community near his home of Bussum, Holland, was called "Walden," named after Thoreau's book for which he had much admiration. Van Eeden's Walden was a success, or was headed to being successful, when Dr. van Eeden became involved in a railroad union strike in Amsterdam. He became its director of some 70,000 members. The union fell on difficult financial times, and van Eeden used up much of his fortune before he resigned its leadership. Walden was auctioned off to settle much of the debt incurred from his time as leader of the railroad union. Dr. van Eeden lost a fortune—$100,000—a huge sum of money at that time and, most likely, a sum that would equal more than a million dollars by today's standards. What a man of character! He made sure that not one poor person whom he had led to strike lost money. Yet, he quietly paid for his decision to lead them to strike and uttered not a whimper for his personal losses and the loss of Walden.

Walden proved that selecting good, hard working, intelligent people was crucial to a successful venture, and he was eager to do the same with MacRae and others in North Carolina. **Mr. William J. Hoggson** sought out other financial investors to buy the land in eastern North Carolina, with the already existing Castle Hayne(s). They began selecting immigrants to come to America. Jan and Willemina van Roekel became one of those immigrant farm families. The Co-operative Company of America was formed with the financial assistance of MacRae and a $25,000 loan from some local banks in Wilmington.

{Numerous Internet links are included in the Appendix on pages 105-106 to explain Van Eeden's perspective: a 1959 article in *The New England Quarterly* about his life; *New York Times* articles, *Happy Humanity*, his presentations at Carnegie Hall and in San Francisco; and a book by Susan Taylor Block, *Van Eeden*, and the complete translation of *Van Eeden Kolonie* by Dr. van Eeden begins on page 161.}

What an exciting time! Jan and Willemina lived with courage, idealism, and tenacity.

There are two things we can only assume to be true since we cannot find supporting documents. First, we can only assume that Dr. van Eeden met

Jewish Refugee Farmers in Van Eeden

The incredible story is true: a Wilmington Episcopalian, Hugh MacRae, and a Nyack, New York, Jew, Dr. Alvin Johnson, partnered to save European Jews in 1939. They obligated themselves to give North Carolina farming jobs to all the Jews they could save. When visas were halted, the flow ended. But 50 to 60 adults and children made it safely. They attended Reform services faithfully in Wilmington. Winslow Wilkings and his son, John, farm the land now. They live in a new house to which two of the original Jewish houses have been appended. Van Eeden lies four miles north of Burgaw in Pender County, NC. From Burgaw, take US 117 north, left on #1347, right on #1315. (Factual details may be found in the book *Van Eeden* by Susan Taylor Block.)

Photo © University of North Carolina, Chapel Hill, NC

Figure 6: Pictured are Max Wolf and David Loeb in Van Eeden II. From *Van Eeden* by Susan Taylor Block.

Herman Vogel with his family.

Herman Vogel during his visits with Hugh MacRae in eastern North Carolina. Dr. van Eeden needed a person to "sponsor" the immigrating Dutch families. He may have asked Mr. Vogel to fill the role of sponsor since we find in the documents from Ellis Island that Herman Vogel was the sponsor of my grandparents, Jan and Willemina van Roekel. We have no proof that it took place this way, but they had no other way of knowing Mr. Vogel.

The second thing we can only assume is how our grandparents heard about the opportunity in America. We can surmise that Jan saw the advertisement in the Dutch newspapers that had been placed by Dr. van Eeden or Hugh MacRae for "intelligent, hard-working Dutch" who would move to America and start a colony that would be somewhat communal in nature.

Jan learned from this business process, and it served him well in his later business, "Say It With Flowers." He mirrored some of MacRae's business ideas of transport to the northern markets by rail. Somehow, I think MacRae must have felt as a parent does when his children do well and his chest swells with pride. Much good was accomplished. Southern agriculturists adopted many of MacRae's ideas, and the South prospered.

As cited later, many individuals who came to America from their native homes did prove that immigration was successful in stimulating the revival of farming in eastern North Carolina, but one must wonder if some of the failure to achieve the larger aspects of the experiment cannot be left with the fact that van Eeden did not personally supervise the overall operation of the Van Eeden experiment for a period of time and, instead, left supervision to others at the colony.

Much more could have been accomplished if certain things had been considered in the beginning, such as more realistic advertising. It also would have been beneficial had the land drained to a standard to sustain truck farming. There should have been more attention given to how the colonies were to exist. The settlers themselves were in such a dire financial position that many felt they had to seek more lucrative employment in urban centers similar to those from which the immigration was to save them. All of these confounders prevented the experiment from becoming the "ideal" to which they were aspiring.

Hugh MacRae
Biography From Frank Ainsley's "Dutch Settlers in the Cape Fear," 1987. Reprinted with permission.

In the early years of the twentieth century, **Hugh MacRae** (1865-1951), a prominent Wilmington businessman, founded the Carolina Trucking Development Company for the purpose of establishing several agricultural colonies in the Cape Fear region. MacRae, from a long line of merchants and entrepreneurs, was educated as a mining engineer at the Massachusetts Institute of Technology (MIT). After a brief stint in mica mining in the Linville area of western North Carolina, MacRae returned to Wilmington to run his father's cotton mill and become the president of the Tidewater Power Company with control of the utilities and street car lines in Wilmington. MacRae was a land developer in the Wilmington vicinity; his projects included several early twentieth century street suburbs, oceanfront developments at Wrightsville Beach, and six regionally unique ethnic European farm colonies.

Hugh MacRae was motivated to the experiments in farm colonization for several reasons. One of his dreams was the solution of the South's labor and economic problems by the establishment of farming colonies. He envisioned these colonies of small intensive farms as the answer to the economic problems in the South. Even though MacRae was an entrepreneurial land development magnate in the Wilmington vicinity, he always maintained an intense interest in the success of the colonists who populated his farm settlements. He liked to take the visitors to the settlements and show off the successes of the residents. MacRae believed that if a person and his family could own and farm their own land (not tenant farm), they would be happy and content.

In 1905, for one or two dollars per acre, MacRae acquired several large tracts of worn out farmlands and woodlands along sections of the Atlantic Coast Line Railroad. His Carolina Trucking Development Company surveyed the land, laid out streets, and subdivided each tract into a townsite and ten-acre farms.

For many years, the President of Carolina Trucking Development Company was Cornelius van Leuven, a man of Dutch heritage who had moved to Wilmington from Kingston, New York. MacRae's colonies were established under a "company-town" concept, each having a company store and commissary, a superintendent who lived in each colony, and a common pool of agricultural implements and equipment from which all the colonist could borrow. Agents were hired on a commission basis to go to Europe and secure colonists. Immigrants from Europe, including those who had settled in the northwestern United States, were actively solicited by promotional brochures that were printed in various languages (Dutch, French, Hungarian, Polish, Italian, Slovak, Czech, and German). After much discussion about the climate of the region, soils, and various bountiful crops, markets, health conditions, roads, and the city of Wilmington, the brochure described the farmlands available, the prices and terms of payment, and deed transactions.

The first colonies established were as follows: (1) St. Helena—Italians; (2) Castle Haynes—Hollanders and Hungarians; (3) New Berlin (now known as Delco)—Germans and Hungarians; (4) Van Eeden—Hollanders; (5) Marathon—Greeks and Poles; and (6) Artesia—Poles and Hollanders.

{Figure 5 on page 18 shows a map of the suggested colonies. Note that a seventh colony, Maraco, is shown but is never mentioned. The colony's name was double underlined on the map, the same as the other six colonies.}

These six communities were anomalies in the rural South due to the fact that most of the deluge of European immigrants who flocked to America in the early 1900s remained in the industrialized Northwest and Midwest. MacRae's experiments in what he termed "human engineering" were rather unique for the early 20th century South.

Other significant people involved in forming the North Carolina colonies and the van Roekel move to America

Herman Vogel

On page 160 in the Appendix is a biography of Herman Vogel. On the previous page is a picture of him with his family as depicted in *The Van Eeden Colony*, written by Dr. Frederik van Eeden. We do not know much about his involvement with the Carolina Trucking Development Company or the Co-operative Company of America, but we do know he was the "superintendent to whom the colonists were to go with their requests for assistance." And we know from the Ellis Island records that he was the sponsor listed by Jan and Willemina when they came through New York.

Dr. Alvin Johnson

Alvin Johnson, (1874-1971) is another key player in the Van Eeden story, but his contribution to Van Eeden was during the 1939-1945 period when MacRae, Johnson, and President F. D. Roosevelt covertly rescued 50 to 60 German and Austrian Jewish adults from the Hitler regime. Dr. Johnson helped found the New School for Social Research in New York.

William J. Hoggson

William J. Hoggson was the proposed Secretary for the Co-operative Corporation of America. Additionally, he acted as an intermediary between Hugh MacRae and Frederik van Eeden. He also published articles praising van Eeden and the experiment. Below and on page 25, you will find the structure of the Co-operative Company of America as proposed by van Eeden and Hoggson to MacRae.

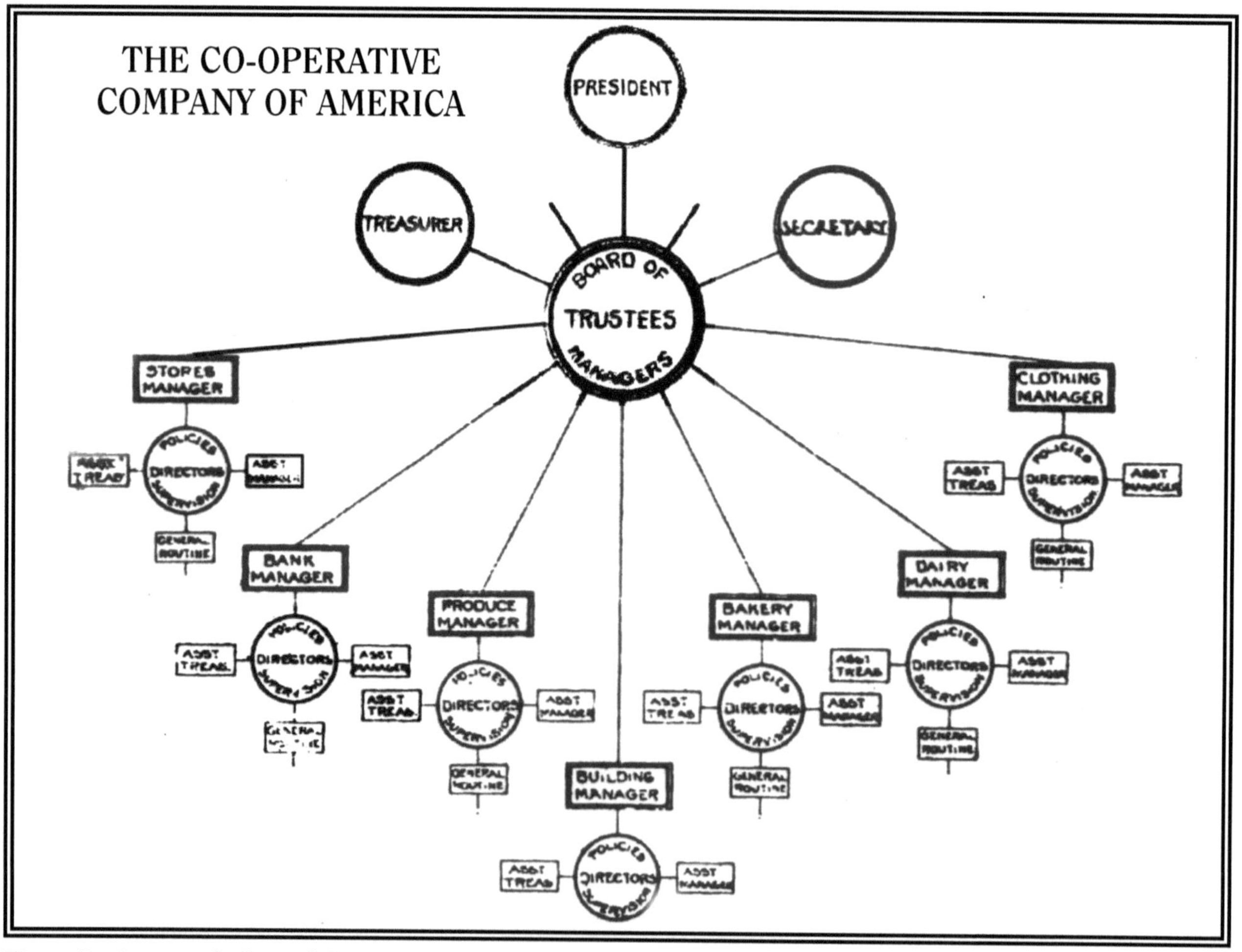

Dr. Alvin Johnson at Van Eeden
Source: Manfred and Ann Loeb Collection: North Carolina Collection, University of North Carolina Library at Chapel Hill.

Figure 7. Structural Chart of the Co-operative Company of America.

STRUCTURE OF THE UNITS IN THE CO-OPERATIVE COMPANY OF AMERICA

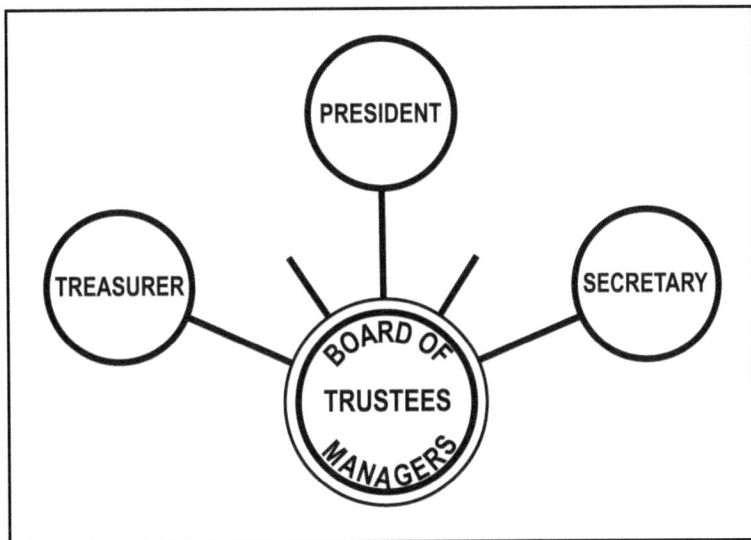

Figure 8. Board of Managers.

Each Department Manager would serve on the Board of Trustees. Each department could follow the same schematics as shown for the Store Manager (Figure 9). The other departments were as follows: Bank, Produce, Building, Bakery, Dairy, and Clothing.

Thus, the seven Managers, the President, Secretary, and Treasurer positions would comprise the Board of Managers (Figure 8). Note: No Vice President is shown, but was proposed in the letter from Hoggson to MacRae.

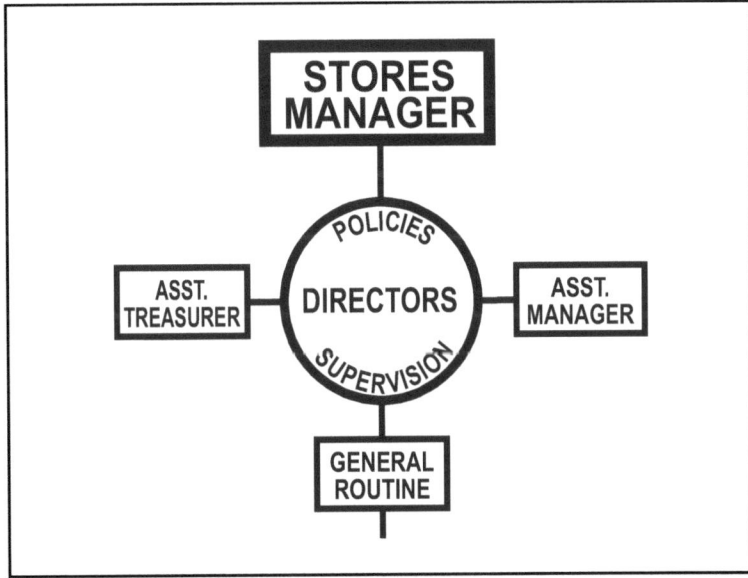

Figure 9. Departments.

Figure 10. Letter from W. J. Hoggson to Hugh MacRae, written onboard the H. M. S. Baltic. (Original letter was too faint to copy.)

Dear Mr. MacRae,

Dr. Van Eeden and I have mapped out here on the steamer an outline of our plan and we enclose it herewith for your consideration.

In the first place, it seems advisable to have a Memorandum containing the points on which we agree and which to the Doctor seem necessary, if the Colony is to be built up on the lines he and I think necessary to make it permanent. Such an Agreement I enclose, endorsed by the Doctor.

I also enclose a draft of what it seems would be a suitable set of by-laws for the corporation, to be submitted to the board, of course, for confirmation.

The title does not seem to suggest itself, but we think the CO-PRODUCING COMPANY might be used. It is assumed that they decided to call it the Co-operative Company of America.

The financial plan for the capitalization I submit for your criticism, taking my figures from what you told the Doctor, of the cost of the land.

The control should, of course, be with you and the Wilmington people; at least, until the preferred stock is redeemed, and we therefore suggest Dr. Van Eeden as President, you as Treasurer and myself as Secretary, with two Wilmington people as the other two directors would compass the matter.

The Doctor's absence from America for the present could be overcome by electing one of those places on the Board to the office of Vice President, and if the Wilmington people were willing, it would appoint Mr. Page or Mr. Holt to the office, provided either of these gentlemen were willing, it would give the movement a great impetus and the opportunity for publicity we never could have otherwise.

The fifth man could be made Assistant Treasurer, if necessary, which would relieve you.

The rules governing the Colony are tentative and will probably have to be revised, but these may be a start.

The selection of the applicants (by) the Doctor is taken care of, and his experience I count invaluable in connection with this work. We may confidently expect results not otherwise attainable.

In laying out the plan in this way, we believe future misunderstandings will be eliminated and with an assurance from you that it will go forward on the lines outlined in the enclosed, (the) Doctor will lend all his energy to getting together the settlers for crossing as soon as the land is ready to receive them. Will you communicate with him at once—and with me, on my return.

You will, of course, understand that all of the above and the enclosed, is submitted by Dr. Van Eeden and me, as suggestions and that any adjustment found necessary and advisable in making the arrangements for Capital, we will of course agree to, provided that they do not conflict with the principles we are striving to establish and maintain. All of which I believe you fully understand.

With Kindest Regards and hoping you are well,

Believe me

Yours truly,

W. J. Hoggson

Figure 11. Retyped letter from the Acting Secretary (not signed). (Copying was not legible.)

7 East 44th Street, New York City

May 5, 1909

A preliminary meeting of the Trustees of the Co-operative Company of America (farming) was held at 7 East 44th Street, New York City, May 3rd, at 4 'clock p.m.

Dr. Frederik Van Eeden addressed the meeting—gave at length the results of his investigation of several localities as a suitable site to start his plan of co-operation in connection with farming, and stated that the soil, the climate, and the marketing facilitation of the tract of land in North Carolina, about 50 miles north of Wilmington, were most satisfactory in his judgment to try the experiment.

His interview with President Taft (President 1909-1912) and Secretary (of Commerce and Labor Charles) Nagel and Secretary (James) Wilson (of Agriculture) and their interest and sympathy, were also reported. The place of the land, soil maps, cost of preparing the land for the colonization, and the probable expense of carrying charges until the land produces paying crops, were fully discussed.

It was decided to prepare a statement containing the necessary data to interest capital, and this will be forwarded to you as soon as prepared.

It is the intention to increase the Board of Trustees, and if you will kindly suggest the name of any persons you think might be interested, either as trustee, or as investors, the matter will be laid before them.

Dr. Van Eeden expects to leave at once for Holland and will look over the field with a view to directing emigrants to the land in the month on which we have an option. In this too we will have the hearty cooperation of the Department of Commerce and Labor.

Meanwhile, it is hoped that anything you can do to assist us to obtain the necessary capital—a part of which is already pledged—will be done, the necessary money will be forth coming and the company incorporated and launched.

Respectfully submitted,

Acting Secretary

Figure 12a. A sample of the sales contract between the Carolina Trucking Development Company and the immigrant purchasers (Page 1).

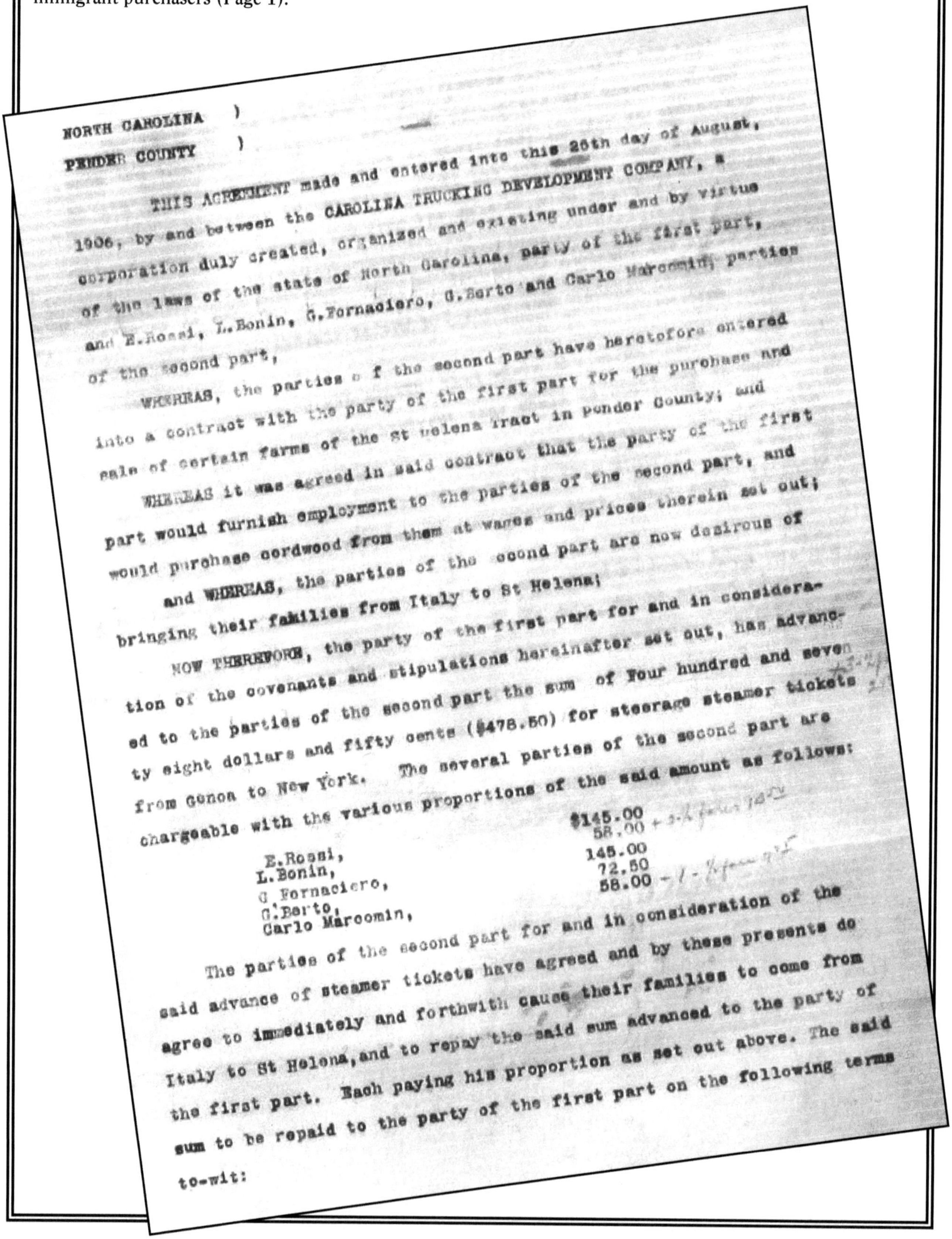

NORTH CAROLINA)
PENDER COUNTY)

THIS AGREEMENT made and entered into this 25th day of August, 1906, by and between the CAROLINA TRUCKING DEVELOPMENT COMPANY, a corporation duly created, organized and existing under and by virtue of the laws of the state of North Carolina, party of the first part, and E. Rossi, L. Bonin, G. Fornaciero, G. Berto and Carlo Marcomin, parties of the second part,

WHEREAS, the parties of the second part have heretofore entered into a contract with the party of the first part for the purchase and sale of certain farms of the St Helena Tract in Pender County; and

WHEREAS it was agreed in said contract that the party of the first part would furnish employment to the parties of the second part, and would purchase cordwood from them at wages and prices therein set out;

and WHEREAS, the parties of the second part are now desirous of bringing their families from Italy to St Helena;

NOW THEREFORE, the party of the first part for and in consideration of the covenants and stipulations hereinafter set out, has advanced to the parties of the second part the sum of Four hundred and seventy eight dollars and fifty cents ($478.50) for steerage steamer tickets from Genoa to New York. The several parties of the second part are chargeable with the various proportions of the said amount as follows:

E. Rossi, $145.00
L. Bonin,   58.00
G. Fornaciero, 145.00
G. Berto,   72.50
Carlo Marcomin, 58.00

The parties of the second part for and in consideration of the said advance of steamer tickets have agreed and by these presents do agree to immediately and forthwith cause their families to come from Italy to St Helena, and to repay the said sum advanced to the party of the first part. Each paying his proportion as set out above. The said sum to be repaid to the party of the first part on the following terms to-wit:

Figure 12b. Sales Contract (Page 2). Our special thanks to Mr. Chuck Riesz of Wilmington, N.C., for locating and providing us with this contract.

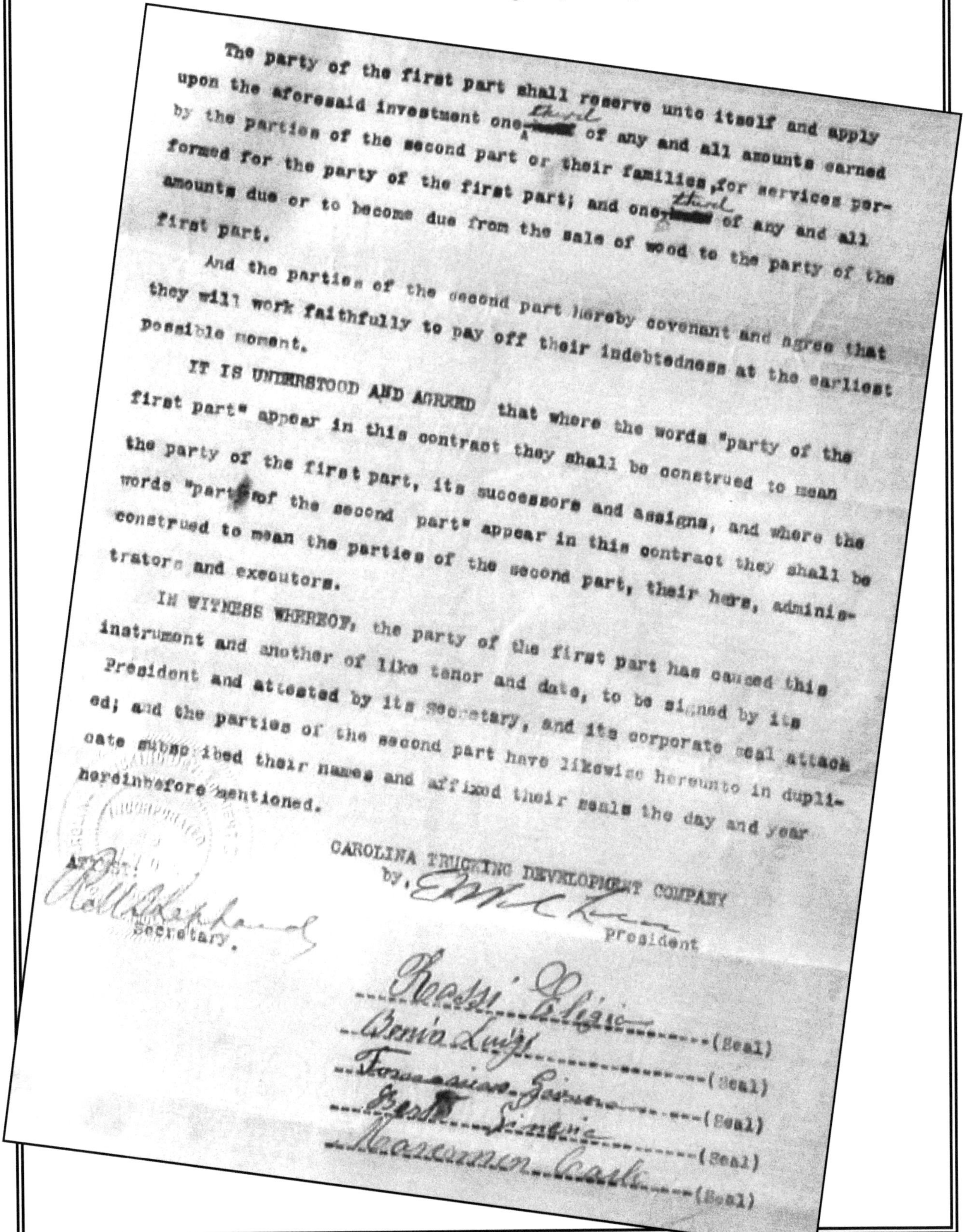

The party of the first part shall reserve unto itself and apply upon the aforesaid investment one-third of any and all amounts earned by the parties of the second part or their families, for services performed for the party of the first part; and one-third of any and all amounts due or to become due from the sale of wood to the party of the first part.

And the parties of the second part hereby covenant and agree that they will work faithfully to pay off their indebtedness at the earliest possible moment.

IT IS UNDERSTOOD AND AGREED that where the words "party of the first part" appear in this contract they shall be construed to mean the party of the first part, its successors and assigns, and where the words "parties of the second part" appear in this contract they shall be construed to mean the parties of the second part, their heirs, administrators and executors.

IN WITNESS WHEREOF, the party of the first part has caused this instrument and another of like tenor and date, to be signed by its President and attested by its Secretary, and its corporate seal attached; and the parties of the second part have likewise hereunto in duplicate subscribed their names and affixed their seals the day and year hereinbefore mentioned.

CAROLINA TRUCKING DEVELOPMENT COMPANY
by _____
President

ATTEST:
_____
Secretary.

_____ (Seal)
_____ (Seal)
_____ (Seal)
_____ (Seal)
_____ (Seal)

Figure 13. Memorandum of Agreement to form a Co-Operative Colony in North Carolina.

Memorandum of Agreement

It is understood and agreed BETWEEN Hugh MacRae of Wilmington, N.C., Dr. Frederik van Eeden of Bussum, Holland, and W. J. Hoggson of New York as follows:

THAT in furtherance of the plan to form a Co-Operative Colony in North Carolina, they jointly and severally agree as follows:

Said MacRae agrees to put up approximately 500 acres of land near Wilmington, and take in payment for same at par 6% Preferred Stock in the Corporation to be formed for the purpose of handling the business of the Colony. Price of the land to be $70.00 per acre, cleared ditched, and plowed. He is also to be a member of the Board of Directors and shall be made Treasurer of said Corporation.

Said MacRae agrees also to represent the Company at Wilmington and to negotiate an arrangement with the Bankers who promise to subscribe capital.

Said Dr. van Eeden agrees to devote his energy to securing colonists and sending them to the Colony, and besides his expenses incurred in this work, to have membership on the Board of Directors and the Presidency of the Corporation.

Said Hoggson agrees to devote his energy to the distribution end of the business, to represent the Company at New York, and to have a membership on the Board and the Secretary-ship of the Corporation.

IT IS AGREED that no acceptance of Colonists and no raising of money, or steps of importance, shall be taken, without the consent of the three parties.

Signed

F. van Eeden

W.J.Hoggson

Date:

The Selling of the Idea

From the *Journal of Cultural Geography*, Vol. 5, No. 2, Spring/Summer 1985, pp. 61-69. Reprinted with permission.

"Own a Home in North Carolina: Image and Reality in Ethnic European Colonies"

W. Frank Ainsley

ABSTRACT. *Between 1905 and 1912, six planned farm colonies were developed in southeastern North Carolina. The dream of Wilmington utilities magnate Hugh MacRae, the colonies were visualized as an experiment in "human engineering" to create a "back to the land" movement as a remedy to the economic ills of the rural South. The six communities (Castle Haynes, Marathon, St. Helena, Van Eeden, New Berlin and Artesia) were anomalies in the rural South in that they were miniature "melting pots" for the flood of European immigrants who flocked to America in the early 1900s. Through the use of documentary photographs, promotional propaganda brochures and oral histories, the material cultural of the colonies is explored and analyzed. The images of the spatial patterns and house types that were created in the minds of the potential colonists by the promotional literature are contrasted with the stark realities of the landscapes that confronted the settlers upon arrival.*

IN THE EARLY YEARS of the 20th century, the South lagged behind other sections of the United States in economic development. Despite many natural advantages in climate, soils and a long growing season, the traditional agricultural base was plagued with the problems of sharecropping and poor farm management. A few visionary entrepreneurs saw the remedy for the South's economic ills in a "back to the land" movement in which intensive capital and labor inputs would be used to convert large tracts of previously unused land into hundreds of small, economically viable truck farms.

The Setting

Hugh MacRae, a Wilmington, North Carolina, businessman, implemented his dream of solving the labor and economic problems of the South by establishing a series of peasant farming colonies in southeastern North Carolina. MacRae had read one of several books

Figure 14. Promotional brochure advertising a 3-room cottage.
Source: Hugh MacRae II Collection, Wilmington, N.C.

Figure 15. The type of dwelling that was to disappear with the immigration of more whites to parts of the South.
Source: *Manufacturers Record* (May 30, 1912), p. 4.

which advocated small scale intensive farming methods. He decided to test the hypothesis set forth in Edmund Morris' book Ten Acres Enough that "the man who industriously and intelligently cultivated 10 acres of land would produce enough each year to support his family and lay up something against the rainy day."

Between 1905 and 1912, the newly formed Carolina Trucking Development company, having acquired large tracts of land along the Atlantic Coast Line Railroad, established six colonies in southeastern North Carolina. MacRae wanted to settle the colonies with European immigrants who might be more familiar with small intensive farms, and who might also be more industrious, frugal, intelligent and orderly than the southern white and Negro tenant farmers (Figure 15). Agents were hired on a commission basis to go to Europe to secure colonists. The company printed promotional brochures in various languages for distribution to potential colonists. The first efforts to entice colonists actually brought families directly from northern Italy; however, this procedure was quickly abandoned as too expensive and the agents shifted their efforts to the large pool of recent immigrants located in the northern cities.

The Ethnic Farm Colonies

The first colonies established and the first European ethnic group to settle in each were as follows: 1) St. Helena—north Italians; 2) Castle Haynes—Hollanders and Hungarians; 3) New Berlin—Germans and Hungarians; 4) Marathon—Greeks and Poles; 5) Artesia—English, Poles and Hollanders and 6) Van Eeden—Hollanders (See Figure 5 on page 18). MacRae's efforts at what he terms "human engineering" were rather unique for the South because most of the immigration of Europeans in the early 1900s remained in the industrialized Northeast and Midwest. The MacRae colonies were anomalous melting pots in the fairly homogeneous cultural landscape of the coastal South.

The overall spatial layouts of the MacRae colonies were very similar. All the settlements were established along two branch lines of the Atlantic Coast Line Railroad with the idea that the truck crops produced in the colonies would be gathered at the central produce sheds and shipped by rail to Wilmington and to northern markets. MacRae hired engineers to survey the large tracts of land and to divide each colony into a town site surrounded by ten-acre farms. A series of streets and roads ran parallel and perpendicular to the railroad and connected all the farms to the colony center. In some cases pre-existing roads were incorporated into the layout. The town blocks shown on the original survey maps contain appellations including "School Lot," "Church Lot," "Reserved—C.T.D. Co." (Carolina Trucking Development Company) and "Park." The St. Helena map dated May 24, 1906 shows symbols for many houses and other buildings and also gives the street names for the early italian colony—running perpendicular to the railroad from north to south were Verona, Sebastian, Garibaldi, Main, Rovigo, Villanova, and Milan Streets. If all the observer had as evidence was the survey map of St. Helena, there would be no question as to the ethnic origins of the initial settlers. This would not hold true, however, for all the other colonies except maybe Marathon in the case of the original Greeks. For example, Castle Haynes, with Hollanders originally, contained streets named Orange, Blossoms, Peachtree, Cedar, Mulberry, Hickory, Holly, Maple, Oak, Poplar, Rosemary, and Castle.

Figure 16. A group of Italians clearing land in St. Helena.
Source: Hugh MacRae II Collection, Wilmington, N.C.

Promotional Literature and Colonists' Perceptions

The purpose of this study is to examine the images portrayed in the promotional propaganda disseminated by the Carolina Trucking Development Company and to compare those images with the reality of the material cultural landscapes of the actual developed colonies. Evidence is available in the form of a myriad of brochures printed in English, German, Italian, French, Greek, Slovak, Polish, Hungarian and several other Slavic languages. Also, hundreds of documentary photographs are available to aid in a reconstruction of the cultural landscapes and spatial patterns of the colonies, especially St. Helena. Interviews with some of the original colonists and their descendants have provided a sense of how well the reality of life in the colonies reflected the images projected by the promotional literature. With such glowing phrases as the "Nation's Garden Spot," or "Small Farms in 'The Great Winter Garden,'" the brochures planted the impression in the minds of many of the immigrants that the colonies represented nothing less than paradise. In 1918, John and Mary Spisak, Slovakian immigrants living in the mining region of Montana, saw a newspaper advertisement and requested by mail a brochure describing St. Helena. After deciding to migrate, Mrs. Spisak had dreams during the week-long railroad journey that the Main Street of the town was lined on either side with rows of orange trees. Upon arrival, her dream images and perceptions faded away, obliterated by the two-fold reality of the unpaved street lined with poplar trees and the lack of a home in which to live.

Napoleon Perseghin, now an elderly man of 98 living in Baltimore, Maryland, originally came to St. Helena in 1907 as an immigrant from San Bellino, near Venice in northern Italy. He recalls his family being visited and shown promotional pamphlets of an agent named Ernesto Valentini. Perseghin's perception was one of fine, fertile farmland, but upon arrival in St. Helena, after what was a terrible ocean voyage on which he became seasick, he was disillusioned to find that in reality almost none of the farmland was cleared. He speaks of "all those woods and stumps" and describes the house he lived in as a shanty. Interviews with descendants of the former residents of St. Helena revealed memories of the back-breaking toil of clearing the woodland, cutting the ties for the railroad and pulling stumps (see Figure 16 on page 32).

House Types in the Colonies

The promotional pamphlets usually began by portraying in glowing language the climate of the region, the bountiful water supply and extremely fertile soils, the expected high yields of the crops, the markets, roads, health conditions, and the nearby larger town of Wilmington. Moreover, general information was provided about the available farms, the prices and terms of payment, deed restrictions and the house types available to the colonists:

> For a limited time, we will build for settlers a comfortable 3 room cottage, at a cost of $240.00 on payment of $90.00 cash, balance in 3 equal yearly payments of $50.00 each, without interest if paid when due.

This comfortable three-room cottage was described in more detail in another brochure entitled "Own a Home in North Carolina" (see Figure 14 on page 31):

> Our company agrees, for a limited time, to build for each settler, when desired, a comfortable 3-room cottage, for $240.00 and allow him to pay for it in installments covering three years. This, we believe is an offer which no other company has ever made. The cuts shown herewith give you a fair idea of the house we offer to build for you. Any slight changes in the plan, or the addition of one or more rooms, would not increase the cost a great deal.
>
> The rooms are either ceiled or plastered, as desired by the purchaser, and when finished they present a very cozy home-like appearance.

The cuts referred to show a front view, a side view, and a floor plan showing some details of the house type. The house is a simple, three-room frame structure with gable sides and a shed room at the rear. The front section contains a living room (11'4" x 13') and a bedroom (10' x 11'4") while the kitchen at the rear measures 9'8" x 9'4". The front and side views show vertical board-and-batten siding and doors with two vertical upper panels and two horizontal lower panels. A shingled stood extends about two feet over the front

Figure 17. A three-room L-shaped cottage.
Source: Hugh MacRae II Collection, Wilmington, N.C.

Figure 18. A company house in St. Helena. Source: Hugh MacRae II Collection, Wilmington, N.C.

entrance. The house is three bays wide with wooden shutters on the windows. There are three entrances 30 inches wide and two capped flues visible on the roof, one at the ridge line above the partition between the living room and the bedroom and the other two at the rear left corner of the kitchen (Figures 18 and 19).

One of the houses proposed according to this L-shaped floor plan was in the Castle Haynes colony. A sketch enclosed in a contract, dated February 26, 1906, shows a house with three rooms (a living room, kitchen and bedroom) and a brief handwritten description which reads:

> Rough ground plan of the house prepared for S. Orlich on farm M at Castle Hayne. To be finished inside with wood ceiling and outside like our other houses at Castle Hayne. House to stand on wooden posts.

A variation of the L-shaped plan, which has three adjacent rooms and no rear extension, was prevalent in the St. Helena colony (Figure 17 on page 33). Only one of these still exists, though in a dilapidated condition, and is still referred to by local residents as a "MacRae House" (Figure 19).

Documentary evidence shows that different house types existed in some of the other colonies. In a pamphlet published in Amsterdam in 1912 by Frederik Van Eeden, the typical cottage of the early Hollander colony is pictured and a sketch of the floor plan shown. The typical Van Eeden house was almost square with a pyramidal roof and two engaged porches, one on either side of a large square front living room. The rear half of the house was the location of a bedroom and a kitchen. The living room doors opened to the sides onto the porches with steps located on either side of the house.

The promotional literature which indicated that these houses were comfortable and either ceiled or plastered was, in the opinion of the daughter of one former resident of Van Eeden, somewhat overrated. She recalls that the cottages were unfinished inside, had no indoor plumbing, and were extremely cold during the winter.

Epilogue

The propaganda literature was just what it was meant to be. Many inconsistencies existed between the images conjured up by the advertisements and the reality of the situation, which the first colonists faced. However, even with the difficulty of finding the anticipated or perceived image in the real world of the six southeastern North Carolina colonies. most of the colonists agreed that MacRae himself was a kind and benevolent, somewhat paternal person who wanted more than anything to see the success of the settlers in his colonies. MacRae's colonies provided an interesting chapter in the agricultural development of the American South in the early 1900s. The settlement by ethnic Europeans was somewhat of a novelty in the region.

Figure 19. A St. Helena house after landscaping and painting. Source: Hugh MacRae II Collection, Wilmington, N.C.

THEY SAID HE WAS CRAZY
But their opinion about Hugh MacRae has changed quite a bit since then

By
JOHN MARSHALL PARHAM

THEY CALLED him crazy twenty-five years ago.

This "Crazy" Hugh MacRae of Wilmington, North Carolina, had decided to virtually "give away" land to farmers emigrated from Europe, and it was hard for some to "see any sense in it."

Mr. MacRae bought large tracts of land near Wilmington, surveyed its agricultural possibilities and carefully set off in metes and bounds the limits of what he called farming communities. Farmers were actually brought from Europe and given farm land for a small down payment, the balance to be paid at convenience.

What to the lay mind represents an absolute right of ownership and what to the lawyer represents a fee simple title was given each tenant in exchange for several notes to be met if possible ... and if not, each tenant should use the money for implements and other farming necessaries.

HUGH MacRAE, of Wilmington, had a vision, and he has lived to see his dreams come true.

The skeptics naturally thought that human nature would prompt every farmer to take advantage of "every loophole," but here's what actually did happen:

During a period when emergency calls for farm relief were being made from every section of the country, the farmers who had settled on these colonies in substantial numbers were paying off not only notes that were due but notes that would not be due until one and two years hence. While the cancerous depression was eating the core out of farming financially and otherwise all over the United States, these colonies were teeming with prosperity in comparison.

These astonishing facts together with other reasons caused the Roosevelt administration to call upon Mr. MacRae for assistance in directing a subsistence homestead project of the Department of the Interior. After a quarter of a century of farm community development, Mr. MacRae has discovered many of the requisites for the successful development of farm life, believed by many to be on the decline in the South. Mr. MacRae says, "I feel sure that we have got to rebuild our economic structure beginning at the base, which means a reshaping of rural life."

These colonies that are green the year through, some four or five in number, recall the old feudal tenures of William the Conqueror in 1066; but with vast differences. These are allodial tenures as opposed to the feudal tenures of William the Conqueror. This means that the tenant is totally independent and free to keep his own accounts, doing homage to no one, directly or indirectly, but buying land "in his own right." The plans of organization is somewhat similar.

Standard purchase contracts are issued to purchasers, stipulating a cash payment of 25 percent and annual installments of 25 percent, payable in one, two, and three years. Notes are issued as security. However, few were able to live up to these contracts. Instead of foreclosing, the settlers were given to understand that they might use their available funds to acquire livestock, farming implements and for conditioning their dwellings. Consequently, most of the settlers made no substantial payments for the first several years after locating in the colony.

Several families of Italian grape growers were the first groups to comprise a community, name "St. Helena Colony" in honor of the Italian queen. Grape culture was carried on extensively until the State Legislature enacted a prohibition law which put an end to the manufacture of wine from these grapes.

Other colonies subsequently sprang up: "Van Eeden" in Pender County, comprised of Hollanders; "New Berlin" in Columbus County, comprised of Germans; Marathon, comprised of Poles and Ruthenians; and Castle Hayne, comprised of Americans, Hollanders, Hungarians and Poles, both these latter groups being situated in New Hanover County. At first, it was thought best to keep the different nationalities set apart in distinct groups, but for purposes of Americanization, it was later decided to mix them.

Since all of these colonies are situated on convenient lines at the Atlantic Coast Line Railroad, passenger, freight and express facilities are available.

On these farms, the most scientific and efficient agricultural methods have been used. In the spring, lettuce, snap beans, English peas, and cucumbers. Summer brings an ample return of corn and forage crops followed by cover crops in the winter. Approximately 250 carloads of fresh vegetables are shipped each year from the Castle Hayne community to northern markets. Something like ten thousand cartons of flowers are shipped abroad each season.

In addition to farming operations, a goodly portion of the settlers engage in dairy farming. The output of milk in the St. Helena group one year was over seven thousand pounds. This output was sold for more than twenty-seven thousand dollars.

Thus, with the financial aid of Hugh MacRae, these farmers have been able to life mortgages from their farms and in addition, it is said, have been able to buy substantial amounts of railroad and industrial stocks in a period of depression.

And they called Hugh MacRae crazy!

JOHN MARSHALL PARHAM, *the author of this article, lives in Charlotte. He is a newspaperman and has written a number of interesting feature articles, as well as handling the usual run of news items.*

From the *Wilmington Morning Star*, May 30, 1983, p. 1D.

MacRae's dream settled area

By Betty Fennell
Staff Writer

ST. HELENA — The first European immigrants that formed six farming colonies in three Southeastern North Carolina counties between 1905 and 1909 paid $240 for a three-room house and $30 per acre for a 10-acre farm.

The immigrants were enticed to the areas because Wilmington businessman Hugh MacRae wanted to introduce innovative farming methods to the South to change a stagnated farm economy, caused by sharecropping and tenant farming, said Dr. W. Frank Ainsley, an assistant professor of geography at the University of North Carolina at Wilmington.

Figure 20. This photo was made in 1908 at the dedication of St. Joseph's Catholic Church in St. Helena.

Ainsley, who is writing a book about MacRae's role in the settlements, spoke Sunday at St. Joseph's Catholic Church in St. Helena to over 100 people, many of them descendants of those first immigrants, who came to hear more about their "roots."

The Catholic Church, which was founded around the colony in St. Helena, the first area settled, is celebrating its 75th anniversary.

Other colonies that developed along the railroad include Van Eeden in Pender County, Castle Haynes and Marathon in New Hanover County and New Berlin and Artesia in Columbus County.

MacRae, who formed the Carolina Trucking Co., printed brochures and hired agents to scout for potential families who would move to the areas, clean the forests, drain the marshlands and grow produce crops that could be shipped north by rail, Ainsley said.

Hugh MacRae II said, "Of all the work (his grandfather) did, he was more proud of this than anything else." MacRae and his sister Marguerite MacRae Boucher of Kent, England, attended the celebration.

Ainsley said that MacRae's firm wanted to insure that the communities would be prosperous and reproductive, so brides were given $5 gold pieces and each child born in the settlements was given $10 in gold.

MacRae's company also loaned families money to buy fertilizer, seeds, equipment and other things needed to farm the land successfully, Ainsley said.

Ainsley showed slides, made from photographs dating from 1905 to the early 1920s, of many of the early buildings, the railroad that ran by the town and some of the many ethnic groups who eventually came to St. Helena.

As industrial jobs drew many of the first settlers to the urbanized areas, Ainsley said other ethnic groups moved in to take their places.

George Spisak, whose parents moved to St. Helena in 1918, continues to farm. Spisak said his family grew many produce crops and owned a dairy until government inspectors put them out of business. The inspectors, Spisak said, came by about 8 a.m. one morning before his family had time to clean the cow barns and refused to let his family sell their milk.

Spisak, who rents part of his land, grows corn and soybeans.

A.L. Leimone, an Italian descendant whose family moved to the area after trying unsuccessfully to farm in South Dakota, said low prices for produce crops and high labor costs have driven many of the farmers to growing grain.

Ann Leimone said the community is dying because much of the land is rented out and many of the young people have moved away, leaving elderly farmers to carry on the tradition.

From the Survey 184855, Volumn XXII, April-October 1909, Pages 743-747, William J. Hoggson as the reference. The Charity Organization Society, 105 East 22nd Street, New York.

THE PROPOSED CO-OPERATIVE COMPANY OF AMERICA

WILLIAM J. HOGGSON

DR. FREDERIK VAN EEDEN, the most prominent scientific and literary man in Holland, whose experiments in social problems have been much discussed in papers and magazines during the last few years, has launched another venture in co-operation. In two recent visits to this country Dr. Van Eeden lectured and wrote about co-operation, and he now proposes a co-operative agricultural colony in North Carolina, the first department of an organization to be known as the Co-operative Company of America.

And an interesting project it is; doubly so, owing to the wide experience that the founder has had in his own country in co-operative work. The outline of the proposed Dutch colony m North Carolina will appear more vital after a brief rehearsal of the founder's work in Holland.

Frederik Van Eeden was born at Haarlem, Holland, in 1860, the son of a bulb grower and botanist of considerable reputation.

He was graduated from the University of Amsterdam in 1883, studied medicine and became a practicing physician in Amsterdam. Later in the same city he established with Dr. Van Renterghem, a regular clinic, where for thirteen years, hypnotic suggestion was successfully applied, not as a cure-all but as a powerful aid in the treatment of disease.

Van Eeden's literary activities have been remarkable. As a poet, dramatist, novelist and essayist, he has been a leader in Dutch literature. His dramas have been produced in Berlin as well as his own country, and two of his books The Deeps of Deliverance and The Guest, have been published in English. Other works are now being translated.

It is, however, in the line of social experiment that Dr. Van Eeden come most famous. In 1889 he bought land near Amsterdam and founded a colony which he called Walden. Here he offered equality of opportunity and individual freedom, but freedom limited by common interest.

Dr. Frederik van Eeden

The divergent views of the various elements gathered together and their unwillingness to submit to sane management and competent leadership, proved to be the rock on which the wreck of the enterprise was accomplished. The bitter lesson learned, the community reorganized and began again and a dozen other co-operative centers were established on its model, all bound together in a "union for the common ownership of the soil.

In 1903 several thousand families were made destitute in Amsterdam by the failure of a railroad strike and Dr. Van Eeden was appointed the head of a committee of relief for the unemployed. Believing that co-operation instead of charity should be the medium, he established co-operative stores and factories, and gave employment instead of distributing alms.

The plan was successful. It aimed at purity of goods, standard prices, would greatly increase its value and the security would constantly become better. The stock of the company would be divided into common and preferred. The former for tenants and the latter for prospective customers. Tenants may he eligible as stockholders only on recommendation of the general manager and acceptance by the board of trustees. They may then acquire stock representing ownership in the company, by purchase, or have stock set aside for them, to be paid for out of the earnings.

The entire details are not yet decided on, but the idea is that if the company furnishes land, houses, seed and implements, the settler shall put up a certain

---

The photographs of farms accompanying this article are from the Italian colony of St. Helena, only a few miles from the proposed colony.

Figure 21. Winter lettuce under cloth.

Figure 22. An alfalfa field.

Figure 23. Italians in the berry fields. Photos from Susan Taylor Block's *Van Eeden*.

Figure 24. Typical farm at St. Helena. Photo © UNC, Chapel Hill, NC

amount of money toward his maintenance, farm supplies and as an evidence of good faith. He will cultivate his land, "his crops will be marketed, and the proceeds, less a certain percentage, will be placed to his credit. This percentage will "be held by the company for a sinking fund for future extensions, or for carrying along the colonists over a possible crop failure.

The financial plan on which it is expected to base the new corporation is as follows: There will be two kinds of stock, preferred seven percent (not cumulative) for consumers and trustees, and for tenants and employees, common stock will be issued, receiving the entire benefits beyond interest on bonds and dividends on preferred stock. First mortgage bonds five percent, secured by land, improvements and all the assets of the company, win be offered to investors. The capital of the company will be $500,000, divided equally between common and preferred stock, but it is expected to make a start on 1,000 acres of land and test the idea before going further. This will require $100,000.

The cost of the 1,100 acre tract, of getting the organization in smooth running order, of preparing the land, building the cottages and buildings, together with the seeds, implements, supplies and mules, and of advancing supplies to colonists for a part of two years has all been carefully computed. The office expenses, and the cost of the incidentals such as taxes, etc., have been anticipated, and it is estimated that the amount mentioned ($100,000) will safely take care of everything until the returns from the crops begin to come in.

The income to be derived will be from the rent of the farms, the commissions on supplies furnished, and the handling and marketing of the products of the farms. Estimated on a basis of fifty families there should be, at least, a gross income of $12,250. The running expenses, consisting of the managers' salaries, both local and at the selling end, and incidental costs should not be over $6,750, which would leave a net return of $5,500 with which to pay interest on the bonds.

These figures are based on fifty families, occupying only about half the land. With tile addition of forty or fifty famines, which the land will support, without materially increasing the expenses, the net income by the time the entire tract is settled should be between $15,000 and $20,000.

By vote of the common stockholders (e.f the tenants and employees) a certain percentage of the amounts passing through the books as receipts for produce could be diverted into an account for dividends, which would even up the chance for entire loss on a crop to any single tenant.

Dr. Van Eeden has already investigated a large number of applicants, and out of one hundred and fifty families applying, it is believed that more than fifty will be found up to the standard. These families are all Dutch, who are known as among the best intensive farmers in the world, the thought being to inaugurate a standard of efficiency that shall be high, and maintain it. The accompanying chart indicates the produce department as one only of many activities which it is proposed to engage in, provided, of course, the initial enterprise proves the success anticipated. Each department will be distinct, controlled by the advisory board, but having its own local management.

The land it is proposed to settle first is in Fender County, North Carolina, on the Atlantic Coast Line

Railroad, about thirty miles north of Wilmington. An option has been obtained on 10,000 acres, though one tract of about 1,000 acres will be utilized for the proposed colony. The government and other reports on the soil of this section show it to be of the finest character to grow peas, beans, cabbage, lettuce, cauliflower, eggplant, corn, beets, celery, radishes, potatoes, strawberries, figs, grapes, asparagus, tomatoes, carrots, peppers, turnips, squash, onions, kale, alfalfa, vetch, clover, etc. The climate is healthful and admits of farming operations the year around, thereby adding greatly to the possibilities of the crop returns. The rainfall is plentiful and evenly distributed through the year.

Transportation facilities are excellent, and the farmers being able to market produce from this section much earlier than northern growers, the prices obtained are among the highest. The feature that the company will emphasize will be the co-operative marketing and distribution of the products. Combining these ideas with the savings effected in the purchase of supplies, great saving is expected. That such a colony should succeed is to a large extent guaranteed by what already has been done by individuals in this same section and on the same types of soil. Within a few miles of the proposed Dutch colony Lioba is the thriving Italian colony of St. Helena. The capabilities of the land have not yet been fully developed, but the results so far have been most satisfactory. There are other colonies of Poles, Dutch, and mixed races, but in none of them has been tried the co-operative principle, and it is believed that this is what is needed to bring about the best results.

The success of the new company depends on competent farmers, good land and climate, market facilities, able and honest management, and the necessary capital to purchase the land and build houses, a store, an assembly hall, and to carry the enterprise until after the first crop has been marketed. The architectural features of the houses and the attractiveness of the surroundings will receive careful attention. The settlers are ready, the land is under option, a local manager is available, and a general manager can be secured. Only the capital is needed to start work this fall ready for next spring's planting.

That the plan of operation is feasible has already been proved, for a corporation on exactly the same lines is already in existence in New York City and has been running successfully for some years.

Dr. van Eeden expects to live in the colony and to utilize the great amount of experience he has had in co-operative work by instructing the colonists in co-operative methods and aiding the management in every way possible to make a success of the movement.

Figure 25. The type of dwelling that was to disappear with the immigration of more whites to parts of the South. Source: *Manufacturers Record* (May 30, 1912), p. 4.

THE CASTLE HAYNE(S) COLONY

The Castle Haynes area of northern New Hanover County was one of the six farm colonies. For years, the area had been an old, over-used plantation until MacRae purchased the land to use for his agricultural experiment. His idea was to divide the colony into a town site surrounded by ten acre farms, thus making available small tracts of land to the individual owners who would, with pride, raise produce on their own land. The European immigrant settlers in the Castle Haynes region consisted primarily of Dutch, Greeks, Hungarians, and Poles. These settlers, seeking a new life in America, brought with them a diverse and rich cultural heritage.

In 1908, a nursery called the Horticultural Company was established on a fifty-acre plot at Castle Haynes by J. Hondius, A. van Leeuwen, and Hugo DeWitt. This company raised and imported fruit, bulbs, and ornamental shrubs and trees. In 1909, the Holland Nursery was founded by H. van Ness and E.I. Tinga. By 1912, Tinga left the Holland Nursery and moved a few miles south to form the thirty-acre Tinga Nursery at Wrightsboro. These nurseries became the foundation of the flower and bulb industry of the Castle Haynes area (the "s" was dropped from the spelling of Castle Haynes by the Railroad).

Several former residents of the Netherlands started growing bulbs. At first they had imported the bulbs from Holland via New York. These men, A. Ludek, E.I. Tinga, Dirk Boet, and Peter Buis, soon realized that by selling flowers rather than bulbs, and by selling directly to New York, they could make much more profit. The North Carolina Bulb and Flower Growers Association was founded in 1928. In 1946, a horticultural research station was established at Castle Hayne. During some of the peak production years in the 1950s, approximately 1,500 acres were planted in flowers (mostly gladiolas, daffodils, and irises), and the growers brought in about $3 million annually.

One of the most successful growers was Adrain Ludeke. Ludeke, a former butler from The Hague, came to New Jersey in 1907. Tiring of city life, he moved to Castle Haynes in 1911, and bought a ten-acre farm and house. Ludeke began selling vegetables, and by 1920 had become very successful. Much of his success came from his discovery of how to "trick" his flowers into blooming earlier or later by adjusting the temperatures of his cold storage plant. According to Ludeke, the key to success was "hard work, economical living, and using sense."

Another nurseryman from Boskoop, Holland, Hadrian Verzaal, learned horticulture under a distributive education program in Holland. A few years after coming to Castle Haynes in 1916, he became manager of MacRae's Audubon Nursery (which was formerly located in Audubon Park at the corner of Floral Parkway and Park Avenue behind Hanover Shopping Center). After a few years, Verzaal bought the nursery from MacRae and continued to run it successfully until early 1930s.

Surnames of Dutch Immigrants in Castle Hayne(s)

Boet	Mijers
Braak	Dosterwyk
Drevyn	Tinga
Grott	van Bavel
Hondius	van de Kalie
Langenburg	Verzaal
Ludeke	Vogels

THE VAN EEDEN COLONY

Van Eeden was one of MacRae's colonies, a Utopian-type venture done in partnership with the Dutch physician, poet, writer, and dreamer, Dr. Frederik van Eeden who wanted to establish a "Walden" in America—Waldens, as Henry Thoreau's Walden, and van Eeden's Walden in Bussum, Holland. According to Dr. van Eeden, the underlying principle of the colony was to be the common ownership of the soil. All colonists would be equal and all would work for the common good.

This cooperative colony was established in 1909 in Pender County just two miles south of Watha, N.C. Van Eeden's promotional book, *Van Eeden Kolonie*, described the area as never being too hot, never too cold, never too wet, and never too dry. He was obviously stretching the truth when he claimed that as many as seven consecutive crops could be grown there in a single year.

By 1912, the first Dutch colonists began arriving on the newly cleared ten-acre tracts, and soon after, many new families lived in Van Eeden. These Dutch families faced some hardships such as harsher winters than they had expected and very poor drainage in the Van Eeden area.

By 1939, most of them had moved on to Wilmington or to some more distant places, and for a few months the farm community was used as a settlement site for Jewish refugees from Europe. Only remnants of the street patterns and some vague outlines of the ten-acre farm survey pattern can be discerned at the site today.

Hugh MacRae had seen that the answer to the rural farm problem in the South was to bring in from the outside a class of motivated, industrious farm workers. His solution was to bring European farmers as independent and, therefore, prideful landowners of their own ten-acre farms. Due to MacRae's dreams and efforts in agricultural colonization, many Dutch families decided to come to Castle Haynes and Van Eeden, and eventually became prosperous and prominent citizens of the Cape Fear Region.

Surnames of Dutch Immigrants in Van Eeden

Bosma
De Jong
De Rueter
Dijkers
Dviksen
Koen
Kuyl
Leeuwenberg
Mol
Peterson
Plevier
Riesz
Meier
Rond
Schoctenhuis
Sluyter
Smit
Snyder
Swart
van Roekel
van Till
Vanderwall
Wilderboer
Blom
Bennik
Dersen

End of citation from Dr. Frank Ainsley

EXAMPLES OF HOMES IN THE VAN EEDEN COLONY

Figure 26. A house freshly purchased for the 1939 settlement from the original Dutch Van Eeden tract. Photo from *Van Eeden* by Susan Taylor Block. Source: Manfred and Ann Loeb Collection: North Carolina Collection, University of North Carolina Library at Chapel Hill.

William Robert van Roekel, a son of Jan and Willemina, identified the house in Figure 26 as being similar to the home he remembered as a boy in Van Eeden.

Figure 27. Van Eeden tracts with houses.

VAN EEDEN TODAY

Figure 28. All of the homes are now gone in Van Eeden. Many were moved to other locations. These two pictures show Van Eeden as it is today.

Life in America

Jan and Willemina build their lives in the new country.

I guess we have all heard stories of someone being sold swamp land. This is another of those stories, but it was not intended to be that way.

Unfortunately, everything does not always work out the way it was intended. Susan Block's book shows the Dutch immigrants digging the drain fields. The drainage efforts worked well for Penderlea, but we are told that before World War I began, steam shovels were used to dig the drainage systems. For reasons that are unclear, the digging stopped on the advent of the war and never resumed again, mainly because so many of the inhabitants of Van Eeden had moved on to neighboring towns to find work. Immigrants are resourceful people. They had to find a way to feed themselves and their families. There were not many handouts in those days.

Jan and Willemina Leave North Carolina

Eight months after landing in Van Eeden-Watha, Jan and Willemina were blessed with a baby boy, William Robert van Roekel. Some time later when they could no longer endure the hardships in Van Eeden, they moved to South Carolina, either Sumpter or Charleston. Jan found work as a tenant farmer growing vegetables. The work was very hard, the hours were long, and the pay was meager. While they were there, Jan contracted either yellow fever or scarlet fever and was hospitalized for several weeks. We have no idea how Willemina and the child survived during that time, but survive they did.

One of the acquaintances they had made on the voyage from Holland got word of their difficult times and invited Jan and Willemina to join them in the Athens-Battle Creek area. So off they moved, yet again, to Michigan. My dad said he thought the name of the family they moved near was "Scalpel" or "Scapel." He was not sure of the spelling or even if that was exactly that name.

Jan was not afraid of hard work, even though he preferred to be the supervisor if at all possible. He was the designer, creator, initiator type. Dad said Jan liked being the "director."

He took a job as a night watchman at the Kellogg Sanitorium. Dr. Harvey Kellogg started a health spa and became quite renowned for advocating yogurt enemas and a lifestyle of complete celibacy, even among marrieds. He was 100 years ahead of his time in promoting colonics. A movie was made several years ago called "Wellville" that portrayed some of their practices. Anthony Hopkins played the part of Dr. Kellogg.

Grandpa worked at the sanitorium at night and farmed during the day. My dad recounts being "directed" at the age of four to go to the large fields and pick the worms off the cucumber plants and put them in a can of oil. That was hard work for a tot of only four. Grandma was a maid in the Kellogg household, presumably the Dr. Harvey Kellogg family.

Jan, we are told, would plant the crops at the time they would have been planted in Holland, which was much too early for the Michigan area. The crops would come up and then freeze, and he would have to replant.

The winters there were difficult. Harsh winter storms would create roof-high walls of snow between the barn and the house during the winter. It was in these conditions that Willemina delivered their second son, Hendrick (Henry) John van Roekel on February 21, 1918. It was a bitter cold,

24-degree morning when Henry was born.

Jan became discouraged with the crop failures and the night work. He wrote to either Hugh MacRae or Herman Vogel in 1920 asking if there were any opportunities there in Watha-Van Eeden. They informed Jan that they had developed a contact in the Wilmington area that would take all the milk that Jan could produce if he would move back. The company wanting the milk was the White Milk and Cream Company.

I can hear Grandpa now, "Well, Honey, we're selling the farm and moving back to that warm country of North Carolina."

Life Back in North Carolina

We are not sure where Jan settled his family when they returned to North Carolina, but Dad was old enough to remember that they had a nicer house than the one they lived in before in Watha-Van Eeden. Jan purchased cows from some of the other settlers who were moving on and set up a dairy. Not long after the dairy was in operation, Jan was told that White Milk and Cream Company did not need as much milk as they had thought, and he would need to find another source for distributing his milk supply. Things don't always turn out the way you expect. Sigh ... sigh.

A friend named Mr. Johnson (we are not sure if this was Alvin Johnson) at a local store heard of Jan's plight and told him that he had a friend in Belfast, North Carolina, north of Goldsboro, who had an empty barn. Johnson thought his friend would let Jan use the barn until things got a bit better. We can only suppose that the farmer allowed them to live in a house on the farm. Jan put the cows on the train and headed to Belfast.

Things finally got better, and Jan bought a refrigerant device from Dillard Device Company to artificially refrigerate milk, and ice would no longer be needed. Jan was apparently the first dairyman to buy such a device, and it gave him a competitive edge over the other farmers since it kept the milk cool longer. Quality control in those days was not what it is today. The inspector would hold the bottle up and look for any dirt in the bottom of the bottle.

After a few years, things improved enough that Jan was able to move once more, this time to an area near what was the old airport near the community of Grantham. Seymore Johnson Air Force Base is not far from there now. Jan bought the Dewey Brothers Farm, and their third child, Otiena Hendrika, was born there on April 22, 1924. Otiena was my mother.

[Note: My mother, Otiena, and my father were divorced when I was a small child. They had one more child, a son, before their divorce. Otiena was unable to provide for all of her children by herself, so she permitted me to be adopted by her brother and sister-in-law, William and Mary Elizabeth Howard van Roekel, who had no children. They were Dad and Mom to me.]

With the help and hard work of his son, William (my dad), then an eleven-year-old young man, Jan built a prosperous, thriving dairy and milk delivery business. Dad told me of getting up between four and five o'clock in the morning to milk the cows, and then he and Jan delivered the milk to homes in the area.

Forty years after he sold the dairy, Dad found a milk bottle with dried milk in it on a "getting place" (trash pile). The milk bottle was from his dad's dairy. We have kept it as a gift to remember the past years of hard work of my forefathers.

Jan's family was complete with the birth of John William (Johnnie) on February 20, 1926. But Jan was restless to move on to other things. He sold the dairy in 1928 to a Mr. Sasser. Dad said Mr. Sasser never fully paid for the dairy because of the depression that came in 1929.

Figure 29: Brogden Middle School, Dudley, North Carolina, across the street from the van Roekel home.

Figure 30: First location of Van Roekel Florist, corner of Chestnut and James Streets.

Figure 31: Earlene Culbreth van Roekel, John William's wife.

The Founding of Van Roekel Florist

After selling the dairy, the van Roekel family moved to Dudley, North Carolina, about five miles south of Goldsboro. Dudley physically resembles the Lunteren area of Holland. The house they purchased is still there, across the road from Brogden Middle School (see Figure 29), which was a high school for many years. The house was purchased from Mr. Tom Nallwood, a banker for Nations Bank in Goldsboro. Mr. Nallwood had a peach orchard there called "Peacharena" that had to be destroyed after a disease infected the peach trees.

Jan bought the house and started a new and different business venture. He became a large volume flower farmer and a participant in the Flower Growers' Association. He rented and leased as much land as possible and grew flowers for shipment to New York and other markets. I have fond memories of walking through the fields there near their home.

The name of the new company was "Say it with

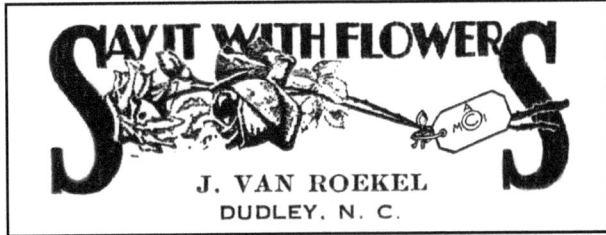

Figure 32: The Van Roekel Florist logo, "Say It With Flowers," from an old postcard. (See Appendix, page 134.)

Flowers." Grandpa used the logo for forty or more years before FTD began using it (See Figure 32 below.) (See copy of envelope on page 134 in Appendix.)

The move to Dudley was the final move that my grandparents made. They had found a place that felt like their home in Holland. It was the next best thing to going home, which they had desired to do at different times in their lives. When Jan became old and senile, the local people would find him walking down the road trying to find his way back to the "ol' country."

Jan's last business venture began in the 1940s. The story goes that Jan sent William, his eldest son, to a training course on how to arrange flowers. William returned and taught the rest of the family what he had learned. That was the beginnings of Van Roekel Florist. It is a testament to resourcefulness, hard work, and family unity.

The first building that housed Van Roekel Florist was located on the corner of Chestnut and James Streets in Goldsboro (see Figure 30 above). That building has now been torn down. I have many memories of being in that florist shop when I was a little tot, three to five years old. I remember Grandma giving us a few coins to go up the street to the drug store or the hardware store to buy a box of Cracker Jack, caramel coated popcorn treats. I can still picture her sitting there in her wheelchair chattering away as those gnarled fingers and hands

Figure 33. Second location of Van Roekel Florist, corner of Ashe and Slocum Streets.

Figure 34: Van Roekel Florist as it is today at the same location in Goldsboro.

swirled stems of flowers onto sticks that would soon be used in the flower sprays. Grandma had developed rheumatoid arthritis, which affected her severely in her elbows, hands, hips, knees and feet. She became an invalid in later years.

When Jan passed away, the florist business was left to his youngest son, John William. John grew and diversified the business, eventually moving it to its present location on the corner of Slocum and Ashe Streets. (See Figures 33 and 34 above.) Ironically, this location is only a few blocks from Willowdale Cemetery where Jan and Willemina are interred, as well as their daughter, Otiena, and their daughter-in-law, Earlene Culbreth van Roekel, John William's first wife (Figure 31 on page 47).

Jan and Willemina returned to Holland only once, in May 1931, to sell the farm to his friend A.J. Bos. Willemina was thrilled to see her family one more time. Truly, had their sons, William and Henry, not been left behind in America, she would have stayed in Holland. She wanted to be home with her family. Figure 43 on page 52 is a letter that Willemina wrote to her family in Hollard six weeks after their return to America. Figure 44 on page 52 is a depiction of the ship that carried them home.

Willemina was the first to pass away, on June 7,

Figure 35: The van Roekel home in Dudley, North Carolina, Highway 117, across from Brogden Middle School.

1969. Jan, senile and lonely, died almost six months later on December 6, 1969. Their passing left a hole in the hearts of all who loved them, but it also left a legacy, a proud and rich legacy of two phenomenal Dutch immigrants. We miss them.

Some years after Jan and Willemina passed on, my mother, Otiena, purchased their house from John William. She completely remodeled the inside of the house. Much of the outside was left as it was in the 1950s, except she added the front porch rail and took down all of the outside buildings to the left of the house. (See Figure 35 above.)

The Legacy

Jan and Willemina ... A love story ... A story about overcoming the odds ... A story of dreamers leaping out to make their dreams come true ... A story of the hardships of millions of immigrants who came to America to seize the opportunities ... A story of hard work, over achieving, and making a valuable contribution to what is America—a land of opportunity ... A story of reaching beyond, in faith, to levels their families would say, even now looking back ... it is a remarkable story ...

Thank you for your legacy, your investment in those of us who are left—your descendants.

Their journey ended on December 6, 1969. What of them have we taken with us? We honor them when we are reasonable risk takers who take a leap of faith and overcome, and when we have a faith in the Creator and faith in ourselves.

Willemina must have had some clairvoyant insight that the young man she saw standing across the way in Arnhem that warm August day was such a man of faith, risk, firmness, values, and passion. She balanced all that about Jan with her own faith, lovingkindness, patience, dedication, and wisdom.

Thank you, God, for their lives!

WILLOWDALE CEMETERY, Goldsboro, North Carolina

Figure 36: Entry gate into Willowdale Cemetery, Goldsboro, N.C., where Jan and Willemina are interred.

Figure 37: Grave stones of Jan and Willemina van Roekel. Side by side for eternity.

Figure 38: The grave stone of Jan van Roekel. The actual dates should be Aug. 24, 1885 and Dec. 6, 1969.

Figure 39: Grave stone of Willemina van Deelen van Roekel—12/31/1887-6/7/1969. We believe there are three discrepancies on her stone: 1) the spelling of her name was Willemina, not Wilhelmina. 2) The spelling of her maiden name was van Deelen, not Van Daleen. 3) She was born in 1887, not 1882.

Figure 40: Grave marker of Otiena van Roekel Bradbury, Jan and Willemina's daughter.

Figure 41: Grave marker of Otiena's second husband, James Thomas Bradbury.

Figure 42: Death certificates for Willemina and Jan. As on the grave stones, we believe some of the information is incorrect on Willemina's death certificate. See Figure 39 on page 50 for details.

Above right, Willemina van Roekel's Memorial Obituary.

A TRIBUTE published in the pages of THE GOLDSBORO NEWS ARGUS GOLDSBORO, N.C.

JUN 9 1969

Memorial Obituary

Entered Into Eternal Rest
Saturday, June 7, 1969

MRS. WILHELMINA VAN D. VAN ROEKEL

Funeral services for Mrs. Wilhelmina Van Dalen Van Roekel, 86, of Rt. 1, Dudley, who died Saturday night, will be held tomorrow at 4 p.m. at Seymour Funeral Home Chapel by the Rev. Jean Hood and Rev. Donner Lucas. Burial will be in Willow Dale Cemetery.

Surviving are her husband, J. Van Roekel; three sons, Johnny and Henry Van Roekel of Goldsboro, and William Van Roekel of Wilson; one daughter, Mrs. Otina Bradbury of Rockville, Md.; 10 grandchildren and three great-grandchildren. Her grandsons will serve as pallbearers.

Figure 43: Translated letter from Willemina to the family in Holland in 1932. See original copy in Appendix.

Dear Brother and Sister and children,

We are back home again for about 6 weeks. We were thinking of visiting you once more before leaving, but traveling from one place to the other was difficult with the 2 children. [Otiena and John Willam accompanied their parents on the trip while William was left on the farm in Dudley and Henry was left with friends in Baltimore.]

We are happy though that we could see you all, some for the first time. We enjoyed it very much and we thank you for your hospitality in your cozy home. Do you know how mother is doing?

Jan has visited her a few times, and she was still the same. How are you all, healthy we hope? How are Otina and the others? Please write us a long letter. We love to hear from Holland and how Jan's mother is doing. Aunt, I am happy that I have been to Holland once more and that I could visit with you all. I only knew a few of Jan's relatives. Jan wants to know how Bart is. Please send us his address, so we can write to him. Please Aunt, don't wait too long with sending us a letter. When we left you we visited Jan and he recognized Jan immediately and we stayed with them for a while. Then Jan joined us and we went to Henry's and we stayed overnight there. I think they are doing very well; her husband is a very nice man.

The next day we went by train to Hoenderloo and a week later Jan went again to Jans, and he got the flu there, but he is ok now. Jan tells me that he also saw Gerrit van de Woert, who visited Jan to meet Jan again and he looked great.

Although we are far away we think a lot about you and how nice it was to be with you and talk and Jan upstairs with Gijs. Jan has been seasick for half a day, but the children and I had no problem. When I was home for a week it got very hot here, it is a bit cooler now, but no frost during the night like in Holland. Our flowers are still beautiful.

Now I will end with sending you our warmest greetings also from Jan and the children to all of you, also Tina and Jan and Ger. And Gijs.

Mina

Figure 44: Postcard of the TSS Statendam, the ship used in Jan's and Willemina's passage back to America in 1931. It was sent back to Holland to Hendricus's family after their arrival back home in North Carolina.

Jan and Willemina with son, William Robert.
(Photo provided by Henni Buitenhuis, a cousin in Holland, son of Aunt Ger [Grace].)

Jan and Willemina at home in Dudley, North Carolina, the later years.

Jan van Roekel was a handsome specimen in his distinguished Yellow Riders uniform.

Jan van Roekel:
8-24-1885 – 12-6-1969

History of the Man and the Name

Jan van Roekel served his required military duties in the Gele Rijders, an elite division of the Dutch military. He was assigned to the Korps Rijdend Artillerie (Gele Rijders), a part of the Mobile Artillery Corps and 4th Field Artillery Regiment (Veldartillerie) from March 1905 until July 13, 1913. Jan saw no actual conflict because Holland declared itself a neutral power and was not directly involved in World War I. They were, however, on alert status.

It should be noted that Jan was discharged one year after he moved to America. We believe he was detained at the hotel at Ellis Island for an extra day because he was still enlisted in the military. Immigration authorities were prompted to hold him an extra day to ensure that he was not Absent Without Leave (AWOL). See Appendix (154-155) for letters from Rijksarchief and Landmacht concerning Jan's military records.

Figures 46 and 47 on pages 56 and 57 are photocopies of Jan's officer placement in Arnhem and his registration in the regimental roll of the Korps Rijdende Artillerie (Gele Rijders / Yellow Riders).

Jan was a risk taker. He enjoyed being the director. Some thought he liked being the director too much. He did have a tender side about him, even though much of the time he was all about business.

Unfortunately, he was an older man when I could truly understand who he was. He was 62 when I was born. It is difficult to comprehend how much he had done in his lifetime.

Jan was a religious man. He had a Dutch commentary from which he studied the Bible in detail to prepare his "brush arbor" evangelistic rallies. He built several churches. Oak Heights is one church we can identify that he built. He and Grandma were members of the Oak Street Pentecostal Holiness Church until they died. That church is known today as the First Pentecostal Holiness Church. It was one of the very first churches of that denomination, which is now worldwide.

Figure 45: Statue of Gele Rijder in Arnhem, Holland.

Jan is pronounced as Yan (not with a "J" sound) in the Dutch language. He was a physical specimen even at age 84. He had a full head of hair and could have been thought to be only in his 60s. He would eat up to 12 to 18 raw eggs a day to give him plenty of protein. I think he had learned in the military that lots of protein would keep him strong, and it worked for him. Jan was only 5'6" and had a solid frame with no fat on it.

I can clearly remember watching my grandfather tussle with my sister, Katherine Fredricka

(Kay). She would relent to his strength, and two minutes later, they would be tussling again. I remember this 6-feet 3-inch, 180-pound young man having his hand shaken by that "old man." Jan would just grin as I went to my knees with that powerful grip. If I did not give up with the simple handshake, he would grab his own thumb to use as leverage to grind his knuckles into the back side of my hand. If neither of these tactics worked, then he would head-butt me in the chest. It did not take long to realize he was not a man with whom to tussle.

My fondest memories of Jan were when he would take Dad and me out into the field and cut a bouquet of flowers for us to take home. We went to Goldsboro from where we lived in Wilson about every third Sunday. I remember with fondness anticipating the cleanly raked driveway all along the house. I particularly remember the huge fields of dahlias of all sorts and colors. That smell always takes me back to their home in Goldsboro. I lived two houses down from them the first four years of my life.

Jan became senile in his 60s. After Grandma passed away, Jan became a lonely old man with only distant memories. The night he died, he was walking along the highway, "going to the ol' country," when he stepped into the path of a car. The doctor who attended to him said he had the heart and lungs of a 50-year-old man. Maybe hard work is good for you. He died on December 6, 1969, due to the accident.

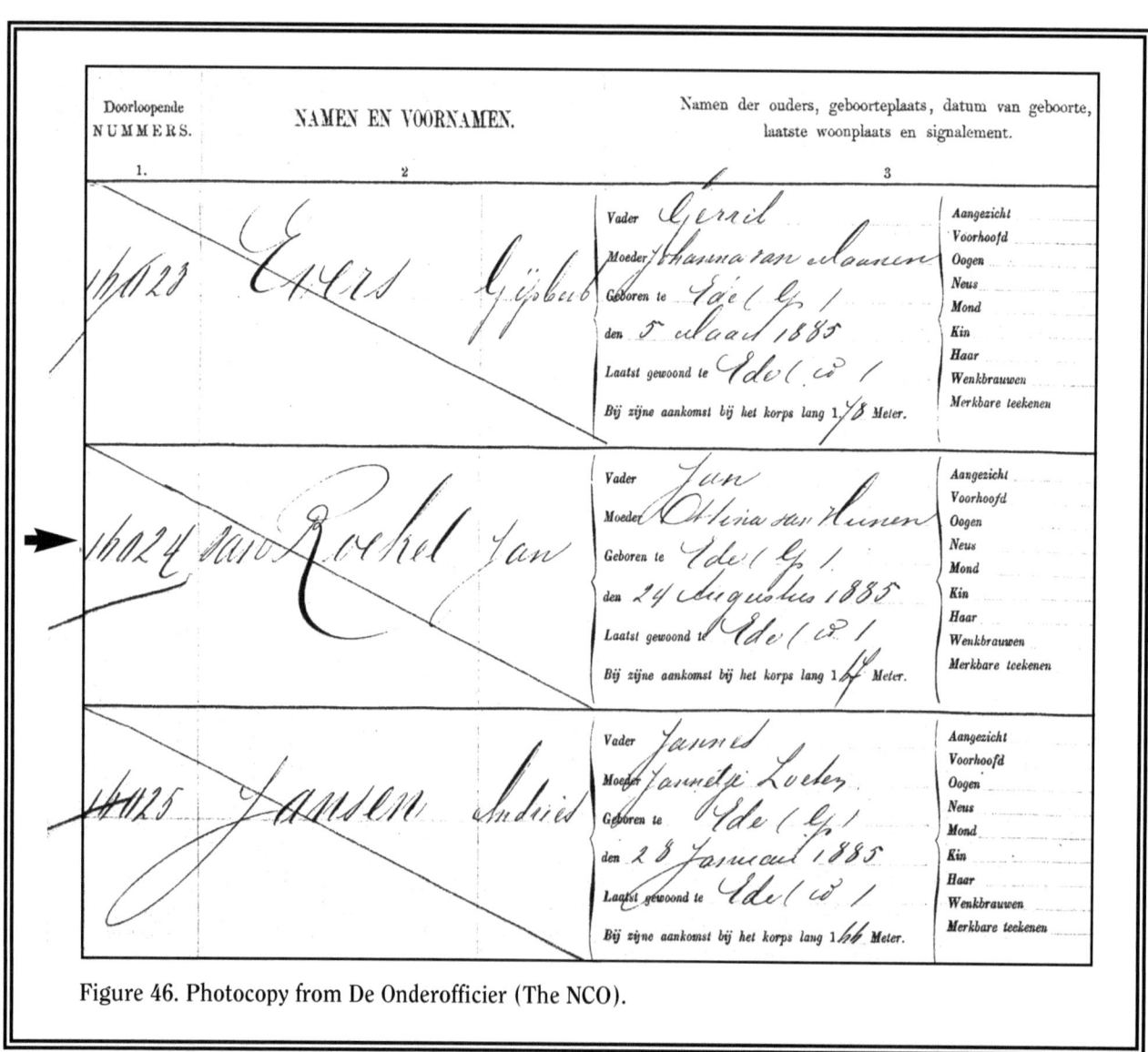

Figure 46. Photocopy from De Onderofficier (The NCO).

The Name "van Roekel"

All van Roekels are most likely related. Even though several branches seem unattached, they probably have some relative who is common to all. The three branches are Arnhem, Wageningen, and Bennekom. The Bennekom branch is found near Eed, which is also near the towns of Lunteren, Otterlo, and Roekel. It is believed that all of the branches are related because of a subtle reason: the branches were all bakers by trade. (The names Backer and Bakker will be discussed later.) It is also relevant to note that these towns are reasonably close to each other in the Gelderland area of Holland.

The village of Roekel has been shown on maps as far back as the 1700s. Roekel was located just west of the town of Otterlo. The village or hamlet that stood there in the early 1900s no longer exists. There is just an open field surrounded by forest. One can find three roads there with Roekel in their names: Roekels bossum, Roekeles Weg, and RoekelZand.

From the history section on Gijsbertus's website, we learn that "in 1811, upon the introduction of the official civil registration by Napoleon Bonaparte, everyone had to take a last name." This was a period of time when Napoleon had control of Holland. The last name was most often derived from either the location of the person's residence or from their profession.

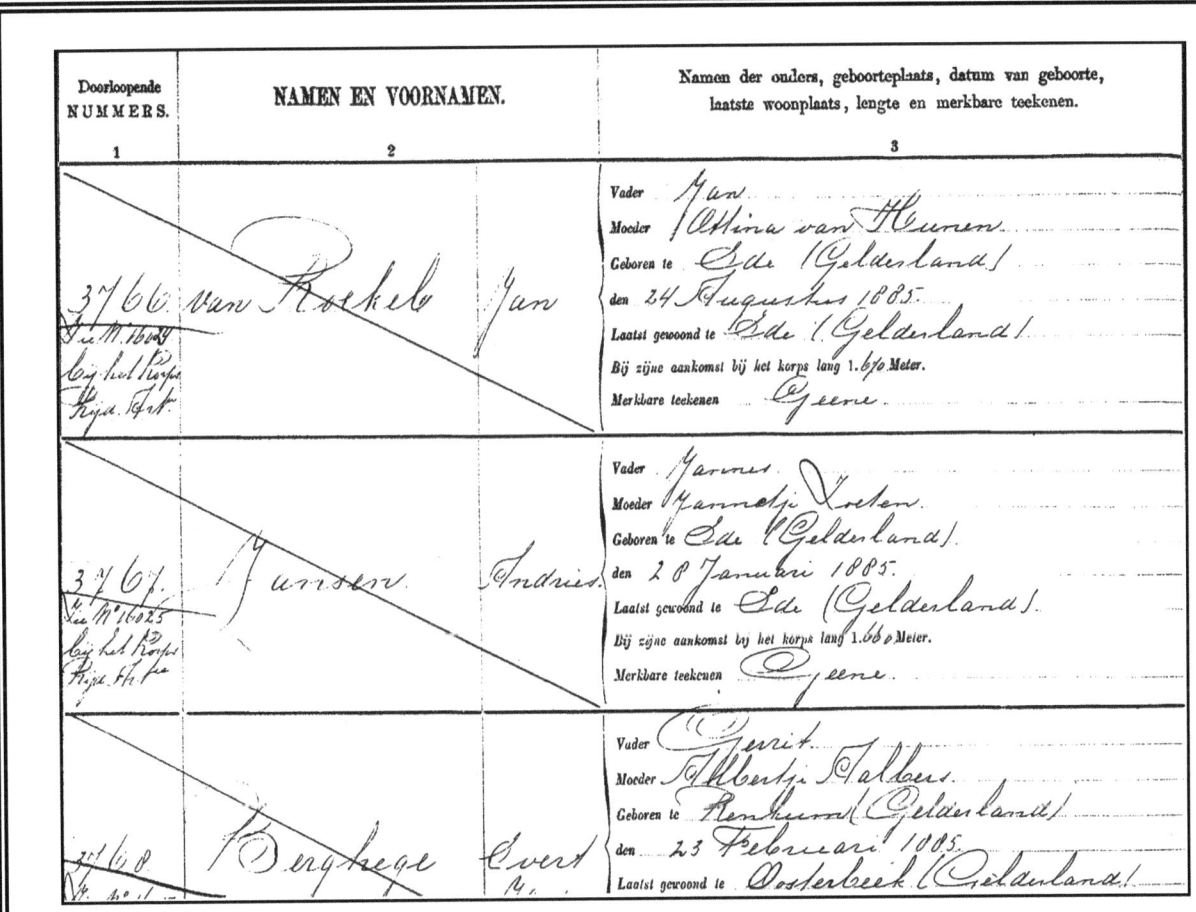

Figure 47. Photocopy from Prins Willem-Alexanderhof accompanying copies of the registration of Jan van Roekel in the regimental roll of the Korps Rijdende Artillerie (Gele Rijders / Yellow Riders) from March 1905 and —since April 1911 in the regimental roll of the 4th regiment Valdartillerie (Field Artillerie. He left the army on July 31, 1913.

The name "van Roekel" came into being when Napoleon, the occupying ruler, decreed that everyone was to have a surname. The van Roekels lived on the edge of a small forest. The "Roek" comes from the root word for a blackbird, or a "rook." The "el" is a new Dutch word for "forest." "Van" is the Dutch word for "from" and is usually used in the lower case. Thus, the name "van Roekel" (Roek-el) means "from the place where the rooks roost in the forest," in the Hoge Veluwe Wild Life preserve.

The Hamlet of Roekel

From page five of the book, *The Family van Roekel*, we find a pencil drawing of "Roekel at the end of the 19th century." Roekel was a hamlet surrounded by farms, fields, and forests, in the middle of a rugged area. From the hamlet's name came the names "Roekels' Forest" and "Roekels Dunes." Dunes in the area were called "bunts." Together with the nearby Gijsselt, the former hamlet of Vinckelt near the village Kootwijk and Mossel, Roekel is part of the late medieval forest names, which are combinations of bird names with "Loo" for forest. "Loo" was old terminology that was later changed to "el," meaning "forest." Even though there is no early mention of the forest Roekel, there is a 1328 registration of a family named Rokel and a few maps from the 17th century that show Rokel." View the pencil drawing of a farm in Roekel in Figure 48 below.

Figure 48: Roekel community in Holland near Otterlo in 1900, by S. Mesda-van Houten. The drawing is found on page five of *The Family van Roekel*. Municiple Museum in Arnhem, inventory #GM 8805, Print # 45.

More historical information found in "The van Roekel Family in the Gelderland"

In the property tax listing of the Veluwe date 1328, we find the first mention of the name van Roekel. It speaks of a property owner named Johan van Roekel (or Rokel). This tax listing gave the name of the principle owner of the property. Johan is among those whose names are related directly to the modern Roekel, Mossel.

In Whitkamps *1877 Geographic Dictionary*, we read, "Roekel, Hamlet in the village of Ede, Providence of the Gelderland, surrounded by farm, fields, and forests in a rugged area.

The forest mentioned in 1877 is still in existence today as Roekels' forest. This forest originally contained 15 farms, as written in the 19th century. These farms together formed the forest marked as the Roekels' forest. The overseer, the man in charge (feudal lord), of this area was the Baron van Heeckeren to Wassenaer to Twickel, as the master of the house of Kernhem.

The oldest van Roekels

We have already mentioned the first person of record, Johan van Roekel. In the same 14th century, we find van Roekels in the city of Arnhem. Arnolds van Roekel and his wife, Bessela, transferred ownership of some rental property on 24-11-1353. In the 15th century we find the following accounts:

01/08/1409 Goiswyn van Roekel and his wife transfer rental property.
01/03/1414 The same as mentioned earlier, Johan van Roekel and his wife Alyt in 1414, settle the property of a deceased Woude van Roekel in Arnhem.
00/00/1415 Again Johan van Roekel is mentioned as a property owner.
00/00/1424 We find the widow of Johan van Roekel mentioned as the mother of Styn van Roekel who is married to Roloff.
18/03/1427 Transfer of some property by Aleyt van Roekel to her son, Hendrick van Roekel. She transferred ownership of a house and farm in Rijnstreet.
00/00/1432 Alyet transfers about 32 acres of land to a monastery of St. Nicholas in Arnhem.
13/01/1446 Styne van Roekel told that the financial obligations for her home is paid off.

Van Roekels in Wageningen

Much more recently, we have accounts of van Roekels in the town of Wageningen. They were known as van Roekel(t)s.

I have been told that the "t" at the end of many surnames was really a cross, indicating that they were Christian.

22-01-1714 There was a transfer of the estate of Jan van Roekel, namely, to his brothers Steven and Hendrick Kemp van Roekel. The two are mentioned with Jan concerning land situated in Wageningen. They also sold a home in the Hoogstreet (Highstreet) area. The same Jan sells a parcel of land to his brother, Steven. A parcel belonging to his brother, Hendrick, is mentioned as being adjacent to the land being sold.
09/07/1711 Hendrick van Roekelt and his wife, Eizabeth, from Brummenkt sell a parcel of farm land.
02/07/1712 Jan sells land in Wageningen again.
17/09/1728 Jan appears to have died. His wife, Catrijn Schreaet, sells the land on Buijse steeg.
24/07/1722 Steven van Roekel has rental debt of 162 guilders and 10 nickles.

It is interesting to follow the entries from the books of the bakers guild in Wageningen. We find the following entries: In 1772 and 1740, Hendrick van Roekelt is a guild member, and in 1742, 1761, 1781, and 1789, Willem van Roekelt is shown as a member.

So what can we do with these "oldest van Roekels"? The van Roekels in Arnhem are undoubtedly descendants of the van Roekels mentioned in the 4th century, Johan van Roekel. It could be, however, that this line died out.

The van Roekels of Wageningen and Bennekom can be established. For one, they had the same profession—bakers. They also had the same name.

Here is the hypothesis of how it may have been: N.N. (No Name) van Roekel(t) about 1615 is possibly the same person as Derck van Roekel. Willem Derks or Willem Baker was forefather of the family van Roekel from the Bennekom area (Bakers in Bennekom). N.N. van Roekel(t) was forefather of the Wageningen branch (Bakers in Wageningen).

Van Roekel Heraldry

Figure 49: Colorized graphic artist rendition of the van Roekel Coat of Arms. Produced from the data supplied by Gijs van Roekel.

Van Roekel Coat of Arms or Wapen (weapon)

Figure 50: The van Roekel crest found in the Posthumous section in the Central Agency for Genealogy in The Hague.

Having a coat of arms is not the sole right of the noble families. In the Netherlands, about 25,000 coats of arms of the original families are known. Most of the original crests can be found in the Central Agency for Genealogy in The Hague. A van Roekel crest was found there but in a completely different location from the usual. The van Roekel crest was found in the Posthumous section. See Figure 50 above.

The description of this coat is as follows: Three gold stars within a silver heart-shaped shield in a red field. Furthermore it states: In the first quarter of the silver are 3 red otellens, vertical bars, horizontally in line. In the second quarter, there are three red medallions. The shield is diagonally bisected. The helmet symbol is a star. Above is a rendition of this coat of arms.

A second coat of arms was found as well from a gentleman from Groningen. The origin is unknown. The description is as follows: A diamond shaped shield, bisected. The right side contains a left facing upright lion. The left side has three flowers, two above and one below. Between the flowers is a ring. The helmet signal is a French lily. See figure 51 below for a rendition.

We have included both renditions of the coat of arms, even though we obviously cannot say for certain which is the authentic one. Our preference, however, is for the one in Figure 49 that came from the CAG in The Hague because it has a sure historical background.

Figure 51: A wapen of unknown origin provided by a gentleman from Groningen.

Willemina Hendrika van Deelen van Roekel, age 21, a beautiful young woman.

Willemina Hendrika van Deelen van Roekel:
12-31-1887 – 6-5-1969

History of the Lady and the Name

Willemina. What a stunning woman she was! Her immigration papers showed her height as 5-foot 7-inches, but those who knew her when she was younger knew she was much taller. All of her children and most of her grandchildren got their 6-foot frames from her. I think she was closer to 5-foot 9-inches in her youth.

Willemina was a typical Dutch woman, a bit big boned, but not large. A fine lass she was. It is no wonder Jan could not take his eyes off her that warm August day in 1911 when they first met.

Her family nickname was "Mies," even though she often signed her correspondence "Mina." She truly exemplified what a Christian woman should be. Any qualities that Jan may have been a bit short in, she had. Like Jan, she was intelligent, and her caring was immersed in sincere warmth. The joke of the family was that as Jan was counting his savings and trying to invest in other ventures in the back bedroom, Willemina was in the living room being philanthropic. She would have given you the shirt right off **Jan's** back.

She was stricken with rheumatoid arthritis in her fifties and later with congestive heart disease. She was wheelchair bound from her fifties to mid sixties. Then she became bedridden for the rest of her life. An amazing thing about her was that in all of those years, I never heard her complain about her condition or about her pain in those gnarled hands and feet. What a courageous, industrious, caring grandmother.

Willemina was smart and curious. She knew everything that was going on from Dudley to Goldsboro, and yet she never left her bedroom. She was intellectually sharp until the day she died at age 81 on June 5, 1969.

She always kept a "broken English" accent. My nickname was "Herbie," but, she pronounced it "hubby." I can still hear her say, "Hubby, you be a good boy, and do what your mommy and daddy tell you to do."

She sent me one letter when I was in college. It had no capital letters and no punctuation, just a string of words. I had to figure out what she was saying. What a precious letter. Somehow it has become lost, but it's not lost in my heart.

Grandma had a special quality about her. Even though she had four children and nine grandchildren, she would make each one feel as if they were the "special one." What a wonderful grandmotherly way to be. Yet, she was the "special one." I truly miss them both.

Willemina and Jan are buried at Willowdale Cemetery off of Williams Street in downtown Goldsboro, North Carolina. Their daughter, Otiena, who is my mother, is interred about a block away, as is her daughter-in-law, Earlene Culbreth van Roekel. (See photos on page 50.)

The Name van Deelen

The van Deelens were named for the community bearing that name just three miles south of Hoenderloo. The "van" means "from" in the Dutch language. In 1811, when Napoleon was in control of Holland, he decreed that each Dutch individual was to have a surname, and many of those surnames had to do with where they were located. Thus, Willem "from" Deelen became Willem van Deelen. The Deelen community exists to this day. There are about six to eight homes, a community fire station, and a community center. We met Hendrick van Roekel in Deelen when we went to Holland. He was the second person on our list of van Roekels to meet.

Willemina (R) and her sister Ger (Grace).

Figure 52: Site of the birthplace of Willemina in the Hoge Veluwe.

The van Deelens as Royalty

There had been rumors that the van Deelens were of royal lineage. Looking back over the centuries, there may have been van Deelens who were from royalty. Two of the family crests do have a crown either affixed to the shield or on the person who is sitting behind the shield. (See the van Deelen family crests on pages 66 through 68.)

Many thought Willemina's name, being the same as the Queen of Holland at that time, could be an indication that there were royal lines. There were numerous Willeminas of that day, and there was a castle near Hoenderloo known as the Deelen Castle. It has no connection to the van Deelens. The owner's name may have been spelled "Deeler" at one time. A wealthy German Earl from North Germany, bought a large tract of land in the area of Deelen. He built a large home that was as big as a castle. His family lives there to this day. Some of the castle was destroyed during World War II.

The truth be known, however, the van Deelens were good, hard working, common people who may have had royalty in their family in a very distant line. This van Deelen family was not close to those royal individuals. There were those in the family who had hoped that Willemina would marry up the social ladder instead of marrying a poor peasant farm boy. There was some disappointment in that decision that lingered for decades.

Hoenderloo: Hometown of Willemina van Deelen

In the early 1800s, there were just a few houses in the area that was to become the community of Hoenderloo. The Willem van Deelen family moved about a mile to Hoenderloo from what was being developed as a nature preserve, De Hoge Veluwe. A marker stands not far from where their house once stood about a mile from the eastern entrance on the Hoenderloo side.

A protestant pastor by the name of Otto Gerhard Heldring passed through this cluster of homes about every week on his way to Otterlo. When the preserve, Hoge Veluwe, was established, Otterlo was at the western gate and Hoenderloo at the eastern gate. There are only a few miles between the two hamlets.

Reverend Heldring lived in Arnhem. He served at least these two churches in the area. He saw a need for a church and a school to be built, and wells were to be dug for good fresh water. The Heldring Church where the entire van Deelen family attended is still in use today. (See Figure 53 below.) He was a key figure in seeing that Hoenderloo and Otterlo became communities. Baptismal records for Willemina van Deelen and most of her family can be found in the church records. Hoenderloo is about seven miles south of Apeldoorn and three miles from Deelen on Highway 50.

The Hoge Veluwe

The Hoge Veluwe is a pristine national wildlife preservation park. It was the dream of one man, Kroller Muller, a German. He envisioned having a natural habitat park for all the people to come and enjoy. At exactly 2.3 kilometers (almost a mile) from the eastern gate entrance on the Hoenderloo side of the park is a marker siting the families who gave up their homes for the establishment of the preserve. The Willem van Deelen name appears on this plaque. There is a poster explaining the purchase of the land. Tract 1061 was the van Deelen home site. There is a depression in the ground that may be the actual site of the house. Henni Buitenhuis said that Willemina was born there at that location. See Figure 54 for a picture of what the house may have looked like. In the 1850s, the van Deelens moved to their new home, which was located behind the house at 20 Krimweg and the Buitenhuis hardware store. There is a moratorium on construction in Hoenderloo, so this may remain a small community well into the future.

Figure 54: House like those of the van Deelens in the Hoge Veluwe.

Figure 53: Heldring Church in Hoenderloo. Reverend Otto Gerhard Heldring, founder, inset.

Figure 55: The van Deelen family home in Hoenderloo, where Willemina lived.

Van Deelen Heraldry

Figure 56: Colorized graphic artist rendition of the van Deelen Coat of Arms.

66

The van Deelen Coat of Arms

We found four van Deelen coats of arms in our search. We will acknowledge the one found in the Bureau of Genealogies in The Hague as the "certified" coat of arms. The oldest coat of arms, it hangs in the village Museum Nairac in Barneveld. (See Figure 57 below.) The date of this coat of arms is 1687 from the family of Steven van Deelen of Crumseler who joined the knighthood van Veluwe on May 11, 1687. Originally, there was a parcel of land in the vicinity of Barneveld between Arnhem and Eed. In 1379, Brand van Deelen, a forefather, was awarded that land, called Esveld, with this shield, which sealed the deal. It shows a crown behind a silver shield, with a red band dissecting the shield horizontally. On the red band are two silver ram's heads facing to their right.

The second shield from 1586 is found in a picture, presumably of Herman van Deelen, and

Figure 58: Coat of arms dated 1586 in a picture belonging to Herman van Deelen that hangs in the Iconografisch Office in Den Haag.

belonging to the same. (See Figure 58.) The picture hangs in the Iconografisch Office in Den Haag (The Hague). It also has the silver shield with the red stripe and two silver sheep's heads facing to their right. The picture is not clear enough to see the details of the "frills" around the sides and top of the shield.

The third van Deelen coat of arms was awarded by the High Court to the noble Baronnen van Deelen in 1881. It is pictured in Figure 59 below. A white shield traversed horizontally with a red band,

Figure 57: The oldest coat of arms dated 1687, from the family of Steven van Deelen of Crumseler.

Figure 59: This shield was awarded to Baronnen van Deelen in 1881 by the High Court.

with two white sheep's heads facing to their right. The shield is heart shaped. There are two red lions facing each other. A gold knight's face mask sits atop the shield. On top of the helmet is a brown-skinned woman with dark hair. Covering her breast is a green wrap with two white ram's heads facing to their right. Her arms are raised as if to embrace someone. Between the two red lions is a white shield that is also dissected horizontally with a red band with white ram's heads facing to their right. No crown is associated with this coat of arms. This shield was certified in 1881. We tried to communicate with Harry van Deelen in Holland, with no response. We do not understand why there is a dark-skinned lady from an obvious Caucasian family.

The fourth van Deelen coat of arms was found atop the coffee table at the home of Willem van Deelen in Holland. See Figure 60, and please excuse the poor quality of the photograph. Willem was Jopie's brother in Apeldoorn. This shield has qualities similar to the two others that were found. Again, a crown is part of this coat of arms and may have caused the perception that the van Deelens were from royalty. There is a light-skinned blonde woman with a gold crown sitting atop her head. In front of her is a shock of wheat. A red breast wrap with two ram's heads facing to their right covers her breast. The shield is again white with a red band dissecting the shield and with the similar ram's heads facing to their right. There is no frill ornamentation around the shield.

We have chosen to use the orginal coat of arms

Figure 60: Photo of picture on the coffee table at the home of Willem van Deelen's home in Apeldoorn, Holland.

shape and color, the lions of the 1881 rendition, and to incorporate the blonde woman with a crown from Willem van Deelen's coffee table picture. You can see our hybridized version of the van Deelen coat of arms on page 66, Figure 56.

Willemina's Family

Right: Willem van Deelen and Rijke Essenstam van Deelen, Willemina's father and mother.

Willemina's Family: (unknown order) Dirk, Wynand, Willemina, Rijke, Jacoba, Jan Willem, Everdien (Dien), Willem, Albert, Evert, Rijke Essenstam, and Willem van Deelen.

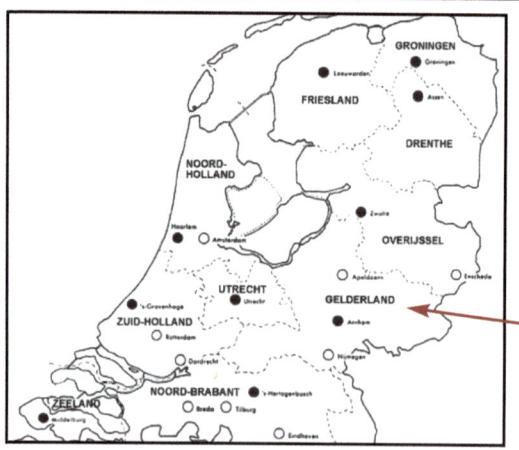

HOLLAND

Figure 61: Amsterdam to Apeldorn, Gelderland. The trip to meet our family and to discover information about our history took us from Amsterdam to Ede, Hoge Veluwe, Roekel, Deelen, Hoenderloo, Lunteren, Veenendaal, Apeldoorn, and Wageningen. The province of Gelderland is one of many provinces in Holland and was the homeland of Jan and Willemina.

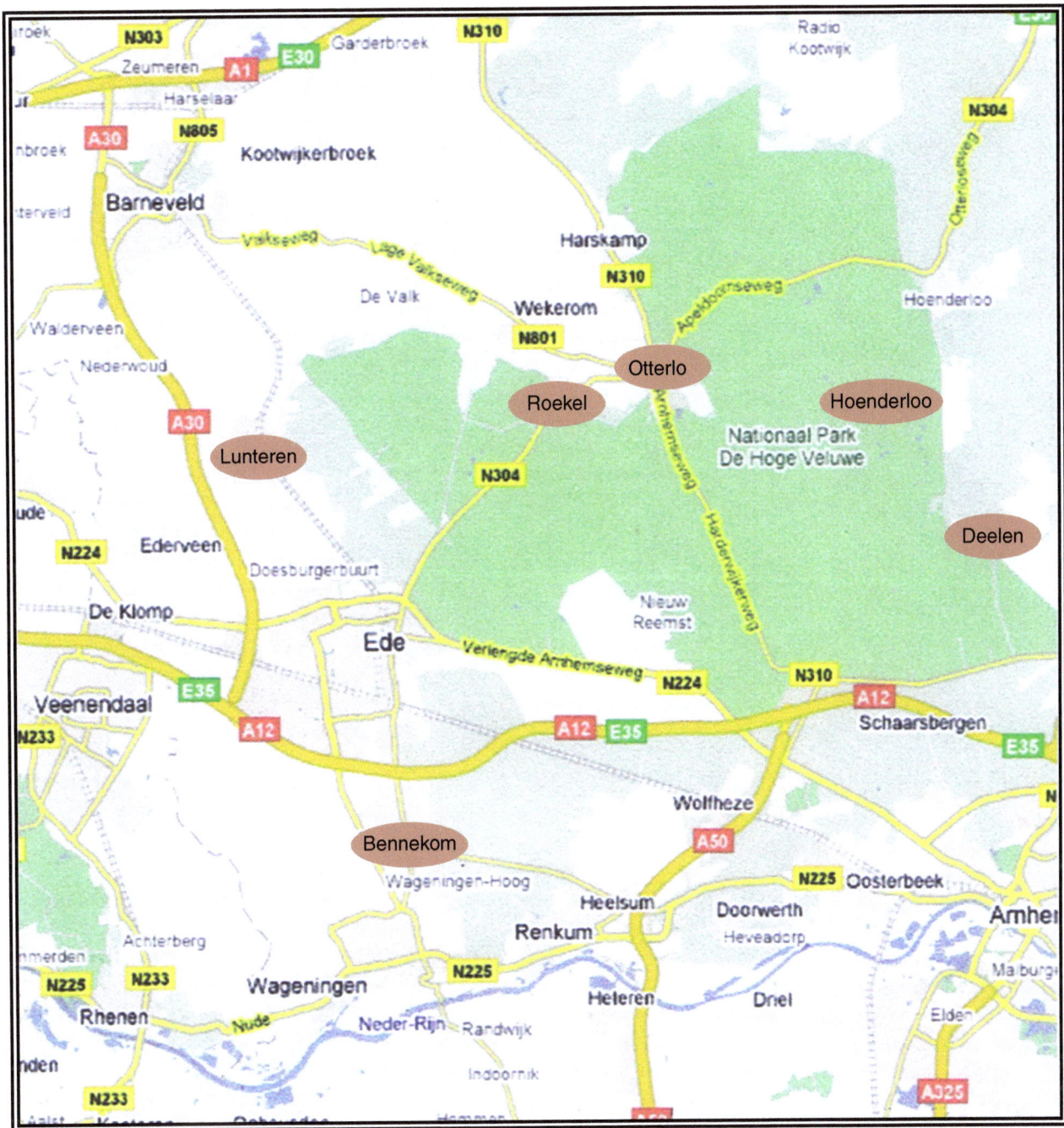

Figure 62: Arnhem, and the Hoge Veluwe. Deelen, Roekel, Hoenderloo, Otterlo, Lunteren, Ede, Bennekom, Veenendaal, and Wageningen. Jan van Roekel was from Lunteren on the west side of the Hoge Veluwe. Willemina was from Hoenderloo on the east side.

The Gelderland province of the Netherlands in 1994 had a population of 1,851,400. It has 1,940 square miles in the east central Netherlands. It borders on Germany in the east. Arnhem, seen on the lower right, which is the capital, as well as Nijmegen and Apeldoorn are the chief cities in the Gelderland. Largely an agricultural region, it is drained by the IJssel River and by the Lower Rhine and Waal rivers, which enclose the Betuwe, a fertile agricultural lowland in the southwest. The Veluwe, west of the IJssel, is an uncultivated, hilly heathland that is popular as a resort area. The region is also used as a military headquarters. Source: "Gelderland." *The Columbia Encyclopedia, Sixth Edition*. 2008. Encyclopedia.com.

John Herbert van Roekel, adopted son of William Robert from his sister, Otiena Hendrika van Roekel Bradbury. Judy Evelyn Taylor van Roekel (wife), Jennifer Deelen van Roekel Strickland (right) and Amanda Carole van Roekel (seated).

Our Trips to Holland

Meeting Relatives and Learning More ...

Judy and I went to Holland in 1976 to research and, hopefully, find genealogical data about the van Roekel name. My dad, William van Roekel, never spoke of Holland. He loved America so much that he wanted me to think of myself as an American and not a Dutch-American.

At the time of our trip, we knew virtually nothing about our heritage. We knew only that we were Dutch and had a cousin in Holland by the name of Jopie van Hunen.

We had one lead to guide us. Jopie van Hunen Blokker, my cousin via my grandmother's sister, Janettje (van Deelen) van Hunen, had sent a note to my mom and dad on her business card. She worked at a craft shop (Het Handwerkhuis) in Apeldoorn, and her business card had the three telephone numbers for the shops in Haarlem, Amsterdam, and Apeldoorn. Another note was written sometime in the late 1950s on what appears to be a scratch pad or stationary from The Handwerkhuis. With no more information than that, we went in search of our family history.

Figure 64: Het Handwerkhuis in Apeldoorn.

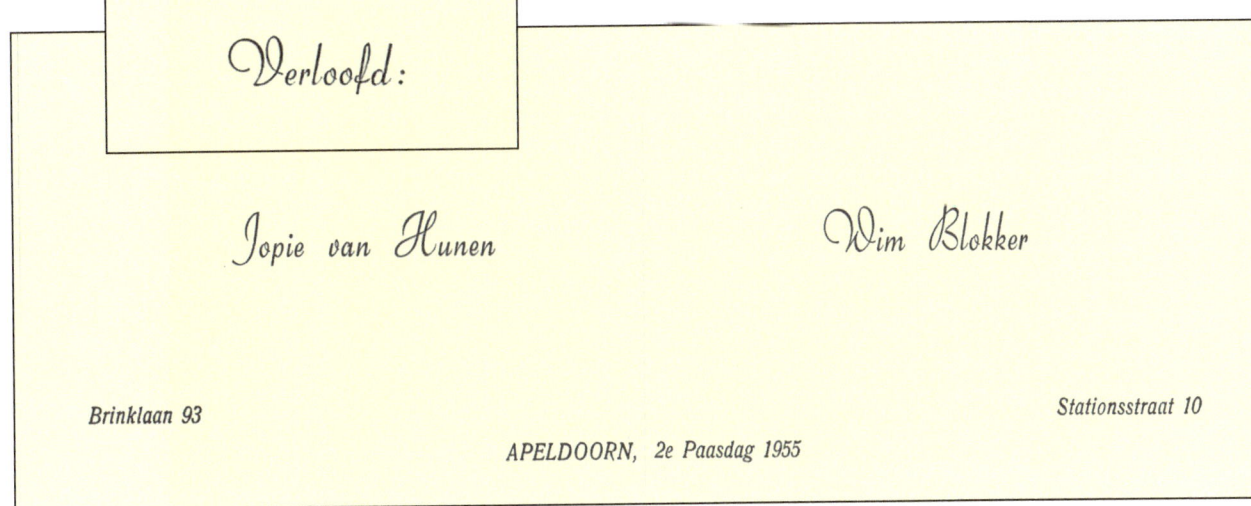

Figure 63: Business card from Jopie van Hunen Blokker. Name from front of card is inset.

Jopie and Wim van Hunen Blokker

Rijke, Ger, and Johanna

When Judy and I planned our visit to Holland and Jopie, we were concerned that once we met "family," it might become difficult to get away to visit the tourist attractions. Because of that concern, we decided to go as tourists before contacting Jopie by telephone. We had sent a letter to her weeks earlier saying that we were coming, but the letter never arrived.

We toured Amsterdam, Volendam, Delft, The Hague, and other sites the first three days of our visit.

On the third day, we finally contacted Jopie and her husband, Wim. Purchasing our train tickets through a coin machine, we left the next day by train from Amsterdam and Apeldoorn. What a ride! We traveled on what is called the "Snail train." We had a private compartment where we could enjoy the beautiful views.

When we got off the train, Judy and I looked at each other with fear and trepidation, realizing that we were now truly in a "foreign land." The metropolitan areas of most countries make you feel less "foreign," but when you get off a train in a more rural location, you sense that "you are not in Kansas anymore."

As it turned out, there was a tourist station near the train station. We got directions to Jopie's shop, which turned out to be only blocks from the train station. Judy and I strolled up the street and stopped at a "Wimpies" hamburger shop for lunch. We continued up the street and had some difficulty finding the shop. We stopped at a sewing machine shop and called Jopie. We were almost right across the street.

Since Jopie had not received our letter telling of our intention to visit, they had little time to prepare for our visit. She and Wim stopped everything they were doing and made us feel very welcome. Holland was experiencing the worst heat wave in history that month. The temperatures were in the 90s. The usual

Willem and Jacoba

Judy van Roekel (right) with the Henni Buitenhuis Family

Bertran and Ger Buitenhuis

temperature that time of year is in the mid to low 70s. They did not have air conditioning, nor do they usually serve ice with the drinks.

Jopie and Wim were superb hosts. We stayed in the apartment above the shop where we enjoyed dinner one evening of smoked herring and beer, a Dutch tradition, I believe.

We learned a great deal about the van Deelens while we were there in 1976, visiting many great aunts, uncles, and cousins on the van Deelen side of the family. We had lunch with grandmother Willemina's sisters—Rijke, Cos, and Johanna. And we made a photo of the van Deelen coat of arms that was on the coffee table of Jopie's brother, Willem.

On the last day that we could investigate the van Roekel heritage, Henni Buitenhuis, the son of Ger, another of Grandmother's sisters, acted as a chauffeur to take us to find out as much as we could about the van Roekels.

We went first to the community of Roekel where we met a quaint old couple sitting in their back yard. They were sporting wooden shoes and shelling early peas. They told us they did not know of any of their family branch going to America, but remembered there were van Roekel's from Mulunteren that had family to go to America near the turn of the century. (Note: It had been 60 years since my grandparents left, yet they remembered.)

We stopped in Mulunteren and asked a farmer standing beside his mailbox, J. Jansen, if he knew anything about Jan van Roekel who went to America. He enthusiastically said, yes. He had known Jan as a young man, and he knew that Jan had served in the Yellow Riders. He also told us that Jan was not from Mulunteren, but was from Lunteren. He also gave us the address of one of Granddad's nieces near Lunteren.

We arrived at the address he gave us and met the niece, Ottina van Roekel Roseboom. Ottina gave

Hendricus and Klaasje Roseboom

Figure 65: Gijs Bos family by the barn that was once the Jan van Roekel (1836) residence and the birthplace of Jan van Roekel (1885). You can see a full color photo of the barn and more information in Figure 1 on page 12.

Figure 66: Gijs Bos family home in 1976. This was once the location of the Jan (1836) and Otina van Hunen van Roekel farm where Jan van Roekel was born in 1885. The photo shows an original thatched roof.

Gijs Bos family. Notice the wooden shoes.

us from memory a family history of birthdays, deaths, and marriage dates of the family. A pastor just out of seminary acted as an interpreter for us. The pastor was her son. (We met with him again on our visit in 1999.) This clergyman was Rev. Henk (Hendricus) Roseboom.

She directed us to the A.J. Bos house located at Smouusewegg 2, Lunteren, Holland. This had been the farm of my great grandfather, Jan van Roekel (1836). My grandfather went back to Holland to sell the farm after his mother, Ottina van Hunen van Roekel, had passed away on August 22, 1930. The children of A.J. Bos still own the farm and live in the house. My grandfather was actually born in what is now a barn there that has wrought iron numbers 1812 over the brickwork. In 1976 the roof was partly thatched. Now the barn has a metal roof. E.G. (Gijs) Bos and his family were very cordial when we met in 1999.

Second Visit to the Fatherland in 1999

In 1999, Judy and I rewarded our daughter, Amanda, for doing well in high school with a trip to Holland. During this visit, we found a plethora of information about the families.

One evening while we were spending some time with Jopie and Wim, Jopie told us that she had some information about a book on the van Roekels. Jimmy van Roekel, my cousin from Dad's brother, Henry, had come to visit Jopie and had shown her the cover of a book he had found in The Hague. He left a few pages from the book with her. The book was titled *The Family van Roekel in the Gelderland*. We asked her for some contacts who might help us find a copy of the book. The book contains the total family history dating back many centuries, and also has a copy of a letter Jan and Willemina sent to the family. Jan's family history can be found on page 40. Pages 42 through 45 show copies of a letter he and Willemina sent to his family. (The translated letter can be found here on page 52, original in Appendix.)

Jopie gave us three "van Roekel" contacts who might help us in our search for our heritage: Willem van Roekel in Veenendaal; Hendrick van Roekel in Deelen; and Henk Roseboom in Bruchem, Holland. Willem is the grandson of Hendricus van Roekel, one of my granddad's brothers.

We went to Veenendal and met with the Willem van Roekel family. While we were there, he gave me a copy of a letter that my sister, Kay Hill Mason, had sent years earlier trying to establish contact with the family. (See Appendix page 144 for a copy of the letter.) Willem's mother, Cornilia Cornelisse van Roekel, was there and shared some pictures my grandmother had sent back to her. She gave us a postcard and some other pictures that Grandma had sent to her.

Willem told us he had a copy of the book we were seeking but did not know where it was. He also gave us an envelope from a letter Granddad had sent to him on Granddad's business stationary. The envelope had the 1927 logo, "Say It With Flowers." Decades later, an FDT floral company uses that logo. (See Figure 32 on page 47 and Appendix page 134.)

We stay in contact with Willem's family through his son, Jan van Roekel. Willem passed away in the spring of 2008.

We left Veenendaal and the Willem van Roekel family to go to Deelen to visit with Hendrick van Roekel. His farm must be the largest in the county. Deelen has only about eight homes, a post office, and a community center. After introductions and conversations, we asked them about the book. Initially, they said, yes, they had the book, but we could not take it to make a copy of it.

We went back to Henni's for dinner. Realizing Henni had a copying machine in his bicycle shop, we asked to go back to request again the opportunity to make the copy. We volunteered to leave Amanda as collateral. They relented without having to leave Amanda. We made the copy of the book and returned the original to them. We do not know how we are related to these van Roekels, but we are assuredly somehow related.

The next day we went to Bruchem and met with Rev. Roseboom. As it turns out, he was the fellow who interpreted the information for us from Granddad's niece back in 1976. He also had additional family genealogy information, which he shared. At our initial meeting, he had just finished seminary and was visiting his mom, Otina van Roekel Roseboom. We have maintained communication with him and his family.

We were so very blessed to get all of this done when we did. Hopefully, we will eventually obtain more information.

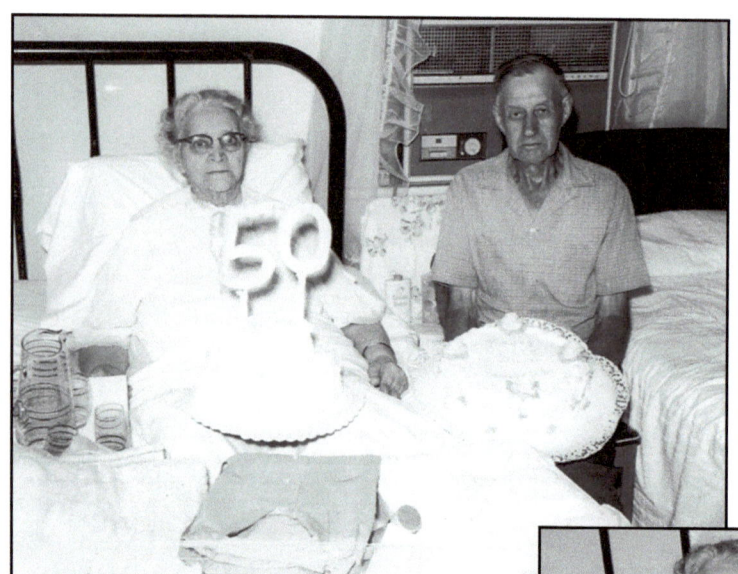

Jan and Willemina celebrated their 50th Anniversary!

Genealogy: Ancestors

Ancestors of Jan van Roekel (1885) and Willemina van Deelen van Roekel

From the book, *The Family van Roekel in the Gelderland*.
(Details of each ancestor follow, beginning on the next page.) Dates are listed as day-month-year.

Dirk Jansz 1440

Jans Dirksz 1470

Jan De Bakker 1499
First Martyr of Holland
It is possible that Jan de Bakker (born Aug.-Sep. 1499), the first martyr of Holland, is Willem Derkson's grandfather. (see Appendix: Jan de Bakker for details)

Derck (van Roekel) Backer 1615

Willem Derksen (Backer) van Roekel 1645	**Jan Evertsen of Roekel(t)**
(Forefather of van Roekels in Bennekom)	His son takes the name, Jan van Roekel.
Backer, indicated their profession: Bakers	(Forefather of the van Roekels of Wageningen)
(Bakers in Bennekom)	(Bakers in Wageningen)
This is our ancestral line.	This branch also multiplied and prospered.

Jacob Willem van Roekel . . . . about 1675

Derk Jacobs van Roekel 24-02-1726

William Derks van Roekel 26-04-1767

Willem van Roekel 28-06-1814

Jan van Roekel 25-12-1836

Jan van Roekel 24-08-1885

Details of Each Ancestor of Jan van Roekel (1885)

Translation of page 11, *The Family van Roekel in the Netherlands. Dates shown as day-month-year.*

Derck (van Roekel) Backer. 1615. No details were found.

Willem Derckson (van Roekel). Born about 1645.
Also known as **Willem Backer**, he married **Jantjen Guertsen**. This Willem Backer is most likely the same person as **Willem Derckson** who, with his wife, **Jantjen Guertsen**, owned a home in the countryside where they were already living in 08-04-1605. It was situated in Wageningen. It had a large stretch of land 1½ "achel gezaais" nearby in Bennekom. Willem was promoted to postmaster in 20-03-1688 in Bovenbuurtin, Bennekom. In 1709 he bought his own plot from the Bennekom Church. It says in his will that he is giving his son, **Gerrit,** the same estate that was given to him by his father, **Derck van Roekel** from about 1615.
   Children: 1- Jacob Willem van Roekel (about 1675) and
             2- Gerrit Willems

Jacob Willem van Roekel (IIa) (Son of Willem Derckson). Born about 1645.
Jacob was a baker in Bennekom. On 17-02-1700 he married **Evertje Jacobs**. He remarried on 13-12-1711 to **Willemtje Gerrits**. He married again on 17-09-1713 to **Trijntje Willems**. He died 13-01-1772. He was also known as Jacob Willems Bakker.
   Children: We have no history of Jacob's first two wives bearing him children. All children were born in Bennekom. *Refer to pages 11 and 13.*
      1- **Willem**, 13-01-1715. No history.
      2- **Jan Jacobs** 13-12-1716. (See section IIIa)
      3- **Gerrits Jacobs** 15-10-1719. IIIb.
      4- **Willemkje**, daughter, married **Tijmen Lubberts** in Bennekom 31-10-1757, born 10-01-1717.
      5- **Evert Jacobs**, born about 1724. See Section IIIC for his genealogy.
      6- **Gerritje**, daughter, 26-04-1753. First married **Class Rijksen van Santen** in 23-04-1753. He was the son of **Rijk Franse van Santen** and **Neeltje Klass Kaay** who were born in Veenendaal about 25-02-1725. She later married again in Veenendaal to **Willem Kool**.
      7- **Hendrikje**, daughter, born 13-06-173(?)
      8- **Derk Jacobs van Roekel** 24-02-1726

Derk Jacobs van Roekel. 24-02-1726. (Page 13, IIId).
Derk was born in Bennekom and died there 31-12-1788. He married **Evertje Jansen** on 04-02-1750. She was born on 04-02-1724 and was the daughter of **Jan Jansen** and **Ariaan Willems**. Derk is mentioned in the tax records as to be successor taxpayer for the Royesnpoll ---------, in Bennekom. We assume all were born in Bennekom.
   Children: 1- **Adreaantje** 06-08-1750. Moved to Ede 17-09-1775. Married 26-03-1775 to **Gerrit Cornelissen van Veldhuizen**. He was the son of **Cornelis Jacobs** and **Lijsbeth Gerrits**. Widowed, and remarried on 26-08-1792 to **Reinder Aarsen**, lived in Ede.
      2- **Trientje**, daughter, 23-04-1752.
      3- **Wouter Derksen** (IVb), 08-02-1754.
      4- **Treintje**, daughter, 29-02-1756. She moved to Ede 11-10-1781. Married **Jacob Hendriks** on 07-09-79. He was born in Ede on 06-05-1751, the son of **Hendrik Jacobs** and **Gertje Teunissen**.
      5- **Jan Derksen** (IVc). Born 12-03-1758.

Details of Each Ancestor of Jan van Roekel (1885) Cont.

6- **Jacobje**, 16-12-1759. Moved to Veenendaal on 12-09-1791. Married **Rijk van Santen**. Born in Veenendaal on 16-01-1757. Parents were **Klass Rijksen van Santen** and **Gerritje Jacobs van Roekel** (IIa).
7- **Gerritje**, daughter, born 16-09-1764. She married **Hendrik Haalboom** in Bennekom on 20-01-1760. She died 28-05-1795; he died 01-09-1831, the son of **Peter Jans Haalboom** and **Teunisje Aarts**.
8- **Willem Derks**, 26-04-1767, (Page 17, IVd).
9- **Derks Dersen**, 26-11-1769, (Page 18, IVe).

Willem Derks van Roekel. 26-04-1767. (Pages 17 & 18, IVd)
Son of **Derk Jacobs**, (IIId). Born in Bennekom. Died 12-07-1841. A farmer. He married **Gijsbertje Gerrits Roseboom**, born in Bennekom on 08-09-1771 and died 15-03-1835. She was the daughter of **Gerrits Everts Roseboom** and **Maria van Leeuwen**. They had 11 children, all born in Bennekom.

Children:
1- **Derk**, 12-01-1793. No history found on him.
2- **Maria Jacobs**, daughter, 17-09-1796. Died in Wageningen 03-08-1831. She married **Jahannes Vonk** in Bennekom 13-12-1817. He was born in Wageningen 31-03-1793 and died there 13-03-1852. He was the son of **Cornelis Vonk** and Maria Uitenbogaard.
3- **Gerrit (Willems),** 12-04-1796. (Page 24. Vh).
4- **Hendrik**, 10-06-1798. (Page 24. Vi).
5- **Evertje**, daughter, 17-05-1800.
6- **Gerritje**, daughter, born 05-06-1802 and died 27-07-1881. She married **Gerrit van Roekel** (Va).
7- **Elisabeth**, 30-11-1804, died 12-03-1824.
8- **Evertje**, daughter, 07-03-1806. Married **Johannes Vonk** on 27-11-1832. He was the widower of her sister, **Maria Jacobs** (see IVd, #2).
9- **Wouter**, 07-03-1810. (Page 26, Vj),
10- **Jacobie**, daughter. Born 30-11-1811. Married **W. van Maanen**.
11- **Willem van Roekel**, 28-06-1814 . (Page 26, Vk).

Willem van Roekel. 28-06-1814. (Page 26, Vk)
Son of Willem Derk (IVd). He was born in Bennekom and died in Ede 06-04-1843. He was a farmer. He married Fijtje van Maanen in Ede on 18-06-1836. She was born in Ede on 20-10-1815 and died there on 13-04-1849. Three children of this marriage.

Children:
1- **Jan van Roekel,** 25-12-1836. (Page 41, VIw). Complete descendants next page.
2- **Willem van Roekel,** 17-01-1839. No family history
3- **Evertje,** daughter, 29-09-1841.

Jan van Roekel. 25-12-1836.
Jan was a farmer in Lunteren. First wife, **Timetje Koudijs**. Born 10-10-1837. Died 05-12-1875. They had eight children. Second wife, **Ottina van Hunen**. Born 15-09-1848. Died 22-08-1930. Married 29-03-1879. They had nine children.

> Details of Jan's family are shown on the next page. His thirteenth child was **Jan van Roekel (1885)** who married **Willemina van Deelen** on 9-9-1911. These were my grandparents, to whom this book is dedicated.
> — John Herbert van Roekel

Family of Origin of Jan van Roekel (1885)

From the book, *The Family van Roekel in the Netherlands*, we find Jan's (1885) family information, page 41.
Dates are listed as day-month-year.

FATHER:

Jan van Roekel	Born in Ede 25-12-1836	Died 22-10-1907	Farmer in Lunteren
First wife, **Timetje Koudijs**	10-10-1837	Died 05-12-1875	Jan married (unknown)
Second wife, **Otina van Hunen**	15-09-1848	Died 22-08-1930	Jan married 29-03-1879

CHILDREN OF FIRST MARRIAGE: Timetje Koudijs

+	1- **Sophia**	Born 15-12-1863	Died 05-04-1928	Copy of Genealogy in the Appendix.
	2- **Reyer**	Born in Ede 22-11-1865		Farmer in Valk. Married at age 50 to Wilhelmina van Wolfwinkle 15-10-1904. Most likely no children.
	3- **Gijsbertie**	Born in Ede 26-08-1867		Daughter
+	4- **Willem**	Born 21-09-1869		(See section XV of the book for descendants page 129-131)
	5- **Evertje**	Born in Ede 14-02-1871	Died 04-02-1872	Daughter (Twin of Gijsbert)
	6- **Gijsbert**	Born 14-02-1871		
	7- **Evertje**	Born in Ede 22-02-1873		Daughter
	8- **Jan**	Born in Ede 27-11-1875	Died 30-11-1875	Lived three days

MOTHER:

CHILDREN OF SECOND MARRIAGE: Otina van Hunen

+	9- **Hendricus**	Born in Ede 04-12-1879		Worked as a farmer Descendants in Appendix
	10- **Hendrikje**	Born 07-01-1881		Daughter
	11- **Jannetje**	Born Ede 19-11-1882		Daughter
	12- **Cornelia**	Born Ede 16-03-1884		Daughter
+	13- **Jan**	Born 24-08-1885	Died 06-12-1969	Immigrated to the US in 1912 Returned to Holland 05-09-1931 to settle his father's estate. Complete genealogy contained in the book
	14- **Cornelisje**	Born 08-12-1887		Daughter
	15- **Bartus**	Born 12-02-1890		Retarded. No marriage and no children
+	16- **Gijsbertus**	Born 13-08-1891		See pages 150 & 153 XXIV of the book van Roekels'
	17- **Evertje**	Born 22-11-1894	Died 09-02-1897	Daughter

+ Descendant's documented genealogy can be found in the Appendix of this book.

Ancestors of Willemina van Deelen

van Deelen ancestors, short version, from Gijs van Roekel in Holland, **Family Tree Maker**.
Dates are listed as month-day-year.

The first Gijsbertsen . . . . about 1570

Tonis Gijsbertsen . . . . about 1595

Jan Tonis Gijsbertsen . . . . about 1625

Gijsbert Jansen . . . . about 1660

Lendert Gijsbertsen 10-08-1699

Tijmen Lendertsen 10-06-1742

Lendert Tijmens van Deelen 02-03-1784

Albert van Deelen 01-26-1823

***Willem van Deelen 08-21-1861

Willem van Deelen 03-19-1907

Willem Rijke van Deelen 12-28-1942

*** *This is the father of Willemina van Deelen, second child with Rijke Essestam.*

See Appendix for details.

Family of Origin of Willemina van Deelen

Paternal Grandparents
Albert van Deelen & Dintje Feriks
Born about 1823   Born 1831
Married: 06-03-1852

Maternal Grandparents
Jacob Essestam & Willempje van der Hoef
Born about 1831   Born 1836
Married: 03-01-1962

FATHER
Willem van Deelen
Born about 1861, Died 08-24-1925

MOTHER
Rijke Essestam
Born 1867, Died 08-09-1940

Married: 01-31-1886

CHILDREN

Everdien (Dien) 06-08-1886

Willemina (Mies or Mina) 12-31-1887

Albert 05-04-1891

Jacoba (Koos) 02-04-1893

Rijke 03-07-1895

Johanna (Jo) 01-08-1898

Jan (Stillborn) 1900

Jantje (Stillborn) 1902

* Jannetje 05-25-1904

Willem 03-19-1907

** Ger (Grace) 03-09-1910

***Jannetje** was the mother of **Jopie van Hunen Blokker**.
****Ger** was the mother of **Henni Buitenhuis**, another cousin with whom we visited in Holland.

Genealogy: Descendants

Descendants of Jan and Willemina van Roekel
Through year 2008.

From Gijs van Roekel in Holland, **Family Tree Maker**

Condensed Presentation of Descendants of Jan and Willemina van Roekel

*William Robert van Roekel (Bill)
  John Herbert (Hill) van Roekel**
    Jennifer Deelen van Roekel Strickland
      Deelen Nicole Strickland
      *Ian Wesley Strickland
      Hannah Lea Strickland
    Amanda Carole van Roekel

*Hendrick John van Roekel, Sr. (Henry)
  *Hendrick John van Roekel, Jr. (Butch)
    Kimberly Ann van Roekel Burkett
      Zachery Ryan Burkett
    Richard Phillip van Roekel, Sr.
      Richard Phillip van Roekel, II
      Katlin Leigh-Ann van Roekel
      Cooper Elton van Roekel
    Cynthia Ashley van Roekel Ullrich Small
      Karen Rachel Ullrich
      Ryan James Ullrich
      Michael John Ullrich
  James Leroy van Roekel
    Heather Lea van Roekel Turner
      Raiford Turner
      Leah Frances Turner
  Teresa Ruth van Roekel Godwin
    Latisha Godwin
    Amanda Nichole Godwin
    Brianca René Godwin

*Otiena Fredricka van Roekel
  *Katherine Hendricka Hill Mason
    Lisa Ann Mason Taylor
      Susan Elizabeth Taylor
      Edward Kent Taylor
    Susan Annette Mason Howell
      Andrew Jordan Howell
      Emilee Kate Howell
    Roy Lee Mason, Jr.
  Thomas Elmer Hill, Jr.
    *Rachelle Marie Hill
    Gregory Thomas Hill
    Nicholas James Hill
    Andrew Wallace Hill
    Nathan Daniel Hill
    Jason Aaron Hill
  John Herbert (Hill) van Roekel**
  William Robert Hill
    Steven Robert Hill
    Susan Anita Hill
    Christina Loraine Hill
    Ryan Wesley Hill

John William van Roekel, Sr.
  John William van Roekel, III
    Candyce Leigh van Roekel
    Jon Eric van Roekel
    Graham William van Roekel

*Deceased
**Adopted by William Robert van Roekel (Bill)

Photo on left: Standing (L-R): John William, Hendrick John (Henry), Otiena Hendrika, William Robert. Seated: Willemina, Jan.

Photo below: Standing (L-R): William Robert and Mary Elizabeth Howard van Roekel; James Thomas (Buddy) Bradbury and Otiena van Roekel Bradbury; Hazel Davis and Hendrick John (Henry) van Roekel; Earlene Culbreth, wife of John William van Roekel (taking picture). Seated Willemina and Jan van Roekel.

Descendants of Jan and Willemina van Roekel

No Name Given van Roekel: Stillborn 04-03-1912. Arnhem, Holland {Record #165-hall of records 1912}. (Note: Although we fully acknowledge and pay homage to this stillborn child as being the first child of Jan and Willemina, we will focus here on their surviving children.)

(I)   **William Robert van Roekel:** 01-10-1913 – 05-04-2000. The first living child of Jan and Willemina van Roekel, William was born in Watha, North Carolina, next to the community of van Eeden. He married **Mary Elizabeth Howard** on 07-10-1938. She was born 12-25-1915 in Dublin County to **Jacob Alonzo** and **Annie Baysden Howard**. There were 12 siblings in her family. Jacob was a pastor in the Pentecostal Holiness Denomination. Elizabeth died 04-09-1994.

    William (Bill) and Mary Elizabeth (Liz) lived in several locations in eastern North Carolina. They settled in Wilson in 1952 and lived happily together for 56 years. Bill worked for B.J. High Home Improvement Company from 1951 until he retired at about age 78. Liz was his homemaker. They were a faithful and loving couple. Bill joined her in her faith later in life.

    Bill and Liz were unable to have their own children. They took the opportunity to adopt John Herbert Hill, their nephew, from Bill's sister, Otiena van Roekel Hill. She was unable to take care of all four of her children after her divorce from Thomas E. Hill, Sr. I am proud to say they were my mom and dad.

    For reasons we will never know, William refused to divulge that his middle name was Robert. We discovered after his death that he had a middle name. He, perhaps, did not want to be called "Billy Bob."

    He and Liz are interred at the Bald Mountain Baptist Church Cemetery on Shumont Road, not far from Lake Lure, North Carolina. It is located about 14 miles south of Black Mountain, North Carolina, off Highway 9.

(I) William, Elizabeth, and (I-A) John Herbert van Roekel. Photo taken in 1960.

(I) William Robert and Elizabeth Howard van Roekel.

(I) William Robert van Roekel (Bill)
Born: 01-10-1913
Died: 05-04-2000

Married 10-07-1938
Mary Elizabeth Howard
Born: 12-25-1915
Died: 04-09-1994

(I-A) John Herbert (Hill) van Roekel (Herb)
Born: 02-28-1947

Married 10-17-1970
Judy Evelyn Taylor
Born: 07-04-1949

(I-A1) Jennifer Deelen van Roekel
Born: 01-31-1975

Married 12-29-1995
Jason Wesley Strickland
Born: 11-15-1973

(I-A1a) Deelen Nicole Strickland
Born: 01-23-1996

(I-A1c) Hannah Lea Strickland
Born: 12-21-2001

(I-A1b) Ian Wesley Strickland
Born: 12-30-1999
Died: 04-13-2000

(I-A2) Amanda Carole van Roekel
Born: 09-30-1981

(I-A) John Herbert (Herb) and Judy Taylor van Roekel with children, (I-A1) Jennifer (L) and (I-A2) Amanda. Taken in 1986.

(I-A) John Herbert (Hill) van Roekel
Descendants and Families of
(I) William Robert van Roekel
First child of Jan and Willemina van Roekel

(I-A1) Jennifer van Roekel and husband, Jason Strickland. Children: (I-A1a) Deelen Nicole (R) and (I-A1c) Hannah Lea Stickland (L)

(I-A2) Amanda van Roekel

Descendants of Jan and Willemina van Roekel Cont.

(II) Hendrick John van Roekel, Sr.: 02-21-1918 – 03-10-1984. The second living child of Jan and Willemina van Roekel, Hendrick John (Henry) was born 02-21-1918 in Athens, Michigan, just outside of Battle Creek. He married **Hazel Davis** on 04-14-1940. He died 03-10-1984 at the Veterans Hospital in Durham, North Carolina.

Henry was a decorated veteran of World War II. He rose to the rank of sergeant in the Infantry, U.S. Army. He fought in the historic Battle of Normandy and the Battle of the Bulge on the Rhine River. He returned from the war and began a career in construction, owning his own company, Van Roekel Constuction Company, from which he retired. Henry was a compassionate man blended with gentle firmness. William said the effects of the war truly changed Henry. I believe the sensitivity he inherited from his mom struggled with the brutality of war. Today, we would say that maybe he suffered from Post Traumatic Stress Disorder.

He loved all of his family, close and extended. I truly enjoyed my visits there during the summers. He allowed the other boys and me the opportunity to help with his business by doing some landscaping at one of his construction sites.

Henry is interred at Wayne Memorial Cemetery on US 117 South, just a few miles north of Dudley, N.C.

(II) Hendrick John van Roekel, Sr., and wife, Hazel Ruth Davis

(II)
Hendrick John van Roekel, Sr. (Henry)
Born: 02-21-1918
Died: 03-10-1984

Married 04-14-1940
Hazel Ruth Davis
Born: 12-19-1922

(II-A)
Hendrick John van Roekel, Jr. (Butch)
Born: 03-28-1943, Died 04-18-1988
Interred Greenlawn Mem Garden, Chesapeake, VA

Married 11-24-1968
Margaret Rose Redman
Born: 06-25-1948

(II-A1)
Kimberly Ann van Roekel
Born: 05-28-1974

Married 08-18-2001
Timothy Burkett
Born: 04-28-1974

(II-A1a)
Zachery Ryan Burkett
Born: 08-22-2005

(II) Hendrick (Henry) John van Roekel, Sr., U.S. Army

(II-B)
Richard Phillip van Roekel, Sr.
Born: 11-18-1946, Goldsboro, NC

Married 08-07-1966
Cynthia Jean Royal
Born: 12-21-1947, Clinton, NC

(II-B1)
Richard Phillip van Roekel, II
Born: 7-04-1969, Goldsboro, NC

Married 07-22-1995
²**Jennifer Leigh Baker**
Born: 05-15-1976

(II-B1a)
Katlin Leigh-Ann
Born: 11-27-2002

(II-B1b)
Cooper Elton
Born: 05-17-2006

(II-B2)
Cynthia "Ashley" van Roekel
Born: 6-29-1973, Goldsboro, NC

Married 5-25-2006
Jimmie Hampden Small
Born: 01-13-1953

(II-B2a)
Karen Rachel Ullrich
Born: 08-16-1988

(II-B2b)
Ryan James Ullrich
Born: 06-07-1994

(II-C)
James Leroy van Roekel
Born: 01-13-1953

Married 10-19-2005
Jean Lilley
Born: 1-22-1969

(II-B2c)
Michael John Ullrich
Born: 04-12-1998

(II-C1)
Heather Lea van Roekel
Born: 08-24-1971

Married 06-26-1993
Vernon Elliott Turner
Born: 12-25-1969

(II-C1a)
Raiford Turner
Born: 08-25-2001

(II-C1b)
Leah Frances Turner
Born: 08-14-2003

(II-D)
Teresa Ruth van Roekel
Born: 02-04-1961

Married 06-14-80
Calvin Lee Peedin Godwin
Born: 02-22-1957

(II-D1)
Latisha Godwin
Born: 01-13-1981

(II-D2)
Amanda Nichole Godwin
Born: 07-31-1989

(II-D3)
Brianca René Godwin
Born: 07-06-1997

Descendants and Families of
(II) Hendrick John van Roekel, Sr. (Henry)
Second child of Jan and Willemina van Roekel

Descendants of Hendrick John van Roekel, Sr. (Henry)

Row 1 - *children seated on ground:* (II-C1a) Raiford Turner; (children of Latisha Godwin Wilkins) James Wilkins, Josh Wilkins, Tyler Wilkins.

Row 2 - *adults and children seated:* Hazel van Roekel (wife of Henry) holding (II-B1b) Cooper van Roekel; (II-d) Teresa van Roekel Godwin holding Allen Wilkins (Latisha's child); Jean van Roekel holding (II-B1a) Katlin van Roekel; (II-C1) Heather van Roekel Turner holding (II-C1b) Leah Turner; (II-B2a) Karen Ullrich.

Row 3 - *standing:* Jennifer van Roekel (wife of Phillip); (II-B1) Phillip van Roekel; (II-D3) Brie Godwin; (II-D1) LaTisha Godwin Wilkins; Chris (friend of family); Calvin Godwin (husband of Teresa); (II-D2) Mandy Godwin; (II-B) Richard van Roekel, (II-B2) Ashley van Roekel Ullrich Small; (II-B2b) Ryan Ullrich; Jimmy Small (husband of Ashley); (II-B2c) Michael Ullrich; Elliott Turner (husband of Heather); (II-C) Jimmy van Roekel; Jean van Roekel (wife of Jimmy).

(II-A) Hendrick John (Butch) van Roekel, Jr.
Descendants and Families of
(II) Hendrick John van Roekel, Sr. (Henry)
Second child of Jan and Willemina van Roekel

(II-A) Hendrick John (Butch) van Roekel, Jr.
03-28-1943 - 04-18-1988

(II-A) Hendrick John (Butch) van Roekel, Jr., with wife, Margaret Rose Redman, and daughter, (II-A1) Kimberly Ann van Roekel

(II-A) Hendrick John (Butch) van Roekel, Jr., with wife, Margaret Rose Redman

(II-A1) Kimberly Ann van Roekel Burkett with husband, Timothy Burkett, and son, (II-A1a) Zachery Ryan Burkett

(II-B) Richard Phillip van Roekel, Sr., with wife, Cynthia Jean Royal; son, (II-B1) Richard Phillip, II; and daughter, (II-B2) Ashley

(II-B) Richard van Roekel, Sr.

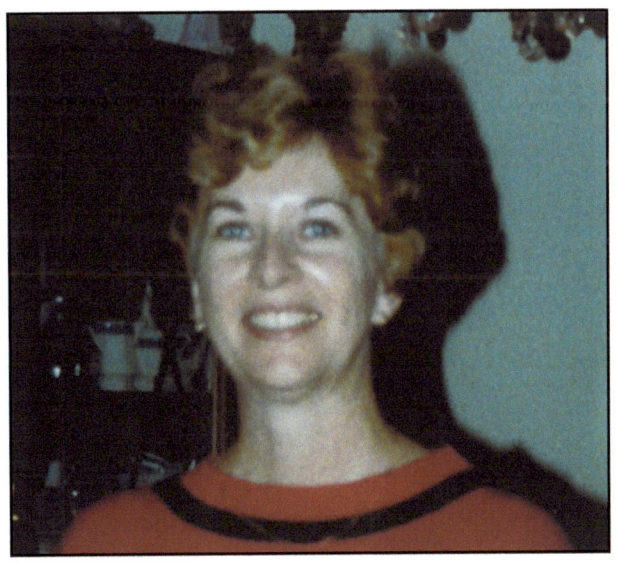

Cynthia "Jean" Royal van Roekel

(II-B1) Richard van Roekel, II

(II-B1) Richard Phillip van Roekel, II, with wife, Jennifer Leigh Baker, and children, (II-B1a) Katlin Leigh-Ann van Roekel and (II-B1b) Cooper Elton van Roekel

(II-B2) Cynthia Ashley van Roekel Small (center back) with children (II-B2a) Karen Rachel Ullrich (L), (II-B2b) Ryan James Ullrich (R), and (II-B2c) Michael John Ullrich (center)

(II-B2) Ashley van Roekel

(II-C) James Leroy van Roekel (Jimmy)
Descendants and Families of
(II) Hendrick John van Roekel, Sr. (Henry)
Fourth child of Jan and Willemina van Roekel

(II-C) James Leroy van Roekel and wife, Jean Lilley van Roekel

(II-D) Teresa Ruth van Roekel Godwin
Descendants and Families of
(II) Hendrick John van Roekel, Sr. (Henry)
Fourth child of Jan and Willemina van Roekel

(II-D) Teresa Ruth van Roekel Godwin with husband, Calvin Lee Peedin Godwin, and childen, (II-D1) Latisha Marie Godwin and (II-D3) Bianca René Godwin

Descendants of Jan and Willemina van Roekel Cont.

(III) Otiena Hendrika van Roekel: **04-22-1924 – 11-15-1998.** The third living child of Jan and Willemina van Roekel, Otiena Hendrika van Roekel was born in Wayne County, North Carolina, on April 24, 1924. She lived in the Dudley area until she was grown. She married Thomas Elmer Hill, Sr., on October 18, 1942.

Otiena and Thomas had four children before they divorced in about 1951. She moved to the Maryland area where she spent most of her adult life raising two of her sons, Thomas E. Hill, Jr. and William Robert Hill.

Otiena then married James Thomas Bradbury, Jr., from Lake Harmony, Pennsylvania, on June 12, 1957. His nickname was "Buddy," and he was born April 14, 1922. Otiena and James moved back to Dudley and purchased the Jan and Willemina home place across from Brogden School in 1975. Otiena worked for the Wayne County government delivering "meal on wheels" to the elderly in the community.

James proceeded her in death in November 1993. Otiena died at Wayne Memorial Hospital on November 15, 1998. She and Buddy are interred at Willowdale Cemetery off Williams street in downtown Goldsboro. She rests just a block away from Jan and Willemina.

(III) Otiena Hendrika van Roekel Bradbury

(III) Otiena Hendrika van Roekel Born: 04-22-1924 Died: 11-15-1998	Married 05-12-1957 ²James Thomas Bradbury, Jr. (Buddy) Born: 04-14-1922 Died: 11-00-1993

(III-A) *Katherine Fredricka Hill (Kaye) Born: 09-23-1943 Died 05-15-1994	Married 10-07-1962 Roy Lee Mason, Sr. Born: 03-29-1940

*Kaye was raised by Jan and Willemina after Otiena's divorce from Thomas Elmer Hill. She was born in Goldsboro, NC, and is interred at the municipal cemetery in Princeton, NC.

III-A1 Lisa Anne Mason Taylor Born: 07-06-1964	Married 04-04-1987 Kent Taylor Born: 1-17-1964	(III-A1a) Susan Elizabeth Taylor Born: 05-24-1993	(III-A1b) Edward Kent Taylor Born: 06-08-1994

III-A2 Susan Annette Mason Howell Born: 07-16-1967	Glenn Kornegay Born: 08-02-1964	(III-A2a) Andrew Jordan Howell Born: 08-03-1992	(III-A2b) Emilee Kate Howell Born: 10-10-1996

(III-A3) Roy Lee Mason, Jr. Born: 01-17-1969	Married 09-25-2003 Denise Waller Born: 1-26-1974

(III-B) *Thomas Elmer Hill, Jr. Born: 12-19-1945	Married 12-19-1970 Rachel Virginia Bryant Born: 06-06-1952	(III-B1) Rachelle Marie Hill Born: 02-15-1971 Died: 02-17-1971

(III-B2) Gregory Thomas Hill Born: 12-04-1972	(III-B3) Nicholas James Hill Born: 09-16-1975	(III-B4) Andrew Wallace Hill Born: 06-05-1980	(III-B5) Nathan Daniel Hill Born: 02-21-1986	(III-B6) Jason Aaron Hill Born: 12-23-1988

(III-C) – (I-A) **John Herbert Hill (van Roekel) To see details, go to I-A under (I) William Robert van Roekel

**John Herbert Hill was adopted by Otiena's brother, William Robert van Roekel, and his wife, Elizabeth, when Otiena was unable to take care of all four of her children after her divorce from Thomas E. Hill, Sr.

(III-D) ^William Robert Hill Born: 04-03-1948	Married 10-17-1981 Sharon May Warnick Born: 03-27-1958

^William and his brother, Thomas, moved to Rockville, MD, with their mother after her divorce from Thomas Elmer Hill, Sr.

(III-D1) Steven Robert Hill Born: 03-05-1972	(III-D2) Susan Anita Hill Born: 06-04-1976	(III-D3) Christina Loraine Hill Born: 02-13-1987	(III-D4) Wesley Ryan Hill Born: 07-14-1994

Descendants and Families of
(III) Otiena Hendrika van Roekel
Third child of Jan and Willemina van Roekel

Descendants of Otiena Hendrika van Roekel Hill Bradbury

(L-R) (III-B) Thomas Elmer Hill, Jr., (III-C) John Herbert (Hill) van Roekel, (III-D3) Christina Hill, (III-D) William Robert Hill, Sharon Hill (wife of William), (III-D4) Ryan Hill, (III-A1a) Lisa Ann Taylor, (III-A1b) Eddie Taylor, Kent Taylor (husband of Lisa), (III-D1) Susan Taylor, (I-A1) Jennifer Deelen Strickland (Herb's daughter), (I-A1c) Hannah Leigh Strickland, (I-A1a) Deelen Nicole Strickland, Joyce C. Taylor (Herb's sister-in-law), Judy T. van Roekel (Herb's wife), Rachel B. Hill (Tom's wife), Jason Wesley Strickland (Jennifer's husband).
Not pictured: (I-A2) Amanda C. van Roekel (Herb's daughter).

(III-A) Katherine Fredricka Hill (Kay)
Descendants and Families of
(III) Otiena Hendrika van Roekel
Third child of Jan and Willemina van Roekel

(III-A) Katherine Fredricka Hill (Kaye)

(III-A) Katherine Fredricka Hill Mason Family (Taken 06-2008):

Kent, (III-A1) Lisa, (III-A1a) Susan, (III-A1b) Eddie Taylor

Glenn, (III-A2) Susan Kornegay, (III-A2a) Jordan Hill and (III-A2b) Emilee Howell

(III-A3) Lee, Denise Mason

(III-B) Thomas Elmer Hill, Jr.
Descendants and Families of
(III) Otiena Hendrika van Roekel
Third child of Jan and Willemina van Roekel

(III-B) Thomas Elmer Hill, Jr. Family: First row (L-R) Rachel Bryant Hill (Thomas's wife); Mrs. Bryant (Rachel's mother); Danielle Hill (Nick's wife). Back row (L-R) (III-B2) Greg Hill; (III-B5) Nathan Hill; (III-B) Tom Hill; (III-B6) Jason Hill; (III-B4) Andrew Hill; (III-B3) Nick Hill.

NOTE: For **(III-C) John Herbert Hill** and his family, see (I-A) on page 88.

(III-D) William Robert Hill
Descendants and Families of
(III) Otiena Hendrika van Roekel
Third child of Jan and Willemina van Roekel

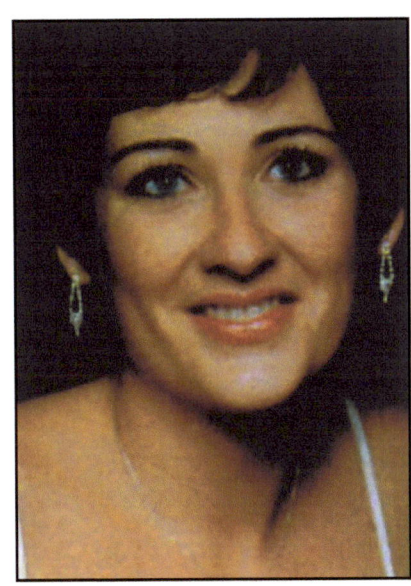

(III-D2) Susan Hill

(III-D) William Robert Hill Family: (L-R) (III-D1) Steven; Sharon (wife of William); (III-D4) Ryan; (III-D) William Robert (Robbie); (III-D3) Christina Hill

Descendants of Jan and Willemina van Roekel Cont.

(IV) John William van Roekel: 2-20-1926 – 05-04-2000. The fourth child of Jan and Willemina van Roekel, John William was born in Goldsboro, North Carolina. He married Earlene Culbreth on 09-11-1943.

John William, whose nickname is Johnnie, also attended the First Pentecostal Church of Goldsboro with his parents. He has served as a Sunday school teacher for more than 20 years. He has been very active in a civic organization, The Shriners, rising to the highest office in the state, Grand Potentate of North Carolina.

Johnnie donated portions of Jan's and Willemina's homestead for the construction of a local meeting place for the Shriners near the family home in Dudley. The Shriners have 19 hospitals for crippled children and 3 hospitals for children who are burn victims. Johnnie has continued the family characteristic of making a difference in the lives of others, as did his mom and dad. He has a great reputation and continues the management of the Van Roekel Florist in Goldsboro, North Carolina.

Johnnie remarried to Mavis Johnson. The Van Roekel Florist has flourished in part because of her determined and unwavering hard work and dedication.

(IV) John William van Roekel (Johnnie)

Earlene Culbreth van Roekel, Johnnie's first wife

| (IV) John William van Roekel (Johnnie) Born: 02-20-1926 | Married 10-07-1938 ¹Earleen Culbreth Born: 11-11-1926 Died: 06-22-1995 | Married Unknown ²Mavis Johnson Born: Unknown |

| (IV-A) John William van Roekel, III (Van) Born: 12-19-1951 | Married 03-27-1978 Beverly Beam Born: 12-09-1953 |

(IV-A1) Candyce Leigh van Roekel
Born: 08-16-1974

(IV-A2) Jon Eric van Roekel
Born: 12-27-1985

(IV-A3) Graham William van Roekel
Born: 12-23-1987

Descendants and Families of (IV) John William van Roekel
Fourth child of Jan and Willemina van Roekel

(IV) John William van Roekel (Johnnie); (IV-B2) Graham William van Roekel; (IV-B) John William van Roekel, III (Van); Beverly Beam van Roekel (Van's wife); (IV-B1) John Eric van Roekel

DIRECTORY: *Van Roekel Descendants • Contacts in Holland*

NAME	ADDRESS	CITY/STATE	ZIP CODE	TELEPHONE	E-MAIL
John H. (Herb) van Roekel	2425 Highway # 9	Black Mountain, NC	28711	828-669-7031	dutchmanjh@juno.com
Jennifer Deelen Strickland	(Contact Herb)				
Amanda Carole van Roekel	(Contact Herb)				
Hazel van Roekel	(Contact Richard)				
Margaret Rose van Roekel	225 Mount Vernon	Portsmouth, VA	23707	757-397-8285	
Kimberly van Roekel Burkett	3715 Western Branch Blvd.	Portsmouth, VA	23707	757-393-0523	
Richard Phillip van Roekel, Sr.	318 Bayleaf Dr.	Goldsboro, NC	27534	919-778-4796	
Richard Phillip van Roekel, II	212 Lee Trace	Smithfield, NC	27577	919-934-8308	
Cynthia Ashley van Roekel Small	P.O. Box 62	Isle of Palms, SC	29451	843-568-8427	
Heather Lea van Roekel Turner	393 Providence Church Rd.	Goldsboro, NC	27530	919-731-3915	
James Leroy van Roekel	(Contact Heather Lea)				
Teresa van Roekel Godwin	910 Institute Rd.	Kinston, NC	28504	Contact Richard	
Latisha Godwin Wilkins		Kinston, NC	28504		
Lisa Mason Taylor	803 Deer Acres Dr.	Goldsboro, NC	27530	919-736-2849	
Susan Mason Kornegay	18 Lassiter Rd.	Princeton, NC	27569	919-396-4062	
Roy Lee Mason, Jr.	210 Cashwell Dr.	Goldsboro, NC	27534	919-736-0963	
John William van Roekel	100 Cassedale Dr.	Goldsboro, NC	27534	919-734-5762	
John William van Roekel, III	218 Sawgrass Lane S.	Lexington, NC	27295	336-956-1927	
William Robert Hill	1220 Emmaus Road	Woodbine, MD	21797	301-854-6542	
Thomas Elmer Hill, Jr.	142 Crest Lane	Front Royal, VA	22630	540-631-0277	

Contacts in Holland (When in Holland, an extra zero is needed in the telephone number. Total of 10 digits.)

Henni and Amy Buitenhuis	Paalberweg 25A	7351 AD	Hoenderloo, NL	011-31-(0) 553-781-754	
René and G. Buietenhuis	Krimweg 22	7351 AD	Hoenderloo, NL	011-31-(0) 553-781-318	
Willem van Roekel	1273 Buurtlaan Oost	3902 DA	Veenendaal, NL	011-31-(0) 318-510-972	
Jan van Roekel	ADSL589299@tiscoli.nl			011-31-(0) 318-561-202	
Gijs and Meinie Bos	Smoussweg Straat 2	6741 NJ	Lunteren, NL	011-31-(0) 318-571-672	
Gijs van Roekel (Genealogist)	Bakkerweg 5	3951 CS	Maam, NL	g.v.roekel@hccnet.nl	
Hendrick and Grada van Roekel	SE 1 (Deelen)	6816 SV	Arnhem, NL	011-31-(0) 264-423-892	
Hendricus Roseboom	Hollandscheveldse Opgaande 60	7913 VE	Hollandscheveld	Ds.HRoseboom@filternet.nl	

Appendix

INDEX

1. **Siblings of Jan van Roekel (1885) and Their Descendants**
   a. Sophia van Roekel (first child) 107
   b. Willem van Roekel (21/09/1869) + Abbreviated version 107
   c. Hendricus van Roekel 108
   d. Gijsbertus van Roekel 109
      Abbreviated version 110

2. **Ancestors of van Roekels**—Family Tree Maker, from Gijs van Roekel in Holland. 111
   a. Family History of van Roekels and van Deelens as written by Willemina on an envelope. 112

3. **Story of Jan De Bakker, the first Dutch martyr** 135

4. **Ancestors of Willemina van Deelen van Roekel**
   a. van Deelen ancestors, document given to us by Jopie and Wim Blokker 141
   b. Hand-wrtten family history of of the van Deelens 142
   c. van Deelen ancestors, long version dating from Tonis Gijsbertsen Abt. 1595 145

5. **Letter from Kaye Mason to Willem van Roekel** (Hendricus' grandson) 144

6. **Letter from Willemina van Roekel to her family in Holland**, handwritten in Dutch 150-151

7. **Copies of documents**
   a. Ellis Island immigration papers (Ship's Manifest) 152-153
   b. Jan's military papers 154-155
   c. Van Eeden Colony Plots Map 156-157
   d. Where is Van Eeden, how do you get there? 158-159
   e. "Say It With Flowers" Postcard, Van Roekel Florist 134

8. **Herman Vogel genealogy** 160

9. **The book, *Van Eeeden Kolonie*, Dr. Frederik van Eeden** (translation included here) 161

OTHER RESOURCES ON THE INTERNET

1. **De Gele Rijders (Rijdende Artillerie) (Yellow Riders) history:** In Dutch:
   http://www.41afdva.net/Rijdende_Artillerie.htm
   Translated into English: http://translate.google.com/translate?js=n&prev=_t&hl=en&ie=UTF-8&u=http%3A%2F%2Fwww.41afdva.net%2F&sl=nl&tl=en&history_state0=

2. **Dr. W. Frank Ainsley Home Page:**
   http://people.uncw.edu/ainsleyf/ainsley.htm

3. ***How the Dutch obtained their Land:***
   http://www.oldandsold.com/articles13/travel-105.shtml

4. **Note:** anyone interested in learning more about MacRae's experiment and similar settlements should track down the following articles: **"A Reconnaissance of Some Cultural-Agricultural Islands in the South,"** by Walter M. Kollmorgen, Economic Geography Vol. 17, No. 4, Oct. 1941, pp. 409-43. In this same publication, Vol. 19, No. 2, April, 1943: **"Agricultural-Cultural Islands in the South—Part II."**

5. **Dr. Frederik van Eeden and His Perspective**

   a. **"Studies Relating to Dr. Frederik van Eeden"** by Dr. J. Glenn Friesen. (see website: http://members.shaw.ca/jgfriesen/Notes/VanEeden.html

   b. **"Walden Goes Wandering: the Transit of Good Intentions."** *The New England Quarterly* article, Vol. XXXII, No. 1, March 1959

   c. ***Van Eeden*** by Susan Taylor Block, 1995. Published by Lower Cape Fear Historical Society. Can be ordered from: http://www.stblock.com/sub/books.html

   d. **"Practical Communism, Work and Bread"** by Frederik van Eeden – An Address Delivered Before the Civic Forum on March 8, 1908 at Carnegie Hall. See website: http://www.archive.org/stream/practicalcommun00eedegoog/practicalcommun00eedegoog_djvu.txt

   e. **"Poet has the Cure for Nation's Ills"** by Frederick Van Eeden. See the *New York Times* article : http://query.nytimes.com/gst/abstract.html?res=9D0CE2D71F3EE233A25756C0A9659C946997D6CF

   f. **"A Leader, Not Law, the Need of Mankind."** Dr. Van Eeden Tells Civic Forum the Time Is Now Ripe for Communism. See article: http://query.nytimes.com/gst/abstract.html?res=9B05E6DF1331E233A2575AC0A9659C946997D6CF

   g. **"Dr. van Eeden's Plan for a Happy Humanity."** Selected by Edwin Markham. The San Francisco Eaminer, 17 August, 1912.

   h. TO TRY FOR INDUSTRIAL UTOPIA IN AMERICA. Dr. **"Frederik Van Eeden Plans a Co-operative Community to be Started in New York—Similar Project in Holland and Its Fate."** By Allan L. Benson, *The New York Times*. Published March 7, 1909.

   i. **"Says Mind Cures More than Drugs,"** Dr. Van Eeden, Dutch Physician, so tells League for Political Education. "Suggestion the Secret." He Answers Many Questions and Warns Hearers Against Faith Healers and Fanatics. *The New York Times*, March 19, 1908: http://query.nytimes.com/gst/abstract.html?res=9805E6DB1639E333A2575AC1A9659C946997D6CF

   j. **"Viewpoint of Frederik van Eeden"** (on dreams). http://www.trionica.com/asp/viewpoints/vanEeden.htm

   k. **"A Study of Dreams"** by Frederik van Eeden: http://www.lucidity.com/vanEeden.html

The Library of the University of North Carolina has an extensive collection of materials about MacRae and the North Carolina colonies, including a thesis by John Faris Corey titled, "The Colonization and Contributions of Emmigrants Brought to Southeastern North Carolina by Hugh MacRae.

Genealogy of Siblings of Jan van Roekel (1885)
Partial list of Siblings and their Descendants • Dates listed as day-month-year

I. Sophia van Roekel (15-12-1863)

First born of Jan van Roekel (25-12-1836) and Timetje Koudjis (10-10-1837). This record from the *Van Roekel Family in The Gelderland* page 41 and also from the records of Hendrick Roseboom, Bruchem, Holland.

I **Sophia van Roekel**, born 15-12-1863 and died 05-04-1928. Married Aibertus Ederveen who was born 1867 and died 05-06-1927. They had four children.

- I-A **J. Ederveen**, married J. Ederveen-van Laar
- I-B **T. Ederveen**, married F. Ederveen-van Zenmeren
- I-C **B. Ederveen**, married J. W. van Maanen
- I-D **J. Ederveen**, married J. ter Maten

IV. Willem van Roekel (21-09-1869)

Fourth child of Jan (25-12-1836) and Timetje Koudijs: Reference in the *Family van Roekel in the Gelderland*, pages 129-131. Descending line XV. Refer to his father, page 41, (VIw) Jan van Roekel. For this genealogical line:

IV **Willem van Roekel**, (brother of my grandfather, Jan (1885). Male, born in Ede 21-09-1869 and died in Breda where he was warden of the federal prison. (Date of Death ?) He married Gerritje van Meerten in Utrecht on 15-06-1898. She was born in Amerongen on 21-07-1871 and died in Breda.

Children:

IV-A **Jan van Roekel**, born 11-04-1898 in Utrecht. Died in Valkenswaard on 09-03-1949. He married on 02-09-1920 to Adriana Prins. She was born 12-04-1900. One son, Willem Antoni.

- IV-A1 **Willem Antoni van Roekel**, son of Jan (11-04-1898) (I-A). Born in Valkenswaard 03-07-1921. Married Aaltje van Wijk on 22-04-1949. She was born in Bergeijk on 23-08-1922. They had one son, Jan Cornelis, born in Waaire 20-06-1954.

IV-B **Tijmen van Roekel**, son, born in Utrecht and died in Breda 05-02-1983. He was a construction supervisor. He married Johanna Hermina Kruijl. She died in Breda 06-05-1986.

Children:
- IV-B1 Johanna Hermina, born in Halsteren 17-07-1932. Married D. van Uittert.
- IV-B2 Hermina Helena, born in Halsteren 17-07-1932. (twins) Married to G. van Groningen who died 17-06-1981.
- I-B3 Gerta, born in Bergen op Zoom on 29-04-1938

IV. WILLEM van ROEKEL – ABBREVIATED VERSION

WILLEM VAN ROEKEL	and	GERRITJE VAN MEERTEN
21-09-1869	15-06-1898	20-10-1871
Jan (11-04-1898)	Tijmen	Dirk Willem (06-07-1905)
Willem (03-07-1921)	1- Johanna Hermina 2- Hermina Relena 3- Gerda 4- W.L (31-22-1929)	Willem (25-08-1932)
		Alida Gerda Carolina (15-09-1938)
Jan Cornelis (20-06-1954)		Irene Jacoba (26-01-1942)
	Paulus (19-09-1956) Willem (24-07-1959) Marcel (18-06-1966)	
		Johanna Carolina (29-06-1964) Saskia Irene Wilhelmina (12-08-1966) Lars Jan Willem (12-08-1970)

Provided by Gijs van Roekel in Holland, **Family Tree Maker**

I-B4 W. L. van Roekel. Son, born in Putte (?) 31-12-1929. He was an electricial engineer. He married 09-06-1955 to Dina Jacoba Snijders. She was born 24-09-1933, the daughter of Arnoldus Snijders and Francina Schoonen.

Children:
- I-B4a Paulus, son, born in Heerien 19-09-1956, a librarian.
- I-B4b Willem, son, born in Heerlen 24-07-1959
- I-B4c Marcel, son, born in Etten-Leur 18-06-1966

I-C **Dirk Willem van Roekel**, born in Breda 06-07-1905 and died in the Hague 19-07-1971. He was inspector for the Federal Acquistions Office. He married Johanna Cornelia Molenaar in Breda 02-05-1929. She was born in Breda and died in Bergen op Zoom 04-01-1937. She was the daughter of Hendrikus Cornelis Molenaar and Elisabeth Christina Weegman. He married again on 15-06-1937 to Carolina Wijkhuizen. She was the daughter of Jacobus Wijkhuizen and Alida Schinkel. She died in Velp on 20-01-1989.

Children:
- I-C1 Willem van Roekel, son of Dirk Willem (IIc). Born in Eindhoven on 25-08-1932. He is a systems analyst. He married in The Hague, Petronella Josina de Munck on 26-10-1961. She was born in Antwerp, Belgium, on 26-08-1940, the daughter of Dingenis Jozias the Munck and Sytske Nieuwenhuis.
- I-C2 Alida Gerda Carolina van Roekel, daughter of Dirk Willem (I-C). She was born in Breda on 15-09-1938. She married Jacobus Willem Vreeke and was a homemaker. He was born 17-12-1937, the son of Johanne Vreeke and Johanna Koeman.

Children:
- I-C2a Johanna Carolina, born in Breda 29-06-1964, married Robert van Osta.
- I-C2b Saskia Irene Wilhelmina, daughter born in Oudenbosch 12-08-1966. She is living with Emile Kersten.
- I-C2c Lars Jan Willem, born in Oudenbosch 12-08-1970.

I-C3 Irene Jacoba, born in Breda 26-01-1942, married W.P. Smit.

IX. Hendricus van Roekel (04-12-1879)

IX **Hendricus van Roekel**, ninth child of Jan (1835) and brother of Jan (1885). Died: 21-11-1955. Married Barendina Bos 24-09-1871.

Children:
- IX-A **Jan van Roekel.** Born 12-08-1905, Utrecht, died 13-07-1970. Married 12-12-1929 to Cornelia Cornelisse. She was born 24-12-1908, and died 04-03-2004. (We met her on the 1999 visit.)

Children:
- IX-A1 Barendina Hendrika 01-06-1930,
- IX-A2 Aletta Willemina 30-12-1931.
- IX-A3 Willem 08-03-1943. Lives in Veenendaal (see Telephone-Address sheet). Married (14-07-1966), Woutrina Hendrika van de Velde, 31-1-1945.

Children:
- IX-A3a Cornelia Maatje Helena (04-01-1967)
- IX-A3b Hendrika Helena (11-08-1970)
- IX-A3c Jan (13-04-1976)
- IX-A3d Engelina Jantine (19-09-1978)

- IX-A4 Cornelia Gijsberta 26-01-1953.

- IX-B **Gijsbert van Roekel.** Born Veenendaal 02-10-1910, died 13-09-1995. Married 07-10-1936 to Catharina van Voorst. Born 22-01-1915. Died 31-03-1990.

Children:
- IX-B1 Hendricus Gijsbertus van Roekel, Born 27-06-1937. Buried in Veenendaal, 24-04-2004. First married Jantje Egbertsen 15-11-1962, She was born 03-02-1941 and died 08-12-1981, buried in Rijssen.

Hendricus van Roekel continued

IX-B1a Gijsbert Williem van Roekel 04-11-1964

IX-B1b Gerald Carle Robert van Roekel 10-07-1967.

Hendricus later married Petonella Catharina Gerritsen 11-05-1988, born 15-06-1958. No children from this marriage.

IX-B2 Jacob Evert Jan van Roekel 24-05-1943.

IX-C **Ottina van Roekel** (04-01-1913) Born in Utrecht, and buried in Ede, 26-06-1991. Married Gijsbert Roseboom 20-05-1931. He was born 13-06-1905, and died 29-03-1934.

Children:
IX-C1 Adriaantje Roseboom (08-09-1937)

IX-C2 Hendricus Roseboom (15-11-1940) Died (03-04-1941)

IX-C3 Hendricus Roseboom (12-02-1947) (Pastor who interpreted the information from his mother, Ottina van Roekel. We met him in 1967 and 1999.) He married Klaasje Hoi. She was born 02-08-1947, From Ede

Children: Rosebooms'

IX-C3a Gijsbert 28-11-1974, Ede (Ederveen)
    IX-C3a1 Hendricus (Enrico)15-08-2001 Hertogenbosch
    IX-C3a2 Florus Jan (Florian) 22-08-2004
    IX-C3a3 Klass Jan (Jannick) 18-06-2007

IX-C3b Florus (11-06-1976) Ede
    IX-C3b1 Hendricus (Rik) (15-07-2004) Harderwijk
    IX-C3b2 Anna Jacoba (Anna) 05-06-2006 Harderwijk

IX-C3c Hendricus (30-03-1980) Amersfort
    IX-C3c1 Hendrik Johan (Iwan) 29-07-2005
    IX-C3c2 Willem Daniel Sheva (Dani) 07-07-2007

IX-C3d Klaasje Melinda (20-04-1982) Apeldorn

IX-C3e KlassOtto (2903-1984) Apeldorn

IX-C3c Willem Marcelis (16-03-1986) Gorinchem

XVI. Gijsbertus van Roekel (13-09-1891)

Gijsbertus van Roekel, born 13-09-1891. Sixteenth child of Jan van Roekel (1836) and Ottina van Hunen. Reference in the *Family Van Roekel in the Gelderland*, pages ISO-153. Descending line XXIV. Refer to page 41, (VIw) Jan van Roekel (25-12-1836.)

XVI. **Gijsbertus van Roekel**, born in Ede 13-09-1891, died in Lunteren 16-10-1972. A farmer. Married Derkje Berkhof 03-04-1915. Born in Ede 21-04-1894 and died in Bennekom 12-02-1977. She was the daughter of Willem Berkhof and Cornelia van de Meent.

Children:
XVI-A **Ottina van Roekel**, born in Ede 20-05-1915. Married Teunis van Ginkel in Woudenberg on 24-11-1939. They had six children.

XVI-B **Willem van Roekel**, born in Ede 30-10-1916 and died on Java 01-01-1947.

XVI-C **Jan van Roekel**, born in Ede 11-04-1918 and died in Ede 18-01-1990. Married Gerritje Hoogeweg in Renswoude 27-03-1946. One son, died in 1990.

XVI-D **Cornelia van Roekel**, daughter, born in Ede 02-08-1919. (Died ?) Married Jan William Berkhof, (Died ?) They had 5 children.

XVI-E **Hendrikus van Roekel**, born in Ede 21-09-1924. Public servant. Married Barendina Klara Pater, born in Renswoude 09-10-1928. She was the daughter of Klaas Pater and Clara van Willigenburg.

Children:
XVI-E1 **Gijsbertus van Roekel**, son of Hendrikus. Born in Woudenberg on 01-05-1949. He is an elementary school principal. He married Everarda Wilhelmina de Ridder in Woudenberg on 04-08-1971. She was born in Woudenberg on 12-12-1947. She is daughter of Martinus de Ridder and Grietje Marie van Wessel.

Children:
XVI-E1a Hendrikus, son, born 16-04-1974 in Doornspijk.
XVI-E1b Martinus, son, born 08-03-1976 in Zwolle.
XVI-E1c Grietje Barendina, daughter, born 09-08-1981 in Apeldorn.
XVI-E1d Klass Jan, son, born 21-06-1983 in Apeldorn.

Genealogy of Siblings of Jan van Roekel (1885)

XVI-E2 **Clara van Roekel**, 27-08-1950, daughter of Hendrikus. Born in Woudenberg on 27-08-1950. Married Dick Lokhorts in Woudenberg on 22-12-1971.

Children, surnamed Lokhorts.
XVI-E2a Dick Anthonie, son, born in Woudenberg on 9-11-1974.
XVI-E2b Barendina Klara, daughter, born in Woudenberg on 27-06-1977.
XVI-E2c Hendrikus, son, born in Woudenberg 07-06-1983.

XVI-E3 **Klaas van Roekel**, son born in Woudenberg 24-09-1951.

XVI-E4 **Dirkje Barendina Hendrika van Roekel**, 11-10-1963, daughter of Hendrikus (1924). Born in Woudenberg 11-10-1963. Married Peter Verwoert in Woudenberg on 12-02-1986.

Children, (Surname Verwoert):
XVI-E4a Barendina Klara, born in Woudenberg 19-03-1987.
XVI-E4b Johanna Petronella, born in Woudenberg 17-09-1990.

XVI-E5 **Wilma Korine van Roekel**, born 30-07-1965 in Woudenberg, daughter of Hendrikus. Married Gabriel Bravenboor on 15-04-1987.

Children, (Surname Bravenboor):
XVI-E5a Johanne Joseph, born in Veenendaal 25-07-1988.
XVI-E5b Barendina Margaretha, born in Veenendaal 02-05-1990.

XVI-E6 **Janetta Gerda**, daughter, born in Woudenberg 24-08-1969.

XVI-F **Aartje van Roekel**, daughter, born in Ederveen 23-11-1929. Homemaker. Married on 25-06-1952 in Ede to Gijsbert Snellen. He was born 22-12-1929 in Lunteren, the son of Hendrick Snellen and Jacoba van de Pol.

Children (Surname Snellen):
XVI-F1 Hendrick (15-05-1957)
XVI-F2 Gijsbertus (12-01-1960)
XVI-F3 Jan Willem (15-01-61)

GIJSBERTUS van ROEKEL – ABBREVIATED VERSION

GIJSBERTUS VAN ROEKEL (13-09-1891)	AND (03-04-1915)	DERKJE BERKHOF (21-04-1894)
(1) OTTINA (20-05-1915) (2) WILLEM (30-10-1916) (3) JAN (11-04-1918) (4) CORNELIA (02-08-1919)	(5) HENDRIKUS (IIa) (21-09-1924)	(6) AARTJE (SNELLEN) (IIb) (23-11-1929) HENDRICK GIJSBERTUS JAN WILLEM
GIJSBERTUS (01-05-1949)		HENDRIKUS (16-04-1974) MARTINUS (08-03-1976) GRIETJE GARENDINA (09-08-1981) KLASS JAN (21-06-1983)
CLARA (LOKHORST) (27-08-1950)		DICK ANTHONIE (19-11-1974) BARENDINA KLARA (27-06-1977) HENDRICUS (07-06-1983)
KLASS VAN ROEKEL (24-09-1951)		
DIKJE BARENDINA (VERWOERT) (11-10-1963)		BARENDINA KARLA (19-03-1987) JOHANNA PETRONELLA (17-09-1990)
WILMA KORINA (BRAVENBOOR) (30-07-1965)		JOHANNE JOSEPH (25-07-1988) BARENDINA MARGARETHA (02-05-1990)
JANETTA GERDA (24-08-1969)		

Provided by Gijs van Roekel in Holland, **Family Tree Maker**

Ancestors of Jan van Roekel (1885)

*From Gijs van Roekel in Holland, **Family Tree Maker** • Dates listed as day-month-year*

Generation No. 1

1. **Jan van Roekel**, born 24-8-1885 in Ede. He was the son of **2. Jan van Roekel** and **3. Ottina Van Hunen**. He married **(1) Willemina van Deelen** 9-9-1911 in Ede. She was born Abt. 1888 in Ede. She was the daughter of Willem van Deelen and Rikje Essenstam.

Notes for Jan van Roekel:
GR41: Emigreerde naar US Dudley, bezocht Nederland met zijn vrouw in 1926

Marriage Notes for Jan van Roekel and Willemina van Deelen:
Archieflocatie: Gelderland
Toegangnr: 0207
Inventarisnr: 8253
Gemeente: Ede
Soort akte: HuwelijksaJcte
Nunimer: 87
Datum: 09-09-1911

Generation No. 2

2. **Jan van Roekel**, born 25-12-1836 in Ede; died 22-10-1907 in Ede. He was the son of **4. Willem Willemsen van Roekel** and **5. Fijtje van Maanen**. He married **3. Ottina Van Hunen** 29-3-1879 in Ede.
3. **Ottina Van Hunen**, born 15-9-1848 in Ede. She was the daughter of **6. Hendricus van Hunen** and **7. Hendrikje van Veldhuizen**.

Notes for Jan van Roekel:
GR41 6w(5k): Landbouwer in Lunteren

Marriage Notes for Jan van Roekel and Ottina Van Hunen:
Archieflocatie: Gelderland
Toegangnr: 0207
Inventarisnr: 5290
Gemeente: Ede
Soort akte: Huwelijksakte
Nummer: 12
Datum: 29-03-1879

Children of Jan van Roekel and Ottina Van Hunen:

i. **Hendrikje van Roekel**, born 7-1-1881 in Ede; married (1) **Jacob Bos** 18-1-1912 in Ede; born Abt. 1883 in Ede; married (2) **Florus Blankespoor** 28-11-1919 in Barneveld; born Abt. 1865 in Barneveld.
Marriage Notes for Hendrikje van Roekel and Jacob Bos:
Archieflocatie: Gelderland
Toegangnr: 0207
Inventarisnr: 8253
Gemeente: Ede
Soort akte: Huwelijksakte
Nummer: 4
Datum: 18-01-1912

ii. **Jannetje van Roekel**, born 19-11-1882 in Ede; died 8-12-1966; married **Barend Vink** 12-11-1909 in Renswoude; born Abt. 1883 in Renswoude.
Notes for Jannetje van Roekel:
Begraven AB Renswoude

Marriage Notes for Jannetje van Roekel and Barend Vink:
Archieflocatie: Utrecht
Toegangnr: 263
Inventarisnr: 45
Gemeente: Renswoude
Soort akte: Huwelijksakte
Nummer: 9
Datum: 12-11-1909
Van Renswoude, Lunteren

iii. **Cornelia van Roekel**, born 16-3-1884 in Ede.

1 iv. **Jan van Roekel**, born 24-8-1885 in Ede; married **Willemina van Deelen** 9-9-1911 in Ede.

v. **Cornelisje van Roekel**, born 8-12-1887 in Ede; married **Cornelis Meijer** 24-10-1918 in Amerongen; born Abt. 1880 in Amerongen.

Marriage Notes for Cornelisje van Roekel and Cornelis Meijer:
Archieflocatie: Utrecht
Toegangnr: 263
Inventarisnr: 231
Gemeente: Amerongen
Soort akte: Huwelijksakte
Nummer: 20
Datum: 24-10-1918
Van Amerongen Ede

vi. **Bartus van Roekel**, born 12-2-1890 in Ede; died 15-8-1973.
Notes for Bartus van Roekel:
Begraven AB Bennekom 18-8-1973

vii. **Gijsbertus van Roekel**, born 13-8-1891 in Ede; died 16-10-1972 in Lunteren; married **Derkje Berkhof** 3-4-1915 in Ede; born 21-4-1894 in Ede; died 12-2-1977 in Bennekom.

Notes for Gijsbertus van Roekel:
GR150 24-l(6w): Landbouwer

ENVELOPE FRONT

Daddy father
Jan Van Roekel
Benkom
Lunteren Holland
Mother
Otilena Van Hunen
Lunteren Holland
J. Van Roekel
Lunteren Holland

1. Reiner Van Roekel
2. Willam Van Roekel 30 –
3. Henije Van Roekel
4. Jannie Van Roekel 80
5. Gysbert Van Roekel
6. Gyp Van Roekel
7. Driek Van Roekel
Henije married Job Bos

8 Bart 7 Frank
7 Dina Bos
Hendrik John Gys Bart

(side notes: Daddy 1895 – Lunteren; Moder 1887 Hoorloo)

ENVELOPE BACK

1. Willam Van Dellen
2. Ricky Essendam Hon.
   mother Hon. Daddy
John Van Dellen
Atto Van Hunten mother
Wilhelmiana Van Hunen mother
Albert Van Dellen Ho –
Willem Van Deelen
Dina Van Deelen Coruba H –
Koos Van Deelen
           Van Brink
Kuk Van Deelen
Jo Van Dellen Van Brink
Cido   Van Beekel
Jannie Van Dellen
Joppe — Van Heuten
Grace Van Dullen
Berend Busthuis

Wimpie – Hoenderloo
Koose, adie – Driebergen –
Hoppie Willi, Wilm, John
rib – Apeldorn
Henry Hon.

Family history of van Roekels and van Deelens as written by Willemina on an envelope.

Marriage Notes for Gijsbertus van Roekel and Derkje Berkhof:
Archieflocatie: Gelderland
Toegangnr: 0207
Inventarisnr: 9059
Gemeente: Ede
Soort akte: Huwelijksakte
Nununer: 25
Datum: 03-04-1915

Begraven te Lunteren

viii. **Evertje van Roekel**, born 22-11-1894 in Ede; died 9-2-1897.

Generation No. 3

4. **Willem Willemsen van Roekel**, born 28-6-1814 in Bennekom; died 6-4-1843 in Ede. He was the son of **8. Willem Derksen van Roekel** and **9. Gijsbertje Gerritsen Roseboom**. He married **5. Fijtje van Maanen** 18-6-1836 in Ede.

5. **Fijtje van Maanen**, born 20-10-1815 in Ede; died 13-4-1849 in Ede. She was the daughter of **10. Jan Woutersen van Maanen** and **11. Evertje Toonen Brandsen**.

Notes for Willem Willemsen van Roekel:
DB64: Willem zv Willem van Roekel 47jr en Gijsbertje Rozeboom
GR26, 5k(4d): Landbouwer

Notes for Fijtje van Maanen:
DB65: Fijtje dv Jan van Maanen 28jr en Evertje Toonen GR26

More About Fijtje van Maanen:
Date born 2: 20-10-1815

Marriage Notes for Willem van Roekel and Fijtje van Maanen:
Archieflocatie: Gelderland
Toegangnr: 0207
Inventarisnr: 5298
Gemeente: Ede
Soort akte: Huwelijksakte
Nummer: 30
Datum: 18-06-1836

Children of Willem van Roekel and Fijtje van Maanen:

2 i. **Jan van Roekel**, born 25-12-1836 in Ede; died 22-10-1907 in Ede; married **(1) Timetje Koudijs** 23-5-1863 in Ede; married **(2) Ottina Van Hunen** 29-3-1879 in Ede.

ii. **Willem van Roekel**, born 17-1-1839 in Ede.

iii. **Evertje van Roekel**, born 29-9-1841 in Ede; married **Gerrit van Ginkel** 16-3-1861 in Ede; born Abt. 1838 in Amerongen.

Marriage Notes for Evertje van Roekel and Gerrit van Ginkel:
Archieflocatie: Gelderland
Toegangnr: 0207
Inventarisnr: 5294
Gemeente: Ede
Soort akte: Huwelijksakte
Nummer: 15
Datum: 16-03-1861.

6. **Hendricus van Hunen**, married **7. Hendrikje van Veldhuizen**

7. **Hendrikje van Veldhuizen**

Child of Hendricus van Hunen and Hendrikje van Veldhuizen is:

3 i. **Ottina Van Hunen**, born 15-9-1848 in Ede; married **Jan van Roekel** 29-3-1879 in Ede.

Generation No. 4

8. **Willem Derksen van Roekel**, born 26-4-1767 in Bennekom; died 12-7-1841 in Ede. He was the son of **16. Derck Jacobsen van Roekel** and **17. Evertje Jansen**. He married **9. Gijsbertje Gerritsen Roseboom** 28-4-1792 in Bennekom.

9. **Gijsbertje Gerritsen Roseboom**, born 8-9-1771 in Bennekom; died 15-3-1835 in Bennekom. She was the daughter of **18. Gerrit Everts Roseboom** and **19. Maria van Leeuwen**.

Notes for Willem Derksen van Roekel:
GR17 4d(3d): Bouwman. Woont in 1811 in Bennekom
VG112p39
VG1985p98
VG1985pl03
VG1985pl70
VG1994pl30
VG1996plO
KAG Ede p72: sectie E Maanderbroek, perceel 33bis westelijk van 'het Floddergat'
DB39: Willem zv Dirk Jacobsen en Evertje Jansse
GR17 4d(3d): Farmer. Lives in 1811 in Bennekom
VG112p39
VG1985p98
VG1985pl03
VG1985p170
VG1994pl30
VG1996plO

Ancestors of Jan van Roekel

KAG Ede p72: sectie E Maanderbroek, perceel 33bis westelijk van 'het Floddergat'

Notes for Gijsbertje Gerritsen Roseboom:
GR17
VG112p42
VG1985pl03: lidm. 10-4-1801
VG1985pl70
DB41: Gijsbertje dv Gerrit Roseboom en Maria van Leeuwen

Marriage Notes for Willem van Roekel and Gijsbertje Roseboom:
TB30: Willem Derksz geb en won Bennekom met Gijsbertje Gerritsd geb en won Bennekom

Children of Willem van Roekel and Gijsbertje Roseboom are:

i. **Derk Willemsen van Roekel**, born 12-1-1793 in Bennekom.

   Notes for Derk Willemsen van Roekel:
   DBS 1: Derk zv Willem Derksz en Gijsbertje Gerritsd

ii. **Maria Jacoba Willemsen van Roekel**, born 17-9-1794 in Bennekom; died 3-8-1831 in Wageningen; married **Johannes Vonk** 13-12-1817 in Bennekom; born 31-3-1793 in Wageningen; died 13-3-1852 in Wageningen.

   Notes for Maria Jacoba Willemsen van Roekel:
   DB52: Maria Jacoba dv Willem Derksz en Gijsbertje Gerritsen Rozeboom

   Notes for Johannes Vonk:
   VG1986pl78

   Marriage Notes for Maria van Roekel and Johannes Vonk:
   Archieflocatie: Gelderland
   Toegangnr: 0207
   Inventarisnr: 6268
   Gemeente: Bennekom
   Soort akte: Huwelijksakte
   Nummer: 5
   Datum: 13-12-1817
   TB42: Johannes Vonk 25jr geb en won Wageningen zv Cornelis Vonk won Bennekom en wijien Maria Uittenbogaard met Maria Jacoba van Roekel 24jr geb en won Bennekom dv Willem Derksen van Roekel en Gijsbertje Rozeboom beide won Bennekom

iii. **Gerrit Willemsen van Roekel**, born 12-4-1796 in Bennekom; married **Willemina Tijmessen**
   Notes for Gerrit Willemsen van Roekel:
   D53: Gerret zv Willem Dirksesz en Gijsbertje Garretsz
   GR24, 5h(4d): Landbouwer in de bovenbuurt, Wageningen
   VG1985pl03

   Notes for Willemina Tijmessen:
   GR24

iv. **Hendrik Willemsen van Roekel**, born 10-6-1798 in Bennekom; died 23-8-1873 in Ede; married **Maria Derksen van Roekel** 22-1-1819 in Ede; born 15-3-1799 in Bennekom; died 6-12-1872 in Bennekom.

   Notes for Hendrik Willemsen van Roekel:
   DB54: Hendrik zv Willem Dirksz van Roekel en Gijsbertje Gerritsz Roosenboom
   GR18, 24, 5i(4d): Landbouwer
   VG1985pl03

   Notes for Maria Derksen van Roekel:
   DB54: Maria dv Dirk Dirkzen en Johanna van Zeifhout
   GR18,24
   VG1985pl03

   Marriage Notes for Hendrik van Roekel and Maria van Roekel:
   Archieflocatie: Gelderland
   Toegangnr: 0207
   Inventarisnr: 5300
   Gemeente: Ede
   Soort akte: Huwelijksakte
   Nummer: 1
   Datum: 22-01-1819

v. **Evertje Willemsen van Roekel**, born 17-5-1800 in Bennekom.

   Notes for Evertje Willemsen van Roekel:
   DB55: Evertje dv Willem Dirkse van Roekel en Gijsbertje Roosenboom

vi. **Gerritje Willemsen van Roekel**, born 5-6-1802 in Bennekom; died 27-7-1881 in Bennekom; married **Gerrit Jacobsen van Roekel** 2-5-1823 in Ede; born 4-2-1799 in Bennekom; died 25-8-1862 in Bennekom.

   Notes for Gerritje Willemsen van Roekel:
   DB57: Gerrietje dv Willem Derksz van Roekel en Gijsbertje Rosenboom
   GR18, 20
   VG1985pl03

   Notes for Gerrit Jacobsen van Roekel:
   DB54: Gerrit zv Jacob Gerritz van Roekel en

Ancestors of Jan van Roekel

Rijkje Willems van Maanen GR20, 5a(4a): Timmerman
VG1985p100

Marriage Notes for Gerritje van Roekel and Gerrit van Roekel:
Archieflocatie: Gelderland
Toegangnr: 0207
Inventarisnr: 5300
Gemeente: Ede
Soort akte: Huwelijksakte
Nimimer: 19
Datum: 03-05-1823

vii. **Elisabeth Willemsen van Roekel**, born 30-11-1804 in Bennekom; died 12-3-1824.

Notes for Elisabeth Willemsen van Roekel:
DB58: Elisabeth dv Willem Dirks van Roekel en Gijsbertje Rosenboom

viii. **Evertje Willemsen van Roekel**, born 7-3-1807 in Bennekom; married **Johannes Vonk** 27-11-1832 in Ede; born 31-3-1793 in Wageningen; died 13-3-1852 in Wageningen.

Notes for Evertje Willemsen van Roekel:
DB59: Evertje dv Willem Dirks van Roekel en Gijsbertje Rosenboom

Notes for Johannes Vonk:
VG1986p178

Marriage Notes for Evertje van Roekel and Johannes Vonk:
Archieflocatie: Gelderland
Toegangnr: 0207
Inventarisnr: 5299
Gemeente: Ede
Soort akte: Huwelijksakte
Nummer: 33
Datum: 27-11-1832 wettiging 1 kind

ix. **Wouter Willemseft van Roekel**, born 7-3-1810 in Bennekom; died 1 -5-1891 in Bennekom; married **Gerritje Willemsen van den Elskamp** 27-10-1832 in Ede; born 26-4-1813 in Bennekom; died 10-5-1853 in Bennekom.

Notes for Wouter Willemsen van Roekel:
DB61: Wouter zv Willem Dirkse van Roekel en Gijsbertje Rosenboom
GR26, 5j(4d): Landbouwer
VG1985p103
VG1985p170: overleden 1-5-1892 ?
VG1994p47

Notes for Gerritje Willemsen van den Elskamp:
GR26
VG1985pl70: geb. 29-4 ?
VG1994p47

Marriage Notes for Wouter van Roekel and Gerritje den Elskamp:
Archieflocatie: Gelderland
Toegangnr: 0207
Inventarisnr: 5299
Gemeente: Ede
Soort akte: Huwelijksakte
Nunimer: 28
Datum: 27-10-1832

x. **Jacobje Willemsen van Roekel**, born 30-11-1811 in Bennekom; died 7-7-1842 in Ede; married Wouter van Maanen 15-10-1836 in Ede; born 13-10-1817 in Bennekom.

Notes for Jacobje Willemsen van Roekel:
DB62: Jacobje dv Willem Dirksen en Gijsbertje Roseboom

Marriage Notes for Jacobje van Roekel and Wouter van Maanen:
Archieflocatie: Gelderland
Toegangnr: 0207
Inventarisnr: 5298
Gemeente: Ede
Soort akte: Huwelijksakte
Nummer: 42

4 xi. **Willem Willemsen van Roekel**, born 28-6-1814 in Bennekom; died 6-4-1843 in Ede; married **Fijtje van Maanen** 18-6-1836 in Ede.

10. **Jan Woutersen van Maanen**, born 23-7-1787 in Bennekom. He was the son of **20. Wouter Willemsen van Maanen** and **21. Baatje Gijsbertsen**. He married **11. Evertje Toonen Brandsen** 25-5-1815 in Bennekom.

11. **Evertje Toonen Brandsen**, born 9-11-1797 in Bennekom. She was the daughter of **22. Brand Toonen** and **23. Fijtje Evertsen**.

Notes for Jan Woutersen van Maanen:
DB48: Jan zv Wouter Wilms en Baatje Gijsbertsen

More About Jan Woutersen van Maanen:
Date born 2: Abt. 1787, Bennekom

Notes for Evertje Toonen Brandsen:
DB53: Evertje dv Brand Thoonen en Fijtje Evertse

Marriage Notes for Jan van Maanen and Evertje Brandsen:
TB40: Jan van Maanen 28jr geb en won Bennekom zv Wouter van Maanen won te Bennekom en Baatje Gijsbers overl te Bennekom met Evertje Toonen 17jr

geb en won Bennekom dv Brand Toonen overl en Fijtje Evers wonende Bennekom

Children of Jan van Maanen and Evertje Brandsen:

5   i. **Fijtje van Maanen**, born 20-10-1815 in Ede; died 13-4-1849 in Ede; married **Willem Willemsen van Roekel** 18-6-1836 in Ede.

    ii. **Wouter van Maanen**, born 13-10-1817 in Bennekom; married **(1) Jacobje Willemsen van Roekel** 15-10-1836 in Ede; born 3 0-11-1811 in Bennekom; died 7-7-1842 in Ede; married **(2) Jantje van Otterloo** 4-5-1844 in Ede; born 24-9-1819 in Ede; married **(3) Cornelisje Broekhuis** 6-5-1871 in Ede; born 31-1-1839 in Barneveld; died 7-11-1874 in Ede.

Notes for Jacobje Willemsen van Roekel:
DB62: Jacobje dv Willem Dirksen en Gijsbertje Roseboom

Marriage Notes for Wouter van Maanen and Jacobje van Roekel:
Archieflocatie: Gelderland
Toegangnr: 0207
Inventarisnr: 5298
Gemeente: Ede
Soort akte: Huwelijksakte
Nummer: 42

    iii. **Brand van Maanen**, married **(1) Gerritje Rooseboom** 8-9-1838 in Ede; born 1-9-1819 in Ede; died 11-2-1842 in Ede; married **(2) Johanna van Otterlo** 26-7-1845 in Ede; born 28-3-1817 in Ede.

    iv. **Bart van Maanen**

    v. **Celia van Maanen**, born 23-12-1826 in Bennekom; married **W. van Holland** 14-7-1849 in Ede.

    vi. **Jan van Maanen**

Generation No. 5

16. Derck Jacobsen van Roekel, born 24-2-1726 in Bennekom; died 31-12-1788 in Bennekom. He was the son of **32. Jacob Willems van Roekel** and **33. Trijntje Willems**. He married **17. Evertje Jansen** 1-4-1750 in Bennekom.

17. Evertje Jansen, born 4-2-1724 in Bennekom; died 15-3-1835 in Bennekom. She was the daughter of **34. Jan Jansen** and **35. Ariaan Willems**.

Notes for Derck Jacobsen van Roekel:
DB17: Derck zv Jacob Willemsen Backer en Trijntje Willems
GR13 3d(2a)
VG112pl7, Derk wordt genoemd in het tynsregister als opvolgend tynsbetaler voor de Royenspoll in Bennekom
VG1994pl30: lidmaat Bennekom 1751, begraven 6-1-1789
VG1984p29: Dirk
VG1985p97
VG1994pl30: begraven 6-1-1789
VG1994pl93
DI441: [1789] Vrijwillige giften 1 van de wed: van Dirk Jacobs 25-0-0

Notes for Evertje Jansen:
DB16: Evertje dv Jan Jansen en Ariaan Willemse
GR13
VG112p16
VG1984p29: Evertien
VG1985p97
VG1994p130: Lidmaat 1751
VG1994p193

Marriage Notes for Derck van Roekel and Evertje Jansen:
TB19: Derk Jacobs met Evertien Jans, beiden te Bennekom
Otr 15-2

Children of Derck van Roekel and Evertje Jansen are:

   i. **Adriaantje Derksen van Roekel**, born 6-8-1750 in Bennekom; died in Ede; married **(1) Gerrit Cornelissen van Veldhuizen** 26-3-1775 in Bennekom; born 24-11-1737 in Ede; married **(2) Reinder Aartsen** 26-8-1792 in Ede.

Notes for Adriaantje Derksen van Roekel:
DB30: Adriaantje dv Derk Jacobsen en Evertjen Jans
GR13: Vertrokken naar Ede 17-9-1775
VG1994p130
VG1985p97: lidm. 22-3-1775
VG1994p130
VG1996p7: Adriaantje Derksen

Notes for Gerrit Cornelissen van Veldhuizen:
DE15: Gerrit zv Cornelis Jacobsen en Elisabet Gerritsen
GR13
VG1985p97
VG1994p130
VG1996p7

Marriage Notes for Adriaantje van Roekel and Gerrit van Veldhuizen:
TB26: Gerrit Corneliszen geb en won Ede met Ariaantje Derksen geb en won Bennekom

ii. **Trientje Derksen van Roekel**, born 23-4-1752 in Beimekom; died 14-10-1753 in Bennekom.

Notes for Trientje Derksen van Roekel:
DB31: Trientjen dv Derk Jacobsen en Evertjen Jans
BB: Begraven 17-10

iii. **Wouter Derksen van Roekel**, born 8-2-1754 in Bennekom; died 8-6-1827 in Ede; married **(1) Hendrikje Rijksen** 1-5-1788 in Bennekom; born 18-7-1751 in Bennekom; died Abt. 1794 in Ede; married **(2) Gerritje Hendriks van de Koekelt** 17-5-1795 in Ede; born 24-2-1769 in Ede.

Notes for Wouter Derksen van Roekel:
DB3 2: Wouter zv Derk Jacobsen en Evertjen Jans
GR17 4b(3d): Vertrokken naar Ede 1-5-1788, landbouwer, de familie woont in 1811 in de buurtschap Veldhuizen in Ede
VG50p60, 61, 63, 64, 66, 67, 70, 71, 73, 75, 78, 81
VG112p46, 47, 48
VG1985p97
VG1985p100: Lidmaat 24-3-1790
VG1985p170: Geboren 17-1-1753 ? ws overleden na 8-7-1826
VG1986p278: 1802 Wouter Dirksen, in 1812 Wouter van Roekel
VG1994p130
KAG Ede p77, sectie F Veldhuizen, perceel 20 1.19.60 weiland in 'de Heere Meijen', perceel 45 4.50 hakhout, perceel 46 3.92.30 weiland, p88 perceel 323 17.70 opgaande bomen, 324 50.20 hakhout, 325 99.20 bouwiand, -99.10, 326 6.10 hakhout, 327 30.10 bouwiand alles aan de maanderbuurtweg, p83 perceel 575 2.10 hakhout, perceel 576 19.70 weiland, perceel 577 5.10 hakhout, perceel 595 18.90 weiland, perceel 624 19.70 hakhout, perceel 625 5.32.60 weiland, perceel 626 29.60 hakhout, perceel 627 .62 schaapskooi, perceel 628 2.65.10 weiland, perceel 629 1.58.70 weland, perceel 630 2.65.90 weiland, p84 perceel 658 1.54.90 weiland, perceel 658bis 6.50 uitweg als weiland, p 87 sectie G het Ederveen perceel 83 37.60 weiland, p88 perceel 148 2.12.30 weiland, sectie K het Dorp perceel 665 23.60 bouwiand, perceel 681 15.00 bouwiand, perceel 692 1.40 hakhout, perceel 701 44.00 bouwiand, perceel 702 .31 hakhout, pi 17 perceel 715 40.90 weiland, pi 18 perc 825 2.20 opgaande bomen, perc 826 8.30 hakhout, perc 827 2.70.50 bouwiand, perc 828 4.90 hakhout, perc 832 3.00 hakhout, perc 833 91.50 bouwiand, perc 834 2.60 hakhout, perc 841 29.50 hakhout, perc 842 1.00.10 bouwiand, perc 843 5.80 opgaande bomen, perc 844 28.60 tuin, perc 845 3.40 opgaande bomen, perc 846 26.60 huis en erf aan de Molenweg aansluiting op de Kraats iets ten zuiden van Kemheim

Notes for Hendrikje Rijksen:
DB31: Brantje en Hendrikje kv Rik Bransen en Evertjen Jans
GR17
VG50p60, 61, 63, 64
VG112p46, 47, 48
VG1994p130
VG1985p100: Lidmaat Bennekom 13-4-1781, vertrokken naar Ede 1-5-1788, gedoopt in Bennekom
VG1985p170: Riksen, overleden Ede 1794

Marriage Notes for Wouter van Roekel and Hendrikje Rijksen:
Geen gegevens in TB, TE, TR, TL ???????
VG1994p130:

iv. **Treintje Derksen van Roekel**, born 29-2-1756 in Bennekom; died 22-5-1822 in Ede; married **(2) Jacob Hendriksen van Voorst** 7-11-1779 in Bennekom; born 16-5-1751 in Ede; died 1-10-1794 in Ede.

Notes for Treintje Derksen van Roekel:
DB33: Treintje dv Derck Jacobsen en Evertjen Jansen
GR13: Moved to Ede on 11-10-1781
VG1985p97: Church member Eastern 17-4-1778
VG1985p103
VG1994p72: "Royement van hypotheek ten laste van Evert van Renes"
Notaris Lunteren 29-4-1822 akte 218.
VG1994p130

Notes for Jacob Hendriksen van Voorst:
DE25: Jacob zv Hendrik Jacobse en Gerritje Teunisse
GR13
VG1985p97
VG1994p72
VG1994pl30

Marriage Notes for Treintje van Roekel and Jacob van Voorst:
TB27: Jacob Hendriksen geb en won Ede met Trijntje Derksen geb en won Bennekom
TE40: te Bennekom Jacob Hendriksen geboren en wonende Ede met Trijntje Derksen geboren en wonende Bennekom

v. **Jan Derksen van Roekel**, born 12-3-1758 in Bennekom; died 3-4-1818 in Bennekom;

married **Anneke Hendriksen van Geesink** 25-8-1791 in Bennekom; born Abt. 1765 in Wageningen.

Notes for Jan Derksen van Roekel:
DB35: Jan zv Dirck Jakobsen en Evertjen Jansen
GR17 4c(3d): Bouwman. Zij wonen in 1811 in Bennekom
VG1985p98
VG1985p102
VG1994p130

Notes for Aimeke Hendriksen van Geesink:
VG1977-64
VG1983p60: Annetje Hendriksen van Geesing wordt als echtgenote genoemd ????
VG1985p102: Aaltjen Elberts ?

Marriage Notes for Jan van Roekel and Anneke van Geesink:
TB30: Jan Derksz geb en won Bennekom met Anneke Hendriksd van Geesink geb te Wageningen en won Bennekom
VG1994p130

vi. **Jacobje Derksen van Roekel**, born 16-12-1759 in Bennekom; died in Veenendaal; married **Rijk Klaassen van Santen**; born 16-1-1757 in Veenendaal.

Notes for Jacobje Derksen van Roekel:
DBS 5: Jacobjen dv Derk Jakobs en Evertien Jansen
GR13: Vertrokken naar Veenendaal op 12-9-1791
VG1985p98: Lidmaat 16-4-1784
VG1994p130
VG1995p89

Notes for Rijk Klaassen van Santen:
Niet te vinden in DB, DE, DL, DO, DR.... ?????

vii. **Hendrik Derksen van Roekel**, born 24-1-1762 in Bennekom.

Notes for Hendrik Derksen van Roekel:
DB37: Hendrik zv Dirk Jacobse en Evertje Jansse

viii. **Gerritje Derksen van Roekel**, born 16-9-1764 in Bennekom; died 28-5-1795 in Bennekom; married **Hendrik Petersen Haalboom** Abt. 1786 in Bennekom; born 20-1-1760 in Beimekom; died 1-9-1831 in Bennekom.

Notes for Gerritje Derksen van Roekel:
GR15
VG1985p98: Church member 25-3-1785
VG1994p130
VG1996p10, 145
DB38: Gerritje dv Dirk Jacobse en Evertje Jansse

Notes for Hendrik Petersen Haalboom:
GR15
VG1985p98
VG1994p130
VG1996p145
DB36: Hendrik zv Peter Haalboom en Teunisje Aars

Marriage Notes for Gerritje van Roekel and Hendrik Haalboom:
TB29: Hendrik Haalboom geb en won Bennekom met Gerritje Derks geb en won Bennekom

8 ix. **Willem Derksen van Roekel**, born 26-4-1767 in Bennekom; died 12-7-1841 in Ede; married **Gijsbertje Gerritsen Roseboom** 28-4-1792 in Bennekom.

x. **Derk Derksen van Roekel**, born 26-11-1769 in Bennekom; died Aft. 1816; married **Johanna Gijsbertsen van Silfhout** Bet. 14-8 -31-12-1791 in Bennekom; born 18-9-1768 in Bennekom; died 8-6-1842.

Notes for Derk Derksen van Roekel:
DB40: Dirk zv Dirk Jacobse en Evertje Jansse
GR18, 4e(3d)
VG1985p98
VG1985p103
VG1985p170: overl. na 1816
VG1986p88
VG1994p130
VG1996p10
Naamsaanneming: Roekel van; Derk Derksen; Bennekom;—;Ede

Notes for Johanna Gijsbertsen van Silfhout:
DB40: Johanna dv Gijsbert van Silfhout en Gijsbertje Jansen van Roekel
GR13, 18
VG1985p96
VG1985p103: Silfhout, lidm. 6-4-1792
VG1985p170: over! 8-6-1842 ?

Marriage Notes for Derk van Roekel and Johanna van Silfhout:
TB30: Derk Derkz geb en won Bennekom met Johanna van Silfhout geb en won Bennekom.

18. Gerrit Everts Roseboom, married **19. Maria van Leeuwen** 28-2-1762 in Bennekom.

19. Maria van Leeuwen

Marriage Notes for Gerrit Roseboom and Maria van Leeuwen:
TB22: Gerrit Evertse met Maria van Leeuwen beide Bennekom

Children of Gerrit Roseboom and Maria van Leeuwen:

i. **Willem Robbertsen Roseboom**, born 19-2-1764 in Bennekom; died Bef. 20-5-1809; married **Woutertje Willemsen van den Brink** 1789 in Bennekom; born 27-7-1766 in Bennekom.

Notes for Willem Robbertsen Roseboom:
DB37: Willem Robberts zv Gerrit Roseboom en Maria van Leeuwen

Notes for Woutertje Willemsen van den Brink:
DB39: Woutertje dv Willem Jansse en Arjaantje Hendriks Marriage

Notes for Willem Roseboom and Woutertje den Brink:
TB29: Willem Robbertsen Rooseboom geb en won Bennekom met Woutertje Willemsen geb en won Bennekom

ii. **Lijsbeth Gerrits Roseboom**, born 6-10-1765 in Bennekom.

Notes for Lijsbeth Gerrits Roseboom:
DB38: Lijsbeth dv Gen-it Roseboom en Maria van Leeuwen

iii. **Maritje Gerrits Roseboom**, born 21-12-1766 in Bennekom.

Notes for Maritje Gerrits Roseboom:
DB39: Maritje dv Gerrit Roseboom en Maria van Leeuwen

iv. **Evert Gerrits Roseboom**, born 12-3-1769 in Bennekom.

Notes for Evert Gerrits Roseboom:
DB40: Evert zv Gerrit Evertse Roseboom en Maria van Leeuwen

9 v. **Gijsbertje Gerritsen Roseboom**, born 8-9-1771 in Bennekom; died 15-3-1835 in Bennekom; married **Willem Derksen van Roekel** 28-4-1792 in Bennekom.

vi. **Gerrit Gerrits Roseboom**, born 5-11-1773 in Bennekom.

Notes for Gerrit Gerrits Roseboom:
DB42: Gerrit zv Gerrit Evers Roseboom en Maria van Leeuwen.

20. **Wouter Willemsen van Maanen**, born Abt 1752; died 17-12-1819 in Bennekom. He was the son of **40. Willem Woutersen van Maanen** and **41. Jenneke Evertsen Roseboom**. He married **21. Baatje Gijsbertsen**.

21. **Baatje Gijsbertsen**, born 19-5-1746 in Ede; died Bef. 25-5-1815. She was the daughter of **42. Gijsbert Jansen** and **43. Marietje Rixse**.

Notes for Wouter Willemsen van Maanen:
VG1989p73

Notes for Baatje Gijsbertsen:
VG1981p169
VG1989p73

Children of Wouter van Maanen and Baatje Gijsbertsen:

i. **Willem Woutersen van Maanen**, born 6-8-1780 in Bennekom.

Notes for Willem Woutersen van Maanen:
DB45: Willem zv Wouter Willemsen en Baatje Gijsbertsen

ii. **Marritje Woutersen van Maanen**, born 29-8-1781 in Bennekom; died 7-4-1829 in Ede; married **Antonij Kelderman** 1800 in Bennekom; born 24-10-1779 in Veenendaal; died 1-9-1863 in Ede.

Notes for Marritje Woutersen van Maanen:
DB46: Marritje dv Wouter Willemsen en Baatje Gijsberts
VG1989p72: Gedoopt 2-9

Notes for Antonij Kelderman:
VG1989p72: Landbouwer

Marriage Notes for Marritje van Maanen and Antonij Kelderman:
TB32: Antomij Kelderman met Marietje Wouters geb en won Bennekom

iii. **Gijsbert Woutersen van Maanen**, born 1-5-1783 in Bennekom; married **Aartje Hendriksen** 7-5-1807 in Bennekom; born 6-3-1786 in Bennekom.

Notes for Gijsbert Woutersen van Maanen:
DB46: Gijsbert zv Wouter Willemsen en Baatje Gijsbertsen

Notes for Aartje Hendriksen:
DB48: Artje dv Hendrik Riksen en Neeltje Maassen

Marriage Notes for Gijsbert van Maanen and Aartje Hendriksen:
TB35: Gijsbert Woutersen 23jr geb Bennekom en won Ede met Aartje Hendriks 21jr geb en won Bennekom ouders bruidegom Wouter Willemsen en Baatje Gijsbertsen ouders bruid Henrik Riksen en Neeltje Masen

iv. **Jenneke Woutersen van Maanen**, born 23-5-1785 in Bennekom; died Bef. 9-5-1789.

Notes for Jenneke Woutersen van Maanen:
DB47: Jenneke dv Wouter Willemsz en Baatje Gijsbertsen

10 v. **Jan Woutersen van Maanen**, born 23-7-1787 in Bennekom; married **(1) Jantje van Otterloo**; married **(2) Cornelisje Broekhuis**; married **(3) Evertje Toonen Brandsen** 25-5-1815 in Bennekom.

vi. **Jenneke Woutersen van Maanen**, born 9-5-1789 in Bennekom; married **Herman Woutersen van den Brink** 8-7-1809 in Bennekom; born Abt. 1784 in Ede.

Notes for Jenneke Woutersen van Maanen:
DB49: Jenneke dv Wouter Willems en Baatje Gijsberts

Marriage Notes for Jenneke van Maanen and Herman den Brink:
TB36: Herman Wouters geb Ede en won Bennekom 25jr ouders overl met Jenneke Wouters dv Wouter Willems en Baatje Gijsberts geb en won Bennekom 21jr.

22. **Brand Toonen**, born 2-5-1772 in Ede; died Bef. 25-5-1815. He was the son of **44. Antony Brandsen** and **45. Selia Gerritsen Ras**. He married **23. Fijtje Evertsen** 1795 in Bennekom.

23. **Fijtje Evertsen**, born in Bennekom. She was the daughter of **46. Evert Aartsen van Eck** and **47. Jantje Berendsen van Maanen**.

Notes for Brand Toonen:
DE46: Brandt zv Anthonie Brantzen en Celia Gerritsen

Notes for Fijtje Evertsen:
DB43: Fijtje dv Evert Aartsen en Jantje Barentsen

More About Fijtje Evertsen:
Date born 2: 10-3-1776, Bennekom

Marriage Notes for Brand Toonen and Fijtje Evertsen:
TB31: Brand Toon met Fijtje Derksen geb en won Bennekom

Children of Brand Toonen and Fijtje Evertsen are:

i. **Selia Toonen Brandsen**, born 8-1-1796 in Bennekom; married Peter van Geesink 27-9-1816 in Bennekom; born Abt. 1796 in Rhenen.

Notes for Selia Toonen Brandsen:
DB52: Selia dv Brand Toon en Fijtje Derksen

Marriage Notes for Selia Brandsen and Peter van Geesink:
TB41: Peter van Geesink 20jr geb en won Rhenen zv Hendrik van Geesink en Elizabeth Lasee met Selia Toonen 20jr geb en won Bennekom dv Brand Toonen en Fijtje Evers

11 ii. **Evertje Toonen Brandsen**, born 9-11-1797 in Bennekom; married **Jan Woutersen van Maanen** 25-5-1815 in Bennekom.

iii. **Thonia Toonen Brandsen**, born 16-3-1800 in Bennekom.

Notes for Thonia Toonen Brandsen:
DB55: Thonia dv Brand Thoonen en Fijtje Evertse

iv. **Gerret Toonen Brandsen**, born 21-2-1803 in Bennekom.

Notes for Gerret Toonen Brandsen:
DB57: Gerret zv Brand Thoonen en Fijtje Evers

v. **Jantje Toonen Brandsen**, born 19-9-1806 in Bennekom.

Notes for Jantje Toonen Brandsen:
DB59: Jantje dv Brand Thoonen en Fijtje Eversd

vi. **Willem Toonen Brandsen**, born 13-5-1809 in Bennekom.

Notes for Willem Toonen Brandsen:
DB61: Willem zv Brand Thoonen en Fijtje Everse.

Generation No. 6

32. **Jacob Willems van Roekel**, born Abt. 1675 in Bennekom; died Abt. 1749. He was the son of **64. Willem Dercksen van Roekel** and **65. Jantjen Geurtsen**. He married **33. Trijntje Willems** 17-9-1713 in Bennekom.

33. **Trijntje Willems**, died 13-1-1772 in Bennekom.

Notes for Jacob Willems van Roekel:
GR11: Geboortedatum onzeker, bakker te Bennekom, wordt ook Jacob Willems Backer genoemd.
VG112p10: Jacob Willems Backer, 11, 13, 15, 19, 21: Jacob Willemsen Backer
VG113p3
VG113p8: Weduwnaar Estjen Jacobs
VG113p8: Weduwnaar Willemtje Gerrits
VG1980p133
VG1984p31
VG1985p95
VG1988p11: Jacob Willemsen
VG1994p193

Ancestors of Jan van Roekel

VG1995p388: bakker te Bennekom
DI33: 1713 van Jacob Backer voor Koom f 6-11-0
DI34: 1713 van Jacob Backer voor saat f 9-18-0
DI39: 1715 van Jacob Backer voor de huyshuyr van Anne Everts verschenen Petri 1715 f 7-0-0
DI46: 1717 van Jacob Backer voor den rogh van Evert Gosens de A 1717 f 6-4-0
DI50: A 1719 den 1 Jan[uari] aan Jacob Backer een gedeelte van de camerhuyr van Anne Jans
DI51: [1719] Den 22 Appril aan Jacob Backer betjaald] het graven van den Hoff 1-4-0
DI72: Petri 1722 aan Jacob Backer voor de camerhuyr van de weduwe van Evert Peters f 10-0-0
DI79: Aan Jacob Backer voor de camerhuyr van de weduwe van Evert Peters veschenen Petri 1722 10-0-0

Notes for Trijntje Willems:
GR11
VG112p10, 11, 13, 15, 19, 21
VG113p8
VG1980p133: van Voorst?
VG1984p31
VG1985p95: j.d., lidmaat Bennekom, pasen 1714
VG1988p147: Weduwe 1749, daghuurster 1 3/4 morgenzand.
VG1994p193: Lidmaat 1714, begraven 18-1-1772
VG1995p388
BB: Begraven 18-1-1772

Marriage Notes for Jacob van Roekel and Trijntje Willems:
TB8: Jacob Willemsen, wed Willemtje Gerrits met Trijntje Willems, beiden Bennekom
GR11
VG112p10, 11, 13, 15, 19, 21
VG113p8: beiden Bennekom
VG1984p31: 17-12-1713 ?
VG1985p95
VG1988p11: j.d.
VG1994p193
VG1995p388

Children of Jacob van Roekel and Trijntje Willems:

i. **Willem Jacobs van Roekel**, born 13-1-1715 in Bennekom; died 15-5-1779 in Bennekom.

   Notes for Willem Jacobs van Roekel:
   DB11: Willem zv Jacob Willemsen Backer en Trijntje Willems
   GR11
   VG112p10
   VG1985p95: de vader Jacob Willems Backer
   VG1994p193
   BB: Begraven 19-5

   More About Willem Jacobs van Roekel:
   Fact 1: Also called Backer

ii. **Jan Jacobs van Roekel**, born 15-12-1716 in Bennekom; died 29-2-1784 in Bennekom; married **Maartje Robberts** 2-7-1747 in Bennekom; born Abt. 1702 in Bennekom; died 16-5-1787 in Bennekom.

   Notes for Jan Jacobs van Roekel:
   DB12: Jan zv Jacob Willemsen en Trijntje Willemsen
   GR13: Ook bekend als Jan Jacobs Backer
   VG112p12
   VG113p14
   VG1985p96: geboren 13-12 ?
   VG1994p193
   VG1995p388
   BB: Begraven 14-3
   DI291: [1769] Aan Jan Bakker voor een kar hooy 2-10-0

   More About Jan Jacobs van Roekel:
   Fact 1: Also called Backer

   Notes for Maartje Robberts:
   DB5: Jan Jacobse Bakker getuigt dat zijn vrouw Marritje Robberts geboren is uit Robbert Willemsen en Gijsbertje Wouters (1701-1705)
   GR13
   VG112p5: Volgens redres geboren in 1701-1705, 16, 17: Maritje, 20: wed Joacobus van Leeuwen
   VG113p11: Marritje
   VG113p14
   VG1985p96
   VG1994p193: geb. ea 1702 BB: 16-5-1787 de wed van Jan Bakker begr den 20

   Marriage Notes for Jan van Roekel and Maartje Robberts:
   TB18: Jan Jacobsen Backer met Maartjen Robbers, weduwe Cobus van Leewen

iii. **Gerrit Jacobs van Roekel**, born 15-10-1719 in Bennekom; died 17-8-1800 in Bennekom; married **Willemke Jansen van Hal** 5-12-1762 in Bennekom; born 25-12-1732 in Bennekom; died 3-3-1801 in Bennekom.

   Notes for Gerrit Jacobs van Roekel:
   DB13: Gerrit zv Jacob Willems Backer en Trintje Willemsen
   GR13: Gerrit en zijn kinderen werden vaak 'Bakker' genoemd in plaats van 'van Roekel'
   VG113p22
   VG1984p29

VG1985p97
VG1994p193
BB: Begraven 25-8
DI286: Huishuur van Gerrit van Roekel verschenen Petri 1769 19-0-0
DI287: [1769] Aan Gerrit Bakker voor 19 1/2 el liimen
DI287: [1769] Nog aan denzelven voor 3 1/2 el sakken linnen
DI288: [1769] Gerrit van Roekel 35-12-0
DI299: [1771] Ontfangen van Willem Evertsen voor een guste koe van Gerrit van Roekel 20-0-0
DI305: [1771] Aan Gerrit van Roekel 52-0-0
DI307: [1771] Aan Hermen Hendriksen voor een gedeelte van een kar hooy voor Gerrit van Roekel 2-0-0
DI308: [1771] Aan RoelofKemink voor een melkkoe voor Gerrit van Roekel 31-5-8
DI320: [1773] Aan Gerrit Bakker voor 8 ellen hemdelinnen 4-8-0
DI321: [1773] Aan Gerrit van Roekel 38-1-0

Notes for Willemke Jansen van Hal:
DB20: Willemke dv Jan Wilmsen en Brantje van Doesburg
GR13
VG113p22
VG1984p29
VG1985p97
VG1994p193
BB: 3-3-1801 Willempje Bakker huisvrouw van Gerrit Jacobs van Roekel, begr7

Marriage Notes for Gerrit van Roekel and Willemke van Hal:
TB22: Gerrit Jacobse van Roekel en Willemke Jansse van Hal beide geb en won Bennekom

iv. **Willemke Jacobs van Roekel**, born 13-9-1722 in Bennekom; married **Tijmen Lubberts** 31-10-1751 in Bennekom; born 10-1-1717 in Bennekom.

Notes for Willemke Jacobs van Roekel:
DB15: Willemken dv Jacob Willemsen Backer en Trintje Willems
GR11
VG112pl5
VG1985p95: Born 13-9-1722 ?
VG1994pl93: Born 13-9-1722 ??

Notes for Tijmen Lubberts:
DB12: Tonen zv Lubbert Jansen en Estjen Teunis
GR11
VG1985p95
VG1994p193

Marriage Notes for Willemke van Roekel and Tijmen Lubberts:
TB20: Tijmen Lubberts, wed Willemken Wouters met Wilmijn Jacobs onder Bennekom

v. **Evert Jacobs van Roekel**, born Abt. 1724; married **Geertruij van Ravenswaaij** 9-5-1762 in Veenendaal; born 25-12-1724 in Veenendaal.

Notes for Evert Jacobs van Roekel:
DB: Geen vermelding van Evert gevonden ... ???
GR13, 3c(2a)
VG93Bp144: jm
VG1985p95, laatste van de lijst?
VG1985p98: j.m. van Bennekom
VG1994p193
VG1995p388
DI275: [1767] Aan Evert Jacobse van Roekel voor 54 pond spek voor Jan Hoek 7-8-8

Notes for Geertruij van Ravenswaaij:
GR13
VG93Bp144
VG1985p98
VG1994p193
VG1995p388

Marriage Notes for Evert van Roekel and Geertruij van Ravenswaaij:
TV144: Evert Jacobsz van Roekel jm en Geertruij van Ravenswaaij wed van Gerrit Lucasse

16 vi. **Derck Jacobsen van Roekel**, born 24-2-1726 in Bennekom; died 31-12-1788 in Bennekom; married **Evertje Jansen** 1-4-1750 in Bennekom.

vii. **Gerritje Jacobsen van Roekel**, born 26-2-1730 in Bennekom; married **(1) Klaas Rijksen van Santen** 23-4-1753 in Bennekom; born 25-1-1725 in Veenendaal; married **(2) Willem Gerritsen Kool** 4-9-1785 in Veenendaal.

Notes for Gerritje Jacobsen van Roekel:
DB19: Gerritje dv Jacob Willemse en Trijntje Willems
GR11
VG93Bp181: Gerrigje
VG112pl9
VG113p20:Bennekom
VG1985p95
VG1985p98
VG1988p11: Gerrigje Jacobsz van Roekel
VG1994pl93

Notes for Klaas Rijksen van Santen:
GR11
VG93Bp181

VG113p20: Veenendaal
VG1985p95
VG1985p98
VG1988p10, 11: doop25-l?
VG1994p193

Marriage Notes for Gerritje van Roekel and Klaas van Santen:
TB20: Claas van Zanten Veenendaal met Gerritjen van Roekel Bennekom

viii. **Hendrikje Jacobs van Roekel**, born 13-6-1733 in Bennekom; married **Sander Derksen** 12-5-1754 in Ede; born 26-4-1716 in Hall.

Notes for Hendrikje Jacobs van Roekel:
DB21: Hendrikje dv Jacob Willemsen Backer en Trijntje Willems

Notes for Sander Derksen:
DI227: Een certificatie van Sander Derks van Hall op dato den 8 Maart 1756
VG1985p38

Marriage Notes for Hendrikje van Roekel and Sander Derksen:
TE24: Sander Dirksze geboren te Hall en wonend te Mane en Hendrikje Jacobsz geboren te Bennecum en wonend te Wekerom bevestigt 2 Juny.

34. Jan Jansen, died 21-1-1772 in Bennekom. He married **35. Ariaan Willems** 20-4-1721 in Bennekom.

35. Ariaan Willems

Notes for Jan Jansen:
VG1984p31

Notes for Ariaan Willems:
VG1984p31

Marriage Notes for Jan Jansen and Ariaan Willems:
TB11: Jan Jansse met Ariaan Willems, beiden te Bennekom

Children of Jan Jansen and Ariaan Willems are:

i. **Jan Jansen**, born 19-4-1722 in Bennekom.

Notes for Jan Jansen:
DB15: Jan zv Jan Jansen en Ariantje Willems

17 ii. **Evertje Jansen**, born 4-2-1724 in Bennekom; died 15-3-1835 in Bennekom; married **Derck Jacobsen van Roekel** 1-4-1750 in Bennekom.

40. Willem Woutersen van Maanen, born 1-1723 in Bennekom. He was the son of **80. Wouter Berendsen van Maanen** and **81. Jantje Hendriksen**. He married **41. Jenneke Evertsen Roseboom** 5-1751 in Bennekom.

41. Jenneke Evertsen Roseboom, born 31-8-1732 in Bennekom. She was the daughter of **82. Evert Gerritsen Roseboom** and **83. Lijsbeth Evertsen van Eck**.

Notes for Willem Woutersen van Maanen:
DB16: Willem zv Wouter Berends en Jantje Hendriks

More About Willem Woutersen van Maanen:
Date born 2: Abt. 1724, Bennekom

Notes for Jenneke Evertsen Roseboom:
DB20: Jenneke dv Evert Gerritse en Lijsbet Everts
Marriage Notes for Willem van Maanen and Jenneke Roseboom:
TB20: Willem Woutersen met Jenneken Everts beide te Bennekom

Children of Willem van Maanen and Jenneke Roseboom are:

20 i. **Wouter Willemsen van Maanen**, born Abt. 1752; died 17-12-1819 in Bennekom; married **(1) Baatje Gijsbertsen**; married **(2) Melisje van de Heuvel** 13-4-1810 in Bennekom.

ii. **Lijsbet Willemsen van Maanen**, born 4-7-1754 in Bennekom.

Notes for Lijsbet Willemsen van Maanen:
DB32: Lijsbet zv Willem Wouterse en Jenneke Evers

iii. **Jantjen Willemsen van Maanen**, born 10-4-1757 in Bennekom; married **(1) Derk Cornelisse** 14-11-1779 in Bennekom; born in Ede; died Bef. 6-1794; married **(2) Hendrik Hendriksen** 6-1794 in Bennekom; born in Barneveld.

Notes for Jantjen Willemsen van Maanen:
DB34: Jantjen dv Willem Woutersen en Jenneke Evers

Marriage Notes for Jantjen van Maanen and Derk Cornelisse:
TB27: Derk Cornelisse geb en won Ede met Jantje willems geb en won Bennekom
TE40: 7 nov te Bennekom Derk Cornelisse geboren en wonende Ede met Jantje willems geboren en wonende te Bennekom

iv. **Evert Willemsen van Maanen**, born 8-7-1759 in Bennekom; married **Woutertje Jacobsen** 14-8-1791 in Bennekom; born in Veenendaal.

Notes for Evert Willemsen van Maanen:
DBS 5: Evert zv Willem Wouterse en Jenneken Evers

Marriage Notes for Evert van Maanen and Woutertje Jacobsen:

TB30: Evert Willemsse geb Bennekom en won Ede met Woutertje Jacobse geb Veenendaal en won Bennekom
TE48: 14 aug te Bennekom Evert Willemze geb te Bennekom en won Ede met Woutertje Jacobze geb Veenendaal en won Bennekom.

42. Gijsbert Jansen, married **43. Marietje Rixse**.

43. Marietje Rixse

Notes for Gijsbert Jansen:
VG1981p169
Notes for Marietje Rixse:
VG1981pl69

Child of Gijsbert Jansen and Marietje Rixse is:

21   i.   **Baatje Gijsbertsen**, born 19-5-1746 in Ede; died Bef. 25-5-1815; married **Wouter Willemsen van Maanen**.

44. Antony Brandsen, born 9-5-1734 in Ede. He was the son of **88. Brand Gerritsen** and **89. Hendrikje Teunissen**. He married **45. Selia Gerritsen Ras** 20-9-1761 in Ede.

45. Selia Gerritsen Ras, born 3-3-1737 in Bennekom. She was the daughter of **90. Gerrit Jacobsen Ras** and **91. Jantje Jansen**.

Notes for Antony Brandsen:
DE13: Antony zv Brand Gerritse en Hendrikje Teunisse

Notes for Selia Gerritsen Ras:
DB23: Selia dv Garret Jacobs en Jantien Jans

Marriage Notes for Antony Brandsen and Selia Ras:
TE29: Anthonij Brandsze geb te Veldhuizen en won te Manen met Celia Gerrits geb eb won te Bennekom bev alhier 4 October

Children of Antony Brandsen and Selia Ras are:

  i.   **Jantje Toonen**, born 12-2-1769 in Bennekom; married **Egbert Gijsbertsen** 7-5-1797 in Lunteren; born in Ede.

Notes for Jantje Toonen:
DB40: Jantje dv Toon Brantse en Celia Gerritse

Marriage Notes for Jantje Toonen and Egbert Gijsbertsen:
TL50: Egbert Gijsbertsen wedn van Claartje Janssen geb en won te Ede met Jantje Tonen geb te Bennecum en won te Lunteren

22   ii.   **Brand Toonen**, born 2-5-1772 in Ede; died Bef. 25-5-1815; married **Fijtje Evertsen** 1795 in Bennekom.

  iii.   **Hendrikje Toonen**, married **Hendrik Evertsen**

46. Evert Aartsen van Eck, born 4-3-1746 in Bennekom; died Bef. 13-4-1814. He was the son of **92. Aart Hendriksen van Eck** and **93. Geurtje Evers**. He married **47. Jantje Berendsen van Maanen** 1775 in Bennekom.

47. Jantje Berendsen van Maanen, born 28-1-1748 in Bennekom; died Bef. 13-4-1814. She was the daughter of **94. Berend Woutersen van Maanen** and **95. Gerritje Everts Roseboom**.

Notes for Evert Aartsen van Eck:
DB28: Evert zv Aart Hendriks en Geurtjen Evers

Notes for Jantje Berendsen van Maanen:
DB29: Jantjen dv Beemt Wouters en Gerritjen Evers

Marriage Notes for Evert van Eck and Jantje van Maanen:
TB26: Evert Aartsen geb en won Bennekom met Jantje Barentzen geb en won Bennekom

Child of Evert van Eck and Jantje van Maanen is:

23   i.   **Fijtje Evertsen**, born in Bennekom; married **(1) Brand Toonen** 1795 in Bennekom; married **(2) Jan Brandsen van Bruxvoort** 13-4-1814 in Bennekom.

Generation No. 7

64. Willem Dercksen van Roekel, born Abt. 1645. He was the son of **128. Derck van Roekel**. He married **65. Jantjen Geurtsen** Abt. 1670 in Bennekom.

65. Jantjen Geurtsen

Notes for Willem Dercksen van Roekel:
GR11: Ook wel genoemd: Willem Backer. Stamvader Bennekomse van Roekels. Willem is mogelijk identiek met de Willem Dercksen die met zijn vrouw Jantjen Geurtsen een huis, hofen bouwiand, zoals zij dat al gebruiken, kopen, gelegen onder Wageningen, met een stuk land, groot 1,5 schepel gezaais, nabij de Bennekomseweg in Wageningen (8-4-1695).
Willem wordt op 20-3-1688 genoemd als aftredend buurtmeester van de Bovenbuurt, Bennekom. In 1709 pacht hij een perceel van de Bennekomse kerk. Hij wordt in het pachtregister zowel Willem Backer als Willem Dercksen genoemd. Hij blijft pachter tot 1721. In hetzelfde register staat hij ook borg voor zijn zoon Gerrit, die op zijn beurt weer borg staat voor zijn vader.
VG230Ap185
VG1980p133
VG1985p95

VG1988p15: Willem Derks Bakker
VG1989p82
VG1994p83
VG1994p85
VG1995p391: Willem Dercksen alias Willem Backer, geboren ca 1645, buurtmeester, in 1688 aftredend als buurtmeester van de Bovenbuurt in Bennekom, in 1709 pacht hij een perceel van de Bennekomse kerk, in het pachtregister wordt zowel Willem Backer als Willem Dercksen genoemd, in dit register komt hij voor tot 1721.
KS185
BB34-1685: Willem wordt benoemd tot buurtmeester voor de bovenbuurt.
BB35-1690: Willem is afgaand buurtmeester.

Notes for Jantjen Geurtsen:
GR11: Niet zeker
VG230Ap185
VG1995p392
KS185
Marriage Notes for Willem van Roekel and Jantjen Geurtsen:
VG230Ap185
VG1995p392
KS185

Children of Willem van Roekel and Jantjen Geurtsen:

32 i. **Jacob Willems van Roekel**, born Abt. 1675 in Bennekom; died Abt. 1749; married **(1) Evertje Jacobs** 17-2-1700 in Bennekom; married **(2) Willemtje Gerrits** 13-12-1711 in Bennekom; married **(3) Trijntje Willems** 17-9-1713 in Bennekom.

ii. **Gerrit Willemsen van Roekel**, born Abt. 1680; died 22-1-1757 in Bennekom; married **Anneken Willemsen** 29-3-1705 in Bennekom; born Abt. 1680; died 27-3-1746 in Bennekom.

Notes for Gerrit Willemsen van Roekel:
GR11: Ook bekend als Gerrit Backer.
Zij kopen op 14-5-1736 een huis en hof met de halve sloot in het dorp Bennekom (belandt oostwaerts de straat, westwaerts Geurt Buijs, zuidwaerts Cornelis van Oort en noordwaerts de armen van Bennekom).
Gerrit wordt evenals zijn vader genoemd als pachter van kerkelanden in Bennekom
VG112p7: Gerrit Willemsen Backer
VG113p6
VG230Ap177, 179: begraven 28-1
VG1980p133
VG1994p28

VG1985p96: begraven 28-1 als Gerrit Backer
VG1989p81
VG1994p28
KS2-177, 179: Beg 28-1-1757
BB: Begraven op 28-1
VG1999p165
DI50: [1719] Den 5 Feb[ruari] aan Gerrit Backer voor het bouwen van't lant in den Wageningsen Enck f 0-16-0
DI78: [1724] Aan Gerrit Backer voor het wegbrengen van een arme vrouw 0-10-0
DI100: van Gerrit Backer wegens de corenpagt van Schuyrhoven 1730 en 1731 12-4-0
DI101: van Gerrit Backer eenjaar interesse verschenen den 14 Maart 1731 8-0-0
DI106: van Claas Willemsen en Gerrit Backer wegens Schuerhoven over de jaren 1732 en 1733 38-1-8
DI106: van Gerrit Backer twe[e] jaren interesse verschenen den 11 April 1732 en 1733 te samen 16-0-0
DI111: van Gerrit Backer wegens het land Schuirhoven voor denjare 1734, 35, 36 en 37 38-7-0
DI112: van Gerrit Backer rente 1734, 35, 36, 37 verschenen den 11 April 32-0-0
DI117: van Gerrit Backer de pagt wegens een stuk land Schuerhoven genaamt van hetjaar 1738,1739 en 1740 29-7-4
DI117: nog van denselven de rente van twee hondert gulden van hetjaar 1738 en 1739 versch[enen] d[en] 11 April 16-0-0
DI117: van Gerrit Backer voor het beest van Cornelis Heijnkanip 34-0-0
DI123: van Gerrit Backer 2 jaar rente van 200 g[u]l[den] 40 en 41 vold[aan] 16-0-0
DI123: van Jan Geurtsen pagt van Scheurhov[en] 21-8-0 en van Gerrit Backer van hetselve waarmede hetj[aar] 42 voldaan is 22-3-0
DI128: [1746] 2 jaar rente cap[itaal] 200 [gulden] ten laste v[an] Gerrit Backer 16-0-0
DI132: [1746] van Gerrit Backer 2 jaar rente van 2 hond[erd] g[u]l[den] 10-0-0
DI140: van Gerrit Backer rente wegens cap[i]t[aal] van 200 g[u]l[den] de jaaren 1746, 1747, 1748 voldaan 24-0-0
DI142: aan G. Backer voor 3/4 dack tot de hofstede 4-10-0
DI145: Obl[igatie] van 200 g[u]l[den] ten laste van Gerrit Backer rente 1749 voldaan 8-0-0
DI147: pagt van Gerrit Backer wegens Scheurhoven 1749 en 1750 24-8-8
DI163: Obl[igatie] van 100 g[u]l[den] ten laste van Gerrit Backer 4 percent 1750 en 1751 ver-

scheenen den 11 April voldaan 16-0-0
DI170: 1 1/4 mudde bouland Schuerhoven Pagter Gerrit Backer 1753 7-10-0 1754 9-16-0
Dll 71: Obl[igatie] van 200 g[u]l[den] ten laste van Gerrit Backer 4 p[ercent] 1742,1753 versch[enen] d[en] 11 April 16-0-0
DI178: Schurhoven 1 1/4 mudde Pagters Gerrit Backer 1755 9-10-12 1756 14-13-0
DI180: Oblig[atie] van 200 g[u]l[den] ten laste van Gerrit Backer 1754 d[en] 11 Apr[il] versche[nen] voldaan 8-0-0 DI190: Schuurhoven 1 1/4 Mud Pagter Gerrit Bakker Tjaar 1757 17-2-0 1758 15-15-8 1759 10-13-8
DI193: Een obligatie van 200 g[u]l[den] ten laste van Gerrit Backer a 4 percent Ontfangen in't jaar verschenen 11 April 1755 8-0-0 1756 8-0-0 1757 8-0-0
DI205: Schuurhoven 1 1/4 mud Pagters Gerrit Backer thans Willem Backer Tjaar 1760 9-9-0 1761 8-6-0
DI207: Een obligatie van 200 g[u]l[den] ten laste van Gerrit Bakker thans Cornelis van den Born a 4 g[u]l[den] p[er] cent Ontvangen in 't jaar verschenen 11 April 1758 8-0-0 1759 8-0-0
DI217: Obligatie nr 2
DI234: Een obligatie van 200 guldens ten laste van Gerrit Willemse Bakker thans Cornelis van den Born a 4 guld[ens] percent Ontvangen dejaren verschenen den 11 April 1760 8-0-0 1761 8-0-0 1762 8-0-0
DI249: Een obligatie van 200 guldens ten laste van Gerrit Willemse Bakker thans Cornelis van den Born a 4 guld[ens] percent Ontvangen dejaren verschenen den 11 April 1763 8-0-0 1764 8-0-0 1765 8-0-0 1766 8-0-0

Notes for Aimeken Willemsen:
GR11
VG112p7
VG113p4
VG113p6
VG230Ap178: Begraven 2-4
VG1985p96: Begraven 2-4 de vrouw van Gerrit Backer
VG1989p81
VG1994p28
KS2-178, 179: Begr 2-4-1746
VG1999pl65

Marriage Notes for Gerrit van Roekel and Aimeken Willemsen:
TB6: Gerrit Willemsen van Roekel met Anneken Willems beiden te Bennekom
KS178

iii. **Evert Jacobsen Backer**, died Abt. 1752 in Bennekom.

Notes for Evert Jacobsen Backer:
Duikt op in het diaconieboek van Bennekom, zoon van Derck ????
DI31: 1712 aan Evert Backer f 4-12-0
DI35: 1714 aan Evert Backer f 16-13-0
DI38: 1715 aan Evert Backer f 26-0-0
DI48: 1719 den 12 July wegens de erfenissen van Gerrit [naam doorgestreept] Evert Backer f 7-6-8
DI49: Nogh voor het kostgeld van van der Wijs aan Evert Jacobsen Backer tot den 25 Juny 1719 f 24-6-0
DI49: Nog aan Evert Jacobsen voor kostgeld bet[aald] tot den 16 July 1719 f 3-6-0
DI51: [1719] De 2 Appril aan de huysvrouw van Evert Backer vvor't wassen voor Cornelis van der Wijs en het groef bidden f 1-13-0
DI51: [1719] Den 19 Juny aan Evert Backer voor het schouwmaken van een 1/2 morgen wegens Cnelis van der Wis f 0-15-0
DI56: [1719] voor een beest voor Evert Backer bet[aald] 19-9-0
DI65: [1720] Op rekeninge van deckloon aan Evert Backers huys aan Geurt Dercksen 3-8-8
DI66: [1721] Aan Evert Backer voor 't maken van de schouw 1-10-0
DI66: Evert Backer heeft sedert 1 7br [= September] 1720 tot 1 7br [=september] 1721 genooten 21-0-0
DI66: 1721 Aan Derck Evers voor gras van Evert Backer over den j are 1719 en 1720 betjaald] L.q 8-10-0
DI66: Den 9 7br [= September] voor 31/4 dack aan 't huis van Evert Backer de vim ad 4-15-0 16-12-0
DI72: [1722] Evert Backer f 22-10-0 DI72: [1722] Aan Wouter Reijers voor een halve morgen gras voor Evert Backers f 9-0-0
DI72: [1722] Aan Gerrit van den Bangh voor een varken voor Evert Backer L.q f 3-17-0
DI77: [1723] Evert Backer f 66-10-0
DI79: [1723] Aan Jan Hermens voor en sul aan't huys van Evert Backer l.q 1-4-0
DI85: [1725] Voor Evert Backer voor een varken 8-0-0
DI88: [1725] Evert Backer 19-12-0
DI90: Van Evert Backer voor het gras in de Geer 1726 2-10-0
DI91: [1727] Evert Backer 22-6-0
DI92: [1727] Een varken voor Evert Backer 3-10-0

DI97: Evert Backer 1728 21-14-0
DI103: [1730] Evert Backer so aan gelt als stro en decken op sijn huys en twe[e] varkens 42-9-0
DI108: [1732] Aan Evert Backer 72-11-0
DI114: [1738] aan Eevert Backer 95-8-0
DI115: [1738] voor enige reparation aan het huis van Evert Backer betaalt aan Jan Gerritsen en Geijsbert Petersen en Guert Hendricksen en voor het hecken aan Schuerhoven
DI119: [1740] aan Eevert Backer 103-10-0
DI127: [1743] aan Eever Backer 116-2-0
DI130: [1746] voor de inboel van Evert Backer 42-9-4
DI130: [1746] voor de rog en boekw[eit] Evert Backer
DI131: [1746] Evert Backer en zijn vrouw 142-2-0
DI136: voor Evert Backer aan Jacob Evers waarmede voldaan is voor het kostgeld tot Mey 1748 als hij nog sal ontvangen hebben 23 g[u]l[den] 10 st[uivers] 76-6-0
DI137: [1746] Karsy [= gekeperde wollen stof] voor Evert Backer 0-10-0
DI137: [1746] voor't baart scheeren van Evert Backer 0-15-0
DI137: [1746] voor Ever Backer 2 hembden en maakloon 3-12-0
DI137: [1746] deeken voor Evert Backer 3-19-0
DI137: [1746] voor Evert Backer laken broek en hembden 5-8-4
DI143: [1749] Kostgelt voor Evert Backer voldaan tot May 1749 25-0-0
DI143: [1749] nog kostegelt voor Evert Backer tot korting van hetjaar beginnende met Mey 1749 25-0-0
DI143: [1749] Kostgeld voor Evert Backers vrouw 31-0-0
DI143: [1749] de dood kist 4-10 0
DI144: [1749] [voor het begraven van de vrouw v[an] E. Backer 1-18-0
DI149: 2 jaaren kostgelt voor Evert Backer waarmede voldaan is tot den 1 Nov[em]b[er] 1751 100-0-0
DI149: [1751] voor Evert Backer kiel hoose en slaapmuts 2-15-0
DI166: [1753] voor Evert Backer waarmede voldaan tot zijn dood 104-0-0
DI220: Huis 6
DI221: Landerij 3.

80. **Wouter Berendsen van Maanen**, born 15-12-1709 in Bennekom; died 15-9-1747 in Bennekom. He was the son of **160. Berend Crijnen** and **161. Gerritie Gijsberts**. He married **81. Jantje Hendriksen** 13-3- 1718 in Bennekom.

81. **Jantje Hendriksen**, born Abt. 1685 in Wageningen; died 21-7-1763 in Bennekom. She was the daughter of **162. Hendrik Petersen** and **163. Hendrikje Arissen**.

Notes for Wouter Berendsen van Maanen:
DB8: Wouter zv Bemt Jaspers en Truijtje Wouters
KS2-168
VG1981p168: Begraven 19-9

Notes for Jantje Hendriksen:
KS2-160
VG1981pl68: Begraven 25-7

Marriage Notes for Wouter van Maanen and Jantje Hendriksen:
TB10: Wouter Bemtsen van Manen met Jantje Hendricks

Children of Wouter van Maanen and Jantje Hendriksen are:

i. **Berend Woutersen van Maanen**, born 19-4-1722 in Bennekom; died 18-7-1778; married **(1) Gerritje Everts Roseboom** 14-6-1744 in Bennekom; born 28-2-1723 in Bennekom; died 2-10-1766 in Bennekom; married **(2) Hendrikje Jansen** 26-4-1767 in Bennekom; born in Bennekom.

Notes for Berend Woutersen van Maanen:
DB15: Bemt zv Wouter Bemsen en Jantjen Hendericks
KS2-160: Beg 21-7-1778
VG1993pl87: Landbouwer

Notes for Gerritje Everts Roseboom:
DB15: Gerritje dv Est Gerritsen en Liesbet Everdsen
KS2-16-: Beg 6-10-1766
VG1993pl87

Marriage Notes for Berend van Maanen and Gerritje Roseboom:
TB17: Beemt Wouters met Gerritje Evers beide Bennekom
VG1993pl87: Tot voogden over de kinderen uit het eerste huwelijk werden aangesteld Gerrit Evertsen en Willem Woutersen, het saldo van hun bezittingen bedroeg 99g en 2s, hij had in 1776 een erf en goed gepacht genaamd het Plaatsje aan de Dijkgraafbehorende tot de goederen van Hoekelom

40 ii. **Willem Woutersen van Maanen**, born 1-1723 in Bennekom; married **Jenneke Evertsen Roseboom**

5-1751 in Bennekom.

   iii. **Antonij Woutersen van Maanen**, born 28-11-1729 in Bennekom.

   Notes for Antonij Woutersen van Maanen:
DB18: Antonij zv Wouter Bemts en Jantje Hendericks.

82. Evert Gerritsen Roseboom, born 4-11-1694 in Bennekom; died 20-12-1766 in Bennekom. He was the son of **164. Gerrit Aartsen Roseboom** and **165. Brandje Hendriks**. He married **83. Lijsbeth Evertsen van Eck** 1722 in Bennekom.

83. Lijsbeth Evertsen van Eck, born 24-10-1697 in Bennekom; died 28-6-1779 in Bennekom. She was the daughter of **166. Evert Jacobsen van Eck** and **167. Gerritje Everts**.

Notes for Evert Gerritsen Roseboom:
DB3: Evert zv Gart Aerts en Brantien Hendriks, Hoekelumse brink
KS2-168: Beg 24-12-1766
VG1998p183: wonende Halderbrink

Notes for Lijsbeth Evertsen van Eck:
DB4: Lijsbeth dv Evert Jacobs en Gartien Evertse, Dorp
KS2-168: Beg 2-7

More About Lijsbeth Evertsen van Eck:
Date born 2: 24-9-1697, Bennekom

Marriage Notes for Evert Roseboom and Lijsbeth van Eck:
VG1993p247: Ze kopen 2/3 deel van 3 schepel bouwland gelegen aan het Molenpad te Bennekom voor 75 gld van Hendrik Camp en zijn vrouw Teunisje Breunissen, het resterende deel was eigendom van de diaconie van Bennekom, hun erfgenamen verkopen dit stuk land op 23-2-1780 aan Cornelis Otten en zijn vrouw voor 95gld, tevens verkopen ze een huis en hof gelegen ten westen van de Halderbrink voor 701 gld aan Willemtje Jansen wed van Jan Willemsen

Children of Evert Roseboom and Lijsbeth van Eck:

   i. **Brantje Everts Roseboom**, born 22-10-1726 in Bennekom; died Bef. 31-10-1729.

   Notes for Brantje Everts Roseboom:
DB17: Brantje dv Evert Gerritsen en Lijsbet Everts

   ii. **Jan Everts Roseboom**, born 7-9-1727 in Bennekom. Notes for Jan Everts Roseboom:

   DB18: Jan zv Evert Gen-its en Lisabet Everts

   iii. **Jan Everts Roseboom**, born 19-9-1728 in Bennekom.

   Notes for Jan Everts Roseboom:
DB18: Jan zv Jan Gerrits en Lijsebet Everts

   iv. **Grietje Everts Roseboom**, born 24-4-1735 in Bennekom; married **Jan Willemsen** 21-10-1757 in Bennekom; born 16-5-1723 in Lunteren.

   Notes for Grietje Everts Roseboom:
DB22: Grietje dv Evert Roseboom en Lijsbet Everts

   Notes for Jan Willemsen:
VG1998p182

   Marriage Notes for Grietje Roseboom and Jan Willemsen:
TB21: Jan Willemsen geb Lunteren met Grietjen Evers Bennekom

   v. **Brandje Evertsen Roseboom**, born 31-10-1729 in Bennekom; married **Lammert Petersen** 29-6-1758 in Bennekom.

   Notes for Brandje Evertsen Roseboom:
DB18: Brantje dv Evert Geurts en Lijsbet Evers

   Marriage Notes for Brandje Roseboom and Lammert Petersen:
TB21: Lammert Pietersen met Brentjen Everts

   vi. **Gerritje Everts Roseboom**, born 28-2-1723 in Bennekom; died 2-10-1766 in Bennekom; married Berend Woutersen van Maanen 14-6-1744 in Bennekom; born 19-4-1722 in Bennekom; died 18-7-1778.

   Notes for Gerritje Everts Roseboom:
DB15: Gerritje dv Est Gerritsen en Liesbet Everdsen
KS2-16-: Beg 6-10-1766
VG1993p187

   Notes for Berend Woutersen van Maanen:
DB15: Bemt zv Wouter Bemsen en Jantjen Hendericks
KS2-160: Beg 21-7-1778
VG1993p187: Landbouwer

   Marriage Notes for Gerritje Roseboom and Berend van Maanen:
TB17: Beemt Wouters met Gerritje Evers beide Bennekom
VG1993p187: Tot voogden over de kinderen uit het eerste huwelijk werden aangesteld Gerrit Evertsen en Willem Woutersen, het saldo van hun bezittingen bedroeg 99g en 2s, hij had in 1776 een erf en goed gepacht genaamd het

Plaatsje aan de Dijkgraafbehorende tot de goederen van Hoekelom

41 vii. **Jenneke Evertsen Roseboom**, born 31-8-1732 in Bennekom; married **(1) Willem Woutersen van Maanen** 5-1751 in Bennekom; married **(2) Bessel Willemsen van Remeker** 23-7-1768 in Bennekom.

88. Brand Gerritsen, married **89. Hendrikje Teunissen**.

89. Hendrikje Teunissen

Child of Brand Gerritsen and Hendrikje Teunissen is:

44 i. **Antony Brandsen**, born 9-5-1734 in Ede; married **Selia Gerritsen Ras** 20-9-1761 in Ede.

90. Gerrit Jacobsen Ras, married **91. Jantje Jansen** 26-4-1722 in Bennekom.

91. Jantje Jansen

Marriage Notes for Gerrit Ras and Jantje Jansen:
TB11: Gerrit Jacobsen Rap met Jantjen Jans beiden Bennekom

Children of Gerrit Ras and Jantje Jansen are:

i. **Gerritje Gerritsen Ras**, born 29-11-1730 in Bennekom.

Notes for Gerritje Gerritsen Ras:
DB19: Gerritje dv Gerrit Jacobsen en Jantje Jansen

ii. **Gerrit Gerritsen Ras**, born 1-7-1731 in Bennekom.

Notes for Gerrit Gerritsen Ras:
DB20: Gerrit zv Gerrit Jacobsen Ras en Jantje Jans

iii. **Neeltje Gerritsen Ras**, born 10-10-1734 in Bennekom.

Notes for Neeltje Gerritsen Ras:
DB22: Neeltje dv Gerrit Jacobse Ras en Jantie Jansen

iv. **Jacob Gerritsen Ras**, born 12-7-1739 in Bennekom.

Notes for Jacob Gerritsen Ras:
DB25: Jacob zv Gerrit Jacobsen en Jantjen Jans

45 v. **Selia Gerritsen Ras**, born 3-3-1737 in Bennekom; married **Antony Brandsen** 20-9-1761 in Ede.

92. Aart Hendriksen van Eck, born 20-7-1715 in Bennekom. He was the son of **184. Hendrik Aartse van Eck** and **185. Mary Hennsen**. He married **93. Geurtje Evers** 11-1744 in Bennekom.

93. Geurtje Evers

Notes for Aart Hendriksen van Eck:
DB11: Aart zv Hendrick Aarsen van Eck en Maria Hermens

Marriage Notes for Aart van Eck and Geurtje Evers:
TB17: Aart Hendriks wed Grietje Geriesen met Geurtje Evers beide Bennekom

Children of Aart van Eck and Geurtje Evers are:

i. **Maas Aartsen van Eck**, born 21-1-1748 in Bennekom.

Notes for Maas Aartsen van Eck:
DB29: Maas zv Aart Hendriks en Geurtjen Evers

ii. **Grietje Aartsen van Eck**, born Bet. 6-6 - 30-6-1751 in Bennekom; married **Evert Berendsen van Maanen** 11-8-1771 in Bennekom; born 6-2-1751 in Bennekom; died 13-6-1809 in Bennekom.

Notes for Grietje Aartsen van Eck:
DB31: Grietje dv Aart Hendriks en Geurtje Evertz

Notes for Evert Berendsen van Maanen:
DB31: Evert zv Berend Wouters en Gartien Evertsen
VG1981p169

Marriage Notes for Grietje van Eck and Evert van Maanen:
TB25: Evert Nerents met Grietje Aartsen beide geb en wonende Bennekom

iii. **Hermen Aartsen van Eck**, born 2-6-1754 in Bennekom; married **Hendrikje Jacobsen van Hal** 1-3-1767 in Bennekom; born in Bennekom.

Notes for Hermen Aartsen van Eck:
DB32: Hermen zv Aart Hendriks en Geurtjen Evers

Marriage Notes for Hermen van Eck and Hendrikje van Hal:
TB23: Herman Aartsen van Eck geb Eede en won alhier met Hendrikje Jacobsen van Hal geb en won alhier

46 iv. **Evert Aartsen van Eck**, born 4-3-1746 in Bennekom; died Bef. 13-4-1814; married **(1) Fijtje Hendrikse** 11-5-1766 in Bennekom; married **(2) Jantje Berendsen van Maanen** 1775 in Bennekom.

94. Berend Woutersen van Maanen, born 19-4-1722 in Bennekom; died 18-7-1778. He was the son of **80. Wouter Berendsen van Maanen** and **81. Jantje Hendriksen**. He married **95. Gerritje Everts Roseboom** 14-6-1744 in Bennekom.

95. Gerritje Everts Roseboom, born 28-2-1723 in Bennekom; died 2-10-1766 in Bennekom. She was the daughter of **82. Evert Gerritsen Roseboom** and **83. Lijsbeth Evertsen van Eck**.

Notes for Berend Woutersen van Maanen:
DB15: Bemt zv Wouter Bemsen en Jantjen Hendericks
KS2-160: Beg 21-7-1778
VG1993p187: Landbouwer

Notes for Gerritje Everts Roseboom:
DB15: Gerritje dv Est Gerritsen en Liesbet Everdsen
KS2-16-: Beg 6-10-1766
VG1993p187

Marriage Notes for Berend van Maanen and Gerritje Roseboom:
TB17: Beemt Wouters met Gerritje Evers beide Bennekom
VG1993p187: Tot voogden over de kinderen uit het eerste huwelijk werden aangesteld Gerrit Evertsen en Willem Woutersen, het saldo van him bezittingen bedroeg 99g en 2s, hij had in 1776 een erf en goed gepacht genaamd het Plaatsje aan de Dijkgraaf- behorende tot de goederen van Hoekelom

Children of Berend van Maanen and Gerritje Roseboom are:

   i. **Lijsbeth Berendsen van Maahen**, born 18-10-1744 in Bennekom.

   Notes for Lijsbeth Berendsen van Maanen:
DB27: Lijsbeth dv Berend Wouters en Jantien Evers

   ii. **Jantjen Berendsen van Maanen**, born 3-7-1746 in Bennekom; died 6-7-1746.

   Notes for Jantjen Berendsen van Maanen:
DB28: Jantjen dv Beemt Woutersen en Gerritjen Evers

47 iii. **Jantje Berendsen van Maanen**, born 28-1-1748 in Bennekom; died Bef. 13-4-1814; married **Evert Aartsen van Eck** 1775 in Bennekom.

   iv. **Woutertjen Berendsen van Maanen**, born 16-11-1749 in Bennekom; died 17-12-1751.

   Notes for Woutertjen Berendsen van Maanen:
DB30: Woutertjen dv Beemt Wouterse en Gerritje Evers

   v. **Evert Berendsen van Maanen**, born 6-2-1751 in Bennekom; died 13-6-1809 in Bennekom; married **Grietje Aartsen van Eck** 11-8-1771 in Bennekom; born Bet. 6-6 - 30-6-1751 in Bennekom.

   Notes for Evert Berendsen van Maanen:
DB31: Evert zv Berend Wouters en Gartien Evertsen
VG1981p169

Notes for Grietje Aartsen van Eck:
DB31: Grietje dv Aart Hendriks en Geurtje Evertz

Marriage Notes for Evert van Maanen and Grietje van Eck:
TB25: Evert Nerents met Grietje Aartsen beide geb en wonende Bennekom

   vi. **Woutertje Berendsen van Maanen**, born 4-8-1753 in Bennekom; married **Gijsbert Aartsen van Eck**; born 7-5-1741 in Bennekom.

   Notes for Woutertje Berendsen van Maanen:
DB32: Woutertje dv Beemt Wouters en Gerritjen Evers

   Notes for Gijsbert, Aartsen van Eck:
DB26: Gijsbert zv Aart Hendriks en Grietje Geurssen

   vii. **Wouter Berendsen van Maanen**, born 25-12-1754 in Bennekom; died 11-8-1805 in Bennekom; married **(1) Gijsbertje Willemsen** 6-12-1778 in Ede; born 16-12-1753 in Ede; died 31-1-1785 in Bennekom; married **(2) Janna Willemsen Lieftink** 15-11-1786 in Bennekom; born 17-1-1748 in Oosterbeek; died 13-2-1827 in Bennekom.

   Notes for Wouter Berendsen van Maanen:
DB33: Wouter zv Beemt Woutersen en Gerritje Eversen
KS2-155: Landbouwer, beg 15-8-1805
VG1993p132

Notes for Janna Willemsen Lieftink:
KS2-155: Beg 17-2-1827
VG1993p132

Marriage Notes for Wouter van Maanen and Janna Lieftink:
VG1981p169: Huwelijkse voorwaarden RAV inv nr 548 nr 58 en 59

   viii. **Jacob Evertsen Berendsen van Maanen**, born 28-10-1758 in Bennekom.

   Notes for Jacob Evertsen Berendsen van Maanen:
DB35: Jacob Evertsen zv Bemt Woutersen en Garitien Evers

   ix. **Brand Berendsen van Maanen**, born 8-11-1761 in Bennekom; died Bef. 27-9-1764.

Notes for Brand Berendsen van Maanen:
DB36: Brand zv Berent Wouterssen en Gerritjen Everts

x. **Brand Berendsen van Maanen**, born 29-7-1764 in Bennekom; married Eef|e Jansens van de Grampel 1798 in Bennekom; born in Bennekom; died 25-10-1822 in Bennekom.

Notes for Brand Berendsen van Maanen:
DB38: Brand zv Barent Wouters en Gerritje Everts Roseboom Marriage Notes for Brand van Maanen and Eefje van de Grampel:
TB31: Brand Berends geb en wo Bennekom met Eefje Janssen van de Grampel won Bennekom.

Generation No. 8

128. Derckvan Roekel, born Abt. 1615.

Notes for Derck van Roekel:
Deze genealogie is gebaseerd op 'De Familie van Roekel' by E. de Jonge, L. Overduin, H. J. van Roekel en J. van Roekel [GR]. Er zijn veel wijzigingen en toevoegingen, speciaal van Amerikaanse takken, dank aan Maynard & Clint van Roekel en anderen
Een andere belangrijke bron is het tijdschrift 'Veluwse Geslachten' [VG]
Deze genealogie bevat ongeveer 9000 personen (8-10-2000) maar is met (nooit...?) af
Toevoegingen en correcties graag sturen naar:

Gijs van Roekel
Bakkersweg 5
NL-3951CS Maarn
The Netherlands
Email: g.v.roekel@hccnet.nl
GR9 0: Hypothetische stamvader.
Derck is onze vroegste gemeenschappelijke voorouder. In oude archieven wordt vanaf 1300 afen toe verwezen naar oudere van Roekel's maar hun relatie tot Derck is onbekend.
De naam van Roekel komt van een nog steeds bestaand gehucht Roekel boven Ede, tussen Wekerom en Otterlo op de Veluwe.
Er staan nu nog enkele boerderijen.
De namen Bennekom, Ede, Wageningen, Renkum, Wekerom zijn van plaatsen op de westelijke grens van de Veluwe een heuvelachtig woest gebied in het hart van Nederland.
De plaatsen liggen dicht bij elkaar, Ede ligt 5km ten noorden van Bennekom, Wageningen ligt ongeveer 5 km ten zuiden van Bennekom
De meeste oudere van Roekel's waren boer, sommige van hen ook bakker oftimmerman.

Ze behoorden alien tot de 'Nederduitsch Gereformeerde Kerk', veel gegevens in deze genealogie komen uit de doop-, trouw- en begraafboeken van deze kerk.

Children of Derck van Roekel are:

64 i. **Willem Dercksen van Roekel**, born Abt. 1645; married Jantjen Geurtsen Abt. 1670 in Bennekom.

ii. **Wouter Dercksen van Roekel**

Notes for Wouter Dercksen van Roekel:
BB211: Wouter Dercksz Backer is buurtmeester van de benedenbuurt 1688-1690.

160. Berend Crijnen, born Abt. 1660 in Ede; died 11-4-1748 in Bennekom. He married **161. Gerritie Gijsberts** 23-3-1685 in Bennekom.

161. Gerritie Gijsberts, born Abt. 1660.

Notes for Berend Crijnen:
KS2-177: Beg 16-4

Marriage Notes for Berend Crijnen and Gerritie Gijsberts:
TB2: Beemt Crienen wedn Stijntje Morren Wageningsche buurt met Gerritie Gijsberts wonende Bennekom
VG1994p28: Ze woonden op de Hoekelumse brink

Children of Berend Crijnen and Gerritie Gijsberts:

i. **Stijntje Bemts**, born 10-3-1689 in Wageningen; died Bef. 1716 in Bennekom; married Willem Jansen Veenbrmk 12-4-1711 in Bennekom; born Abt. 1685 in Bennekom; died 31-1-1771 in Bennekom.

Notes for Stijntje Bemts:
VG1989p100

Notes for Willem Jansen Veenbrink:
KS2-169: Begr 7-2
VG1989p100
VG1993p250: Op 8-5-1771 werd een Staat en Inventaris ingeschreven betreffende Willem's nalatenschap, tevens magescheid tussen de erfgenamen

Marriage Notes for Stijntje Bemts and Willem Veenbrink:
TB8: Willem Jansen Veenbrink met Stijntje Bemts beiden Bennekom
VG1993p250: Door aankopen vergroten ze regelmatig hun bezittingen, uit deze aankopen blijkt dat ze in de omgeving van de Halderbrink hebben gewoond

Ancestors of Jan van Roekel

    ii. **Hendrickie Berendsen**, born 8-12-1696 in Bennekom.

        Notes for Hendrickie Berendsen:
DB4: Hendrickie dv Berent Crijne en Gartien Gijsberts, Hoekelumse brink

    iii. Aart Berendsen, born 10-2-1708 in Bennekom.

        Notes for Aart Berendsen:
DB7: Aart zv Bemt Crijnen en Gerritjen Gijsberts

80 iv. **Wouter Berendsen van Maanen**, born 15-12-1709 in Bennekom; died 15-9-1747 in Bennekom; married **Jantje Hendriksen** 13-3-1718 in Bennekom.

162. Hendrik Petersen, born Abt. 1660 in Bennekom; died Aft. 1684. He married **163. Hendrikje Arissen** 5-1-1684 in Bennekom.

163. Hendrikje Arissen, born Abt. 1660 in Bennekom.

More About Hendrik Petersen:
Date born 2: Abt. 1660, Wageningen

More About Hendrikje Arissen:
Date born 2: Abt. 1660

Marriage Notes for Hendrik Petersen and Hendrikje Arissen:
TB1: Hendrik Pessen met Hendrikie Arie, beiden te Bennekom

Children of Hendrik Petersen and Hendrikje Arissen:

81 i. **Jantje Hendriksen**, born Abt. 1685 in Wageningen; died 21-7-1763 in Bennekom; married **(1) Wouter Berendsen van Maanen** 13-3-1718 in Bennekom; married **(2) Hendrik Jansen Slophoos** 18-8-1748 in Bennekom.

    ii. **Reintje Hendriks**, born Bef. 1688 in Bennekom; died 18-1-1746 in Bennekom; married **Jan Hendriks Haalboom** 8-4-1714 in Bennekom; born Abt. 1683 in Bennekom; died 20-11-1756 in Bennekom.

        Notes for Reintje Hendriks:
VG1991p73

        Notes for Jan Hendriks Haalboom:
VG1991p73

        Marriage Notes for Reintje Hendriks and Jan Haalboom:
TB9: Jan Haalboom met Reintje Henderiks beide te Bennekom

    iii. **Arris Hendriks**, born 13-5-1688 in Bennekom.

        Notes for Arris Hendriks:
DB1: Arris zv Hendrik Peters en Hendrikien Ariisen, Hoekelumse brink

164. Gerrit Aartsen Roseboom, born in Ede; died Bef. 1733 in Bennekom. He married **165. Brandje Hendriks** 6-2-1681 in Bennekom.

165. Brandje Hendriks, born Abt. 1660 in Ede.

Notes for Gerrit Aartsen Roseboom:
VG1988pl51

Notes for Brandje Hendriks:
VG1988pl51: jd van de Slunt bij Ede Marriage

Notes for Gerrit Roseboom and Brandje Hendriks:
TB1: Geurt Aartsen tot Bennekom met Breintje Hendriks van de Slunt Ede

Children of Gerrit Roseboom and BrandJe Hendriks:

    i. **Aertie Gerrits Roseboom**, born 1-1-1690 in Bennekom.

        Notes for Aertie Gerrits Roseboom:
DB1: Aertie dv Gerrit Aerts en Brantie Hendriks, Heukelom

    ii. **Willemijntje Gerrits Roseboom**, born 13-12-1691 in Bennekom; married **(1) Willem Hendriksen van Kampen** 19-4-1711 in Bennekom; born Abt. 1680 in Wageningen; died Bef. 18-1-1728; married **(2) Derck Cornelissen** 18-1-1728 in Bennekom; born 4-1-1680 in Rhenen.

        Notes for Willemijntje Gerrits Roseboom:
DB2: Willemijntje dv Garrit Aerts en Brantie Hendriks, Hoekelumse brink

        Marriage Notes for Willemijntje Roseboom and Willem van Kampen:
TB8: Willem Hendriks met Willemijn Gerrits beiden Bennekom

82 iii. **Evert Gerritsen Roseboom**, born 4-11-1694 in Bennekom; died 20-12-1766 in Bennekom; married **Lijsbeth Evertsen van Eck** 1722 in Bennekom.

    iv. **Geurt Gerritse Roseboom**, born Abt. 1700 in Bennekom; died 17-2-1773 in Bennekom; married **Cornelia Everts** 8-2-1728 in Bennekom; born Abt. 1700 in Bennekom; died 1-11-1763 in Bennekom.

        Notes for Geurt Gerritse Roseboom:
VG1985p40
VG1993p248: Te Bennekom aangenomen als lidmaat met Pasen 1757, in 1772 woonde hij op boerderij de Ham

Notes for Cornelia Everts:
VG1985p40

Marriage Notes for Geurt Roseboom and Cornelia Everts:
TB13: Geurt Gerritsen met Cornelia Evers beide won alhier.

166. Evert Jacobsen van Eck, born Abt. 1660 in Bennekom. He married **167. Gerritje Everts** 19-6-1692 in Bennekom.

167. Gerritje Everts, born Abt. 1660 in Wekerom; died 13-10-1742 in Bennekom.

Notes for Evert Jacobsen van Eck:
VG1994p28: Bakker

Notes for Gerritje Everts:
KS2-177: Beg 18-10-1742

Marriage Notes for Evert van Eck and Gerritje Everts:
TB3: Evert Jacobsen met Garritie Evers van Wekerom

Children of Evert van Eck and Gerritje Everts are:

    i. **Jacob Evertsen van Eck**, born 1-8-1694 in Bennekom; married **(1) Hendrikje Wouters van Eck**; died Bef. 21-1-1720; married **(2) Mamjtjen Ebbers** 21-1-1720 in Bennekom.

    Notes for Jacob Evertsen van Eck:
    DB3: Jacob zv Evert Jacobs en Gartje Evers, Dorp

    Marriage Notes for Jacob van Eck and Mamjtjen Ebbers:
    TB10: Jacob Evers wedn Hendrikje Wouters van Eck met Mamjtjen Ebbers beiden Bennekom

83 ii. **Lijsbeth Evertsen van Eck**, born 24-10-1697 in Bennekom; died 28-6-1779 in Bennekom; married **Evert Gerritsen Roseboom** 1722 in Bennekom.

    iii. **Gerritje Evertsen van Eck**, born 17-8-1708 in Bennekom.

    Notes for Gerritje Evertsen van Eck:
    DB7: Gerritje dv Egt Jacobsen en Gerritjen Evers

    iv. **Jan Evertsen van Eck**, born 24-7-1712 in Bennekom.

    Notes for Jan Evertsen van Eck:
    DB9: Jan van Eck zv Evert Jacobs en Gerritjen Evers.

184. Hendrik Aartse van Eck, born 2-2-1690 in Bennekom; died Bef. 22-12-1732. He was the son of **368. Aardt van Eck** and **369. Geessien Everts**. He married **185. Mary Hermsen** 1-5-1712 in Bennekom.

185. Mary Hermsen

Notes for Hendrik Aartse van Eck:
DB2: Hendrik zv Aardt van Eck en Geessien Everts, Halderbrink

Marriage Notes for Hendrik van Eck and Mary Hennsen:
TB8: Henderick van Eck te Bennekom met Mary Hennsen van den Doomwerth Children of Hendrik van Eck and Mary Hennsen are:

92 i. **Aart Hendriksen van Eck**, born 20-7-1715 in Bennekom; married **(1) Grietje Geurssen**; married **(2) Geurtje Evers** 11-1744 in Bennekom.

    ii. **Aart Hendriksen van Eck**, born 17-l-1717 in Bennekom.

    Notes for Aart Hendriksen van Eck:
    DB12: Aart zv Hendrick Jan van Eck en Marritjen Hermens

    iii. **Hermen Hendriksen van Eck**, born 12-11-1724 in Bennekom.

    Notes for Hermen Hendriksen van Eck:
    DB16: Hermen zv Hendrick van Eck en Martje Herms.

Generation No. 9

368. Aardt van Eck, born in Veenendaal. He married **369. Geessien Everts**.

369. Geessien Everts

Notes for Aardt van Eck:
VG1990p253
Notes for Geessien Everts:
VG1990p253

Children of Aardt van Eck and Geessien Everts are:

184 i. **Hendrik Aartse van Eck**, born 2-2-1690 in Bennekom; died Bef. 22-12-1732; married **Mary Hennsen** 1-5-1712 in Bennekom.

    ii. **Annetie Aartse van Eck**, born 25-9-1692 in Bennekom.

    Notes for Annetie Aartse van Eck:
    DB2: Annetie dv Aert van Eck en Geessien Everts, Halderbrink iii. NN Aarts van Eck, born 10-12-1693 in Bennekom.

    Notes for NN Aarts van Eck:
    DB3: .... dv Aardt van Eck en Geertie Everts, Halderbrink

iv. **Martien Aartse van Eck**, born 6-9-1696 in Bennekom.

Notes for Martien Aartse van Eck:
DB4: Martien dv Aert van Eck en Geertien Everts, Hoekelumse brink

v. **Jan Aartse van Eck**, born 1-1697 in Bennekom; married **Elisabeth Drijssen** 17-4-1729 in Bennekom.

Notes for Jan Aartse van Eck:
DB4: Jan Aartse zv Aart van Eck en Geertje Evers

Marriage Notes for Jan van Eck and Elisabeth Drijssen:
TB13: Jan Amtsen van Eck van Bennekom met Elisabeth Drijssen van Achterbergh beyde wonende Bennekom.

Postcard from Van Roekel Florist in Dudley, North Carolina, showing their "Say It With Flowers" logo. See Figure 32 and story on page 47.

The Story of Jan de Bakker, the First Dutch Martyr

Jan de Bakker – Johannes Pistorius Woerdensis
A family legend

Jan de Bakker - Johannes Pistorius Woerdensis
(Illustration from the website of Henry Wagensveld)

In a branch of the Van Roekel family, a story is handed down from father to son that the family descends from Jan de Bakker [=John the Baker], the first Dutch martyr. TAKE DUE NOTE: For the time being, this is NOTHING MORE than a living family legend. Supporting facts from the archives have yet to be found.

From: www.xs4all.nl/~roekelg/genealogie/JanDeBakker.html#engels © Gijs van Roekel, Maarn 2006. Used with permission.

In an email on August 9, 2006, Henry Wagensveld wrote the following:

"On your site I saw the history of the Van Roekel family. It might be interesting to know that in my branch (see: Gerrit van Roekel 1891-1985 was my great grandfather) the story was told from father to son that we descend from Jan de Bakker (Johannes Pistorius Woerdensis), one of the first Dutch martyrs. In the old generations, that never did perform any genealogical research, it was also known that in earlier times the name of the family was Backer.

The story tells that Jan de Bakker (and that is a fact) violated celibacy after he left the Roman Catholic church. He had two children. Also, his father's name (Jan Dirksz) conforms with early Van Roekel first names. According to tradition, Jan's wife found refuge in the hamlet Roekel near Ede. So, in the course of time, the family adopted the name Van Roekel [=from Roekel].

Also see the article on www.wagensveld.tk."

In a following email dated August 14, 2006, Henry added:

"To my knowledge, Jan de Bakker had two children. About this fact the sources contradict. In the archives of the Dom [=cathedral] in Utrecht, two different entries are found. In one document, there is no reference to children, and another document tells us that they [=inquisition] will also prosecute his children until their death. In short, not much is known, only the story that Jan's wife fled to the Veluwe might offer some grip."

In an email dated 5-6-2008, Jacob Slack from the USA posed some interesting questions about a possible connection between Floris Dirksz and Jan Dirksz, the father of Jan de Bakker:

"I am searching for [information about] the father of Floris Dirksz, who lived outside the Woerden city wall in 1463. I read your webpage about the legend of Jan de Bakker. Jan de Bakker was a son of Jan Dirksz, who was Woerden church sexton. Could Floris Dirksz have been a brother of Jan Dirksz? What do you know about Dirk Jansz and his family?

My family name is Slack, derived from Slecht or Slechten. Other members of the Slecht family during the 15th century were church leaders: Tilman Slecht von Elmpt (Germany), Kanunnik of St. Lambert Cathedral in Luik Belgium and Chancelor to Count Carl van Gelre; Heinrich Slecht, Kanunnik and Priest of Borner Kirche near Elmpt; Johann Slecht von Boppard (Germany), Vikar of St. Barbara's Church; Wilhelm Slecht de Elmpt, Kantor of St. Quirin de Neuss (Germany); Henricus Slecht, Abbot of Werden Abbey in Essen Germany; Franziskus Slecht, Priest of Gosseltshausen in Wolnzach Germany; Rheinbold Slecht, Kantor of Straussburg France.

These Slecht men who were church leaders during the 15th century leads me to believe that the family of Floris Dirksz in Woerden also were church leaders, which leads me to ask if Jan Dirksz, father of Jan de Bakker was the brother of Floris Dirksz."

This might possibly imply that Willem Dercksen Backer, our family founder, descends from this Jan de Bakker. The book, *Johannes Pistorius Woerdensis* by J. W. Gunst, reverend in Woerden, published in 1925 by the Uitgeversmaatschappij "De Blauwvoet" Hilversum, is a comprehensive biography of Jan de Bakker. Gunst considers it highly improbable that Jan de Bakker had children, but does not exclude it. Below follows a summary of the story of the life of Jan de Bakker based upon the book of J. W. Gunst. For that matter, this book contains numerous references to the text of Gnapheus [=a friend of Jan] in Haemstede's *Martelarenboek* [=the book of martyrs].

Origin and name

The father of Jan de Bakker was Jan Dirksz, son of Dirk Jansz. Dirk Jansz was an artisan in Woerden who often got assignments of the municipality of Woerden. Probably Jan Dirksz was educated on the school of the "Broeders van het Gemeene Leven" [=Brothers of Common Life, still existing, non-monastic communities] in Deventer. At this school also Desiderius Erasmus was present and most likely Jan Dirksz lived in with the mother of Erasmus who lived in Deventer. Jan Dirksz and Erasmus must have known each other well and possibly were friends. About 1493, Jan Dirksz became sexton of the church of Woerden and, along with that, he also worked as artisan and baker. Unlike many colleagues, he did not become a school teacher. The name of the mother of Jan de Bakker is not known. He had a sister named Cornelia, also known as Neel de Koster. She assisted her father in his activities as sexton. Jan Dirksz is often also known as Jan Koster [=John Sexton] or Jan de Koster. Their son is named Jan Jansz, Jan van Woerden, Jan Coster, Johannes Custodis, Joannes Woerdensis, Johannes Pistorius Woerdensis. The last name Bakker of Pistorius pops up after his death.

Youth and education

Jan de Bakker was born between the end of August and mid-September 1499 in Woerden. So he was a few months older than Karel V, who was born on February 25, 1500 in Gent. In that time, Philips de Schone was count of Holland. Until his 12th year, he visited the only school that existed in Woerden at that time and was educated by "Mister Gerrit." The subjects were reading, writing, calculation, singing, and the "learning of Psalms," probably there was no teaching of Latin. From 1511 to 1514, Jan de Bakker attended the chapter school connected to the Dom [=Cathedral] in Utrecht. The head of this school, the "scholasticus" taught the Quadrivicum: Arithmetica, Musica, Geometrica en Astronomia. Under the scholasticus stood the rector who taught the Trivium: Grammatica, Rhetorica en Dialectica. Jan de Bakker also sang in the Dom choir. It is remarkable that a simple sexton in Woerden sent his son to a school like this.

To the Hieronymus school

In 1514 Jan de Bakker left the chapter school and was found again at the famous Hieronymus school, also in Utrecht. Here he stays for five years. This school was established by the Broeders van het Gemeene Leven [=Brothers of the Common Life] (Geert Grote) and brought forth a number of people inclined to the ideas of reformation. In that time, Hinne Rode is rector of the Hieronymus school, who taught Jan de Bakker "with diligence and punctuality the 'commandments of the Lord' and trained him with respect to his forthcoming priestly office." Willem Gnapheus, born in 1493 in The Hague is a fellow-pupil and friend of Jan de Bakker. In the years that Jan de Bakker attended this school, the reformation broke through and his teacher, Hinne Rode, under the influence of Luther's writings, was one of the first advocates of the reformation. Jan de Bakker and his fellow students were resident pupils of the Hieronymus school, had relatively little contact with other priests of the Dom, and thus were spoon fed with the heretic ideas. The rumors of heresy in the Hieronymus school soon spread in Woerden. Jan presumably was even involved in the diffusion of the "New doctrine." His father, fearing the eventual consequences, drags him away from the school, and he returns to Woerden.

Preacher of the Reformation in Woerden

In 1520 when the reformation started spreading, Jan de Bakker was appointed to the post of sexton by his father. In the accounts of the town of 1520-1521, there was talk of the "jonge Jan Koster." In that position, he actively disseminated the reformation ideas. His message fell in fertile soil among the inhabitants of Woerden, but he was warned by the officials repeatedly. Most likely during this time, the town government appointed him as school master. It is probable that church and government looked at this development with disgust and could not tolerate it, but the town goverment protected him as much as possible under the circumstances. Worden became, thanks to Jan de Bakker, one of the first places in Holland where the "New doctrine" took root.

To the University of Leuven

The father of Jan de Bakker looked for possibilities to educate his son to be a priest. Utrecht was out of the question because of Jan's heretic ideas. It became the university of Leuven where Jan was sent somewhere between the end of 1520 and the beginning if 1521. It was at this university in Leuven where world-famous Erasmus, acquaintance of Jan Dirksz, taught classical languages and Hebrew. Jan stayed in the boarding-school "de Lelie," which belonged to the philosophical faculty. Most likely, he studied philosophy and theology. Jan took lessons for about a year and, in 1522, on urgent request of his father and without having taken a title, returned to Woerden. He did not loose his heretic ideas. During that time at the university of Leuven, the writings of Luther were banned and the persecution of the heretics began. Erasmus did not feel safe in Leuven any more and left for Basel in 1521.

Oud-Woerden.

"Where now is the west wing of the former town hall (now cantonal court), that was added during the restoration at the end of the last century, was situated the house of the married couple *Pistorius*, almost sure, also that of his parents." "The building where Jan de Koster and his son worked, is the present Dutch Reformed Church, which however has undergone a number of modifications."
(Illustration from J. W. Gunst: *Johannes Pistorius Woerdensis*)

Ordination and Parish work

After his return to Woerden, the father and mother of Jan de Bakker insisted on his ordination, most probably because of selfishness. Jan was not very keen about it but, in the end, agreed because of the urgent wish of his parents. The ordination was to take place in Utrecht, but, of course, he was distrusted, being an advocate of the "New doctrine." They required him to abjure Lutheranism, and so he does. After this abjuration and the payment of an amount of money, he was ordinated in Utrecht at the age of 22, then being a priest.

Parish priest in Jacobswoude

In 1522, Jan de Bakker became parish priest of Jacobswoude and preached the "New doctrine" there. Jacobswoude has ceased existence for a long time now; it was situated near the current Woubrugge. It was the first place in Holland where the "New doctrine" was preached from the pulpit. Woubrugge was a remote place already in the process of extinction. The church authorities probably were thinking that Jan de Bakker's evil influence would be limited there. Nevertheless, the heretic message spread rapidly in the direct environment of Jacobswoude: Rijnsaterswoude, Roelofsarendsveen, Rijpwetering, Hoogmade, and Oud-Ade. Very soon, Jan de Bakker stopped celebrating the mass and only gave sermons and

The Story of Jan de Bakker, the First Dutch Martyr

The disappeared Jacobswoude.

"Jacobswoude is the first of all Dutch places, where, in public, an heretic preaching was held, that savoured of Lutheranism by the in Woerden repeatedly warned apostate *Johannes Pistorius*."
(Illustration from J. W. Gunst: Johannes Pistorius Woerdensis)

taught the catechism to the youth. He was warned by the clerical authorities repeatedly. He stays in Woubrugge for less than one year.

Priest in Woerden

In 1523, Jan de Bakker was back in Woerden as a priest. His father had it his way at last, and Jan could assist his father in his tasks as sexton. He was probably called to Woerden to serve as a guild-priest. It might have been that his father, who also was a baker, had a hand in the matter. As guild-priest he celebrated at the guild altar in the church of Woerden. So he was no pastor or chaplain of this church. He continued to spread the heretic message, and the clerus of Utrecht called him to account for this. Jan de Bakker did not respond, so the priests of the bishop-town ordered the castellan of Woerden to arrest him. This was done, and he was thrown into the gaol [jail] of the castle of Woerden. This brought the castellan of Woerden into an awkward position, and a revolt of the population of Woerden was threatened. After some time, the castellan freed the prisoner under the condition that he kept himself available for interrogation. A complaint was lodged against Jan at the Hof of Holland.

Traveling

By this time, the situation in Woerden was becoming dangerous for Jan de Bakker, and he traveled with a colleague (master Aert) to Wittenberg, the stronghold of Luther. There is no agreement about what Jan did in Wittenberg and whether he met the great Luther. After a stay of three monthsh he and his colleague returned to Woerden in the summer of 1523. Soon after their return, the clergy once more called them on account, but, again, they refused to appear. Being absent, thereupon, they were sentenced by the clergy to three years of banishment and a pilgrimage to Rome. Jan de Bakker completely ignored this and continued spreading the "New doctrine" in Woerden. The situation was becoming dangerous again, and he left Woerden and wandered through Holland where he visited and rendered assistance to the new reformed communities.

Marriage

Near the community hall of Woerden stood a few small houses. In one of them lived Jacob Jansz, also named Jacob Jansdochter, suster Jab, suster Jaep. Jan de Bakker secretly married the woman there named Jacoba. She had a normal, neat appearance, not really beautiful nor rich.

She lived beside the house of Jan's parents, so it was not conspicuous that Jan and Jacoba had a relationship. Being a priest, an official marriage, of course, was out of the question. Jan's father had no objections against this marriage. According to J. W. Gunst, it is highly improbable that there were children born from this marriage. Other writers state that in jail he said goodbye to his wife and children.

End of priesthood

At the same time, Jan de Bakker stopped being a priest. He did not shave his head anymore and layed aside his habit. He earned the living for his family just like his father, by baking bread and doing all kinds of work. He also acted as an assistant sexton. He continued his reformation work but no longer as a priest of the Roman Catholic church. He considered himself as minister of God's Holy Word. He opposed the trade of letters of indulgence in Woerden, the consequence being that the normal priests saw their incomes dwindle. Entrance to the church of Woerden was denied him, unless he openly submitted himself to the papal institutions. Then, only once more, he shaved his head and consecrated a mass in the church of Woerden, where he spoke out against the indulgence trade. Because almost all citizens of Woerden were on hand, the local authorities let it happen.

Imprisonment, trial

Jan de Bakker was summoned by the town council and interrogated in the presence of the new pastor of Woerden. The new pastor decided that it had all

Pistorius is led to the scaffold.

"Passing by the Gevangenpoort he looked up to the barred window of the gaol where his friends and fellow-believers were incarcerated, and cried to them: "I take the lead!" It was heard fro]m the gaol: "Our brother! Fight devoutly, we will follow you."
(Illustration from J. W. Gunst: Johannes Pistorius Woerdensis)

gone far enough and lodged a complaint against Jan de Bakker at the governess Margaretha of Austria and the bishop of Liege, Everardus van de Marck, inquisitor general for the Netherlands. The case was sent to the Hof van Holland giving order to arrest Jan de Bakker and bring him to The Hague. Jan de Bakker was arrested and on May 10, 1525, arrived at the Gevangenpoort in The Hague. He stayed there a while, together with his friend Gnapheus who later wrote a comprehensive account about the trial and execution of Jan. He was examined a number of times by the inquisition that repeatedly urged him to revoke his heretic ideas. Jan de Bakker does not budge. He admitted, however, that he was married. He stayed in prison for about four months and celebrated his twenty-sixth birthday there. While in jail, his father visited him a few times. He was also examined by the inquisition. At last, Jan de Bakker was sentenced to die at the stake.

Execution

On Friday, September 15, 1525, Jan de Bakker was brought from the prison to the Prinsenhof [=seat of the government]. Many dignitaries were present, among them governess Margaretha. Jan took his place, in priest's clothes, on a stage, and a priest spoke out a short sermon containing an enumeration of Jan de Bakker's heretical mistakes. Then he was officially desecrated as priest. His priestly clothes are taken off him, and he was dressed in a yellow robe. A yellow cap was put on his head. Next, the judgement of the inquisition was read, whereby Jan de Bakker was being convicted and handed over to the worldly judges.

Pistorius at the stake.

"Pistorius uncovers his chest for the gunpowder that will be put on."
(Illustration from J. W. Gunst: Johannes Pistorius Woerdensis)

Thereupon, all clergymen left the scene. Next, the clerk Sandelijk read over the official sentence and punishment. Then Jan was led to the execution place at the Vijverberg and placed on the scaffold. Gunpowder was put on his chest, the fire ignited, and the executioner strangled him. The fire did the rest. Jacoba, Jan de Bakker's spouse, had to walk in a procession in The Hague and, thereafter, was exposed at the pillory in Woerden. Next, she was banned to the Abdij van Leeuwenhorst near Katwijk where she had to do penance.

Ancestors of Willemina van Deelen

From a document given to us by Jopie and Wim Blokker • Dates listed as day-month-year

Generation No. 1

1. **Willemina van Deelen**, born Abt. 1888 in Ede. She was the daughter of **2. Willem van Deelen** and **3. Rikje Essenstam**. She married **(1) Jan van Roekel** 9-9-1911 in Ede. He was born 24-8-1885 in Ede. He was the son of **Jan van Roekel** and Ottina Van Hunen.

Notes for Jan van Roekel:
GR41: Emigreerde naar US Dudley, bezocht Nederland met zijn vrouw in 1926

Marriage Notes for Willemina van Deelen and Jan van Roekel:
Archieflocatie: Gelderland
Toegangnr: 0207
Inventarisnr: 8253
Gemeente: Ede
Soort akte: Huwelijksakte
Nummer: 87
Datum: 09-09-1911

Generation No. 2

2. **Willem van Deelen**, born Abt. 1862 in Ede. He was the son of **4. Aalbert van Deelen** and **5. Dientje Freriks**. He married **3. Rikje Essenstam** 30-1-1886 in Apeldoom.

3. **Rikje Essenstam**. She was the daughter of **6. Jacob Essenstam** and **7. Willempje van de Hoef**.

Marriage Notes for Willem van Deelen and Rikje Essenstam:
Archieflocatie: Gelderiand
Toegangnr: 0207
Inventarisnr: 6587
Gemeente: Apeldoom
Soort akte: Huwelijksakte
Nummer: 10
Datum: 30-01-1886

Child of Willem van Deelen and Rikje Essenstam is:

1   i.   Willemina van Deelen, born Abt. 1888 in Ede; married Jan van Roekel 9-9-1911 inEde.

Generation No. 3

4. **Aalbert van Deelen**, born Abt. 1823. He was the son of 8. Leendert Timesen van Deelen and **9. Willempje Cornelissen Willems**. He married **5. Dientje Freriks 6-3-1852** in Ede.

5. **Dientje Freriks**, born Abt. 1831. She was the daughter of **10. Willem Freriks** and **11. Gerritje Derksen**.

Marriage Notes for Aalbert van Deelen and Dientje Freriks:
Archieflocatie: Gelderiand
Toegangnr: 0207
Inventarisnr: 5295
Gemeente: Ede
Soort akte: Huwelijksakte
Nummer: 18
Datum: 06-03-1852
Wettiging 1 kind

Child of Aalbert van Deelen and Dientje Freriks is:

2   i.   Willem van Deelen, born Abt. 1862 in Ede; married Rikje Essenstam 30-1-1886 in Apeldoom.

6. **Jacob Essenstam**, born Abt. 1831. He was the son of **12. Jacob Essenstam** and **13. Rikje Jans Stomphorst**. He married **7. Willempje van de Hoef** 1-3-1862 in Renswoude.

7. **Willempje van de Hoef**, born Abt. 1836. She was the daughter of **14. Jan Hendrikse van de Hoef** and **15. Jantje Moriaan**.

Marriage Notes for Jacob Essenstam and Willempje van de Hoef:
Archieflocatie: Utrecht
Toegangnr: 481
Inventarisnr: 918
Gemeente: Renswoude
Soort akte: Huwelijksakte
Nummer: 2
Datum: 01-03-1862

Child of Jacob Essenstam and Willempje van de Hoefis:

3   i.   Rikje Essenstam, married Willem van Deelen 30-1-1886 in Apeldoom.

Generation No. 4

8. **Leendert Timesen van Deelen** He married **9. Willempje Cornelissen Willems**.

9. **Willempje Cornelissen Willems**

Child of Leendert van Deelen and Willempje Willems:

4   i.   Aalbert van Deelen, born Abt. 1823; married Dientje Freriks 6-3-1852 in Ede.

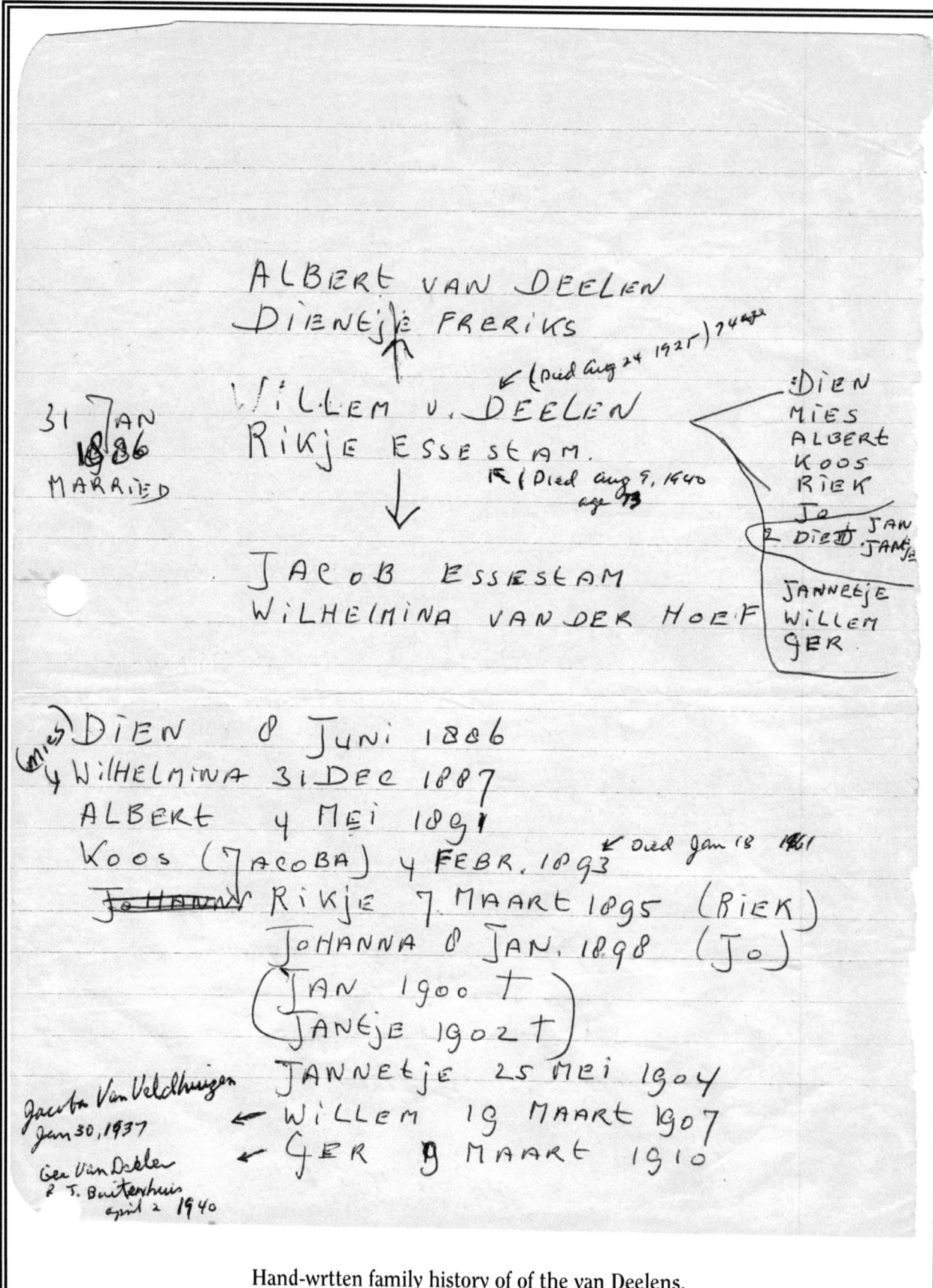

Hand-wrtten family history of of the van Deelens.

10. **Willem Freriks**, born Abt. 1799. He was the son of **20. Breunis Freriks** and **21. Engel Onderstal**. He married **11. Gerritje Derksen** 30-9-1828 in Ede.

11. **Gerritje Derksen**, born Abt 1810. She was the daughter of **22. Jacob Derksen** and **23. Berendina Jans**.

Marriage Notes for Willem Freriks and Gerritje Derksen:

Archieflocatie: Gelderiand
Toegangnr: 0207
Inventarisnr: 5299
Gemeente: Ede
Soort akte: Huwelijksakte
Nummer: 28
Datum: 30-09-1828

Child of Willem Freriks and Gerritje Derksen is:

5   i.   Dientje Freriks, born Abt. 1831; married Aalbert van Deelen 6-3-1852 in Ede.

12. **Jacob Essenstam**, born 21-1-1790 in Beekhuizen. He was the son of **24. Aalbert Essenstam** and **25. Elizabeth Essen**. He married **13. Rikje Jans Stomphorst** 19-3-1819 in Barneveld.

13. **Rikje Jans Stomphorst**, born 4-7-1794 in Ede. She was the daughter of **26. Jan Hindrikzen Stomphorst** and **27. Grietje Rikzen**.

Marriage Notes for Jacob Essenstam and Rikje Stomphorst:
Archieflocatie: Gelderland
Toegangnr: 0207
Inventarisnr: 6431
Gemeente: Barneveld
Soort akte: Huwelijksakte
Nummer: 19
Datum: 19-03-1819

Child of Jacob Essenstam and Rikje Stomphorst is:

6   i.   Jacob Essenstam, born Abt. 1831; married Willempje van de Hoef 1-3-1862 in Renswoude.

14. **Jan Hendrikse van de Hoef**. He married **15. Jantje Moriaan**.

15. **Jantje Moriaan**

Child of Jan van de Hoef and Jantje Moriaan is:

7   i.   Willempje van de Hoef, born Abt 1836; married Jacob Essenstam 1-3-1862 in Renswoude.

Generation No. 5

20. **Breunis Freriks**. He married **21. Engel Onderstal**.

21. **Engel Onderstal**

Child of Breunis Freriks and Engel Onderstal is:

10   i.   Willem Freriks, born Abt. 1799; married Gerritje Derksen 30-9-1828 in Ede.

22. **Jacob Derksen**. He married **23. Berendina Jans**.

23. **Berendina Jans**

Child of Jacob Derksen and Berendina Jans is:

11   i.   Gerritje Derksen, born Abt. 1810; married Willem Freriks 30-9-1828 in Ede.

24. **Aalbert Essenstam**. He married **25. Elizabeth Essen**.

25. **Elizabeth Essen**

Child of Aalbert Essenstam and Elizabeth Essen is:

12   i.   Jacob Essenstam, born 21-1-1790 in Beekhuizen; married Rikje Jans Stomphorst 19-3-1819 in Barneveld.

26. **Jan Hindrikzen Stomphorst**. He married **27. Grietje Rikzen**.

27. **Grietje Rikzen**

Child of Jan Stomphorst and Grietje Rikzen is:

13   i.   Rikje Jans Stomphorst, born 4-7-1794 in Ede; married Jacob Essenstam 19-3-1819 in Barneveld.

Letter from Kaye Mason to Willem van Roekel (Hendricus' grandson), with envelope.

J. Van Roekel
Maanderbuirtsweg 90
Veenendaal, Holland

Kaye Mason
3/75

Dear Family,

It has been quite awhile - Since we have corresponded with any of the family in Holland. I am Kaye Mason. I am Jan Van Roekel's granddaughter. His daughter Oliena was my Mother. I went to live with my grandparents when I was a small girl to help grandmother. I loved my grandparents and I really miss them. I have found a lady here that reads Dutch - So she helped me write your addresses in English. I would like to hear from you. This lady has a husband in service. You don't happen to have any of the family over in the United States. All grandaddy's children are doing fine. His oldest son is in Wilson about (30) miles from here. His middle son is in Mt. Olive he is 30 miles from here. Oliena my mother is in Rockville, Md. This is (360) miles from me, and the youngest son Johnnie is here in Goldsboro - He is still running or operating the florist (flower shop).

My husband is a mechanic. We have been married for 13 yrs in October. We have (3) children. Lisa Anne is 10 yrs old - Susan Annette is 7 yrs old and our son Kay Lee Mason, Jr. is 6 yrs old. I stay at home and keep house and keep a small baby for one of my friend to work.

If there are any of Grandaddy's other relatives living - Please let me know in your letter. I'm praying that everything is well in your house & God will take care of you -

All our love
from our house
to your house,

Kaye, Kay & children

J. Mason
4269 Hwy 70 W.
Goldsboro, N.C.
27530

Air Mail

J. Van Roekel
Maanderbuirtsweg 90
Veenendaal
Holland

Or any living relatives.

Descendants of Tonis Gijsbertsen

van Deelen Ancestors, long version from Tonis Gijsbertsen, Abt. 1595 • Dates listed as day-month-year

Generation No. 1

1. TONIS[1] GIJSBERTSEN was born Abt. 1595. He married NN NN.

Notes for TONIS GIJSBERTSEN:
VG1981p187:

Child of TONIS GIJSBERTSEN and NN NN is:

2. i. JAN TONIS[2] GIJSBERTSEN, b. Abt. 1625.

Generation No. 2

2. JAN TONIS[2] GIJSBERTSEN (TONIS[1]) was born Abt. 1625. He married TIMIETGEN LAMBERTS 12-5-1656 in Barneveld, daughter of LAMBERT PHILIPSEN and FYTJEN JANS. She was born in Barneveld.

Notes for JAN TONIS GIJSBERTSEN:
VG1981pl87: woont 1670 op "Klein Crumseler"

Notes for TIMIETGEN LAMBERTS:
VG1981p187

Children of JAN GIJSBERTSEN and TIMIETGEN LAMBERTS are:

3. i. GIJSBERT[3] JANSEN, b. Abt. 1660, Barneveld.
4. ii. JAN JANSEN, b. Abt. 1660, Barneveld.
   iii. GARRITIEN JANSEN, b. 24-1-1664, Barneveld.

   Notes for GARRITIEN JANSEN:
   VG1981p187

   iv. WOUTER JANSEN, b. 6-8-1665, Barneveld.

   Notes for WOUTER JANSEN:
   VG1981p187: de moeder wordt Timmetje Jansen op Rosilaar genoemd

   v. GRIETIEN JANSEN, b. 10-9-1670, Barneveld.

   Notes for GRIETDEN JANSEN:
   VG1981p187: op Klein Crumseler.

Generation No. 3

3. GIJSBERT[3] JANSEN *(JAN TONIS[2] GIJSBERTSEN, TONIS[1])* was born Abt 1660 in Barneveld. He married FYTJE WILLEMS 28-11-1686 in Barneveld.

Notes for GIJSBERT JANSEN:
VG1981p187: Hiaat doopboek

Marriage Notes for GIJSBERT JANSEN and FYTJE WILLEMS:
VG1981p187: Waarschijniijk heeft dit echtpaar op de boerderij "Klein Krumseler" gewoond, bij het trouwen (Barneveld 11-4-1723) van him zoon Tijmen wordt deze jm van Krumseler genoemd

Children of GIJSBERT JANSEN and FYTJE WILLEMS:

i. JAN[4] GIJSBERTSEN, b. 25-3-1687, Barneveld.

Notes for JAN GIJSBERTSEN:
VG1981p187

ii. GIJSBERT GIJSBERTSEN, b. 18-11-1688, Barneveld.

Notes for GIJSBERT GIJSBERTSEN:
VG1981p187

5. iii. WILLEM GIJSBERTSEN, b. 10-11-1689, Barneveld.

iv. GIJSBERTJE GIJSBERTSEN, b. 6-12-1691, Barneveld.

Notes for GIJSBERTJE GIJSBERTSEN:
VG1981p187

v. HEINTJE GIJSBERTSEN, b. 27-1-1694, Barneveld.

Notes for HEINTJE GIJSBERTSEN:
VG1981p187

6. vi. TUMEN GIJSBERTSEN, b. 2-1696, Barneveld.
7. vii. LEENDERT GIJSBERTSEN, b. 8-10-1699, Lunteren; d. 24-1-1781, Otterlo.

viii. AELTJE GIJSBERTSEN, b. 8-1-1702, Barneveld.

Notes for AELTJE GIJSBERTSEN:
VG1981p187

ix. AELTJE GIJSBERTSEN, b. 18-1-1705, Barneveld; m. CORNELIS GEURTSEN VAN LEEUWEN, 28-4-1731, Barneveld.

Notes for AELTJE GIJSBERTSEN:
VG1981p187

x. TEUNIS GIJSBERTSEN, b. 1-1-1707, Barneveld.

Notes for TEUNIS GIJSBERTSEN:
VG1981p187

xi. IJTJE CIJSBERTSEN, b. 1-4-1709, Barneveld; m. BEERNT JANSE, 12-7-1739, Barneveld.

Notes for IJTJE GIJSBERTSEN:
VG1981p187

Notes for BEERNT JANSE:
VG1981p187: weduwnaar te Harderwijk

Marriage Notes for IJTJE GIJSBERTSEN and BEERNT JANSE:
VG1981p187: otr Barneveld, att naar Harderwijk.

Descendants of Tonis Gijsbertsen

4. JAN³ JANSEN *(JAN TONIS¹ GIJSBERTSEN, TONIS¹)* was born Abt. 1660 in Barneveld. He married GEERTJE GIJSBERTSEN 27-10-1695 m Barneveld.

Notes for JAN JANSEN:
VG1981p187

Notes for GEERTJE GIJSBERTSEN:
VG1981p187

Marriage Notes for JAN JANSEN and GEERTJE GIJSBERTSEN:
VG1981p187: beide wonende op de .... te Barneveld

Children of JAN JANSEN and GEERTJE GIJSBERTSEN:

   i. JAN⁴ JANSEN, b. 19-4-1696, Barneveld Callenbroek.

   Notes for JAN JANSEN:
   VG1981p187

   ii. HENDRIKJE JANSEN, b. 6-8-1699, Barneveld.

   Notes for HENDRIKJE JANSEN:
   VG1981p187

   iii. TUMETJE JANSEN, b. 25-3-1703, Barneveld.

   Notes for TUMETJE JANSEN:
   VG1981p187

   iv. JAN JANSEN, b. 23-11-1704, Barneveld.

   Notes for JAN JANSEN:
   VG1981p187

   v. GERRITJE JANSEN, b. 8-8-1706, Barneveld.

   Notes for GERRITJE JANSEN:
   VG1981p187.

Generation No. 4

5. WILLEM⁴ GIJSBERTSEN *(GIJSBERT³ JANSEN, JAN TONIS¹ GIJSBERTSEN, TONIS¹)* was born 10-11-1689 in Barneveld. He married (1) MELISJE BRANDS 19-6-1718 in Barneveld. He married (2) ELBERTJE HENDRIKS 10-1733 in Barneveld.

Notes for WILLEM GIJSBERTSEN:
VG1981p187

Marriage Notes for WILLEM GIJSBERTSEN and MELISJE BRANDS:
VG1981p187: Wonende in't Garderbroek, att 10-7 naar Garderen

Children of WILLEM GIJSBERTSEN and MELISJE BRANDS are:

   i. GIJSBERT⁵ WILLEMSEN, b. 21-5-1719, Barneveld.

   Notes for GIJSBERT WILLEMSEN:
   VG1981p187:

   ii. AELT WILLEMSEN, b. 21-6-1722, Barneveld.

   Notes for AELT WILLEMSEN:
   VG1981p187

   iii. FYTJE WILLEMSEN, b. 3-10-1723, Barneveld.

   Notes for FYTJE WILLEMSEN:
   VG1981p187

   iv. AERTJE WILLEMSEN, b. 6-2-1730, Barneveld.

   Notes for AERTJE WILLEMSEN:
   VG1981p187.

6. TUMEN⁴ GIJSBERTSEN *(GIJSBERT³ JANSEN, JAN TONIS² GIJSBERTSEN, TONIS¹)* was born 2-1696 in BaRNeveld. He married GRIETJE MAASEN 11-4-1723 in Barneveld, daughter of MAAS GIJSBERTSEN and MARYTJEN ROBBERS. She was born 11-11-1694 in Lunteren.

Notes for TUMEN GIJSBERTSEN:
VG1981p187:

Notes for GRIETJE MAASEN:
VG1981p187
DL11: Grietjen dv Maas Gijsbertsen en Marijtjen Robbers

Marriage Notes for TUMEN GIJSBERTSEN and GRIETJE MAASEN:
VG1981p187: jm van Klein KrumselaarJd uit de Valk

Children of TUMEN GIJSBERTSEN and GRIETJE MAASEN are:

   i. GIJSBERT⁵ TUMENSEN, b. 3-2-1726, Barneveld.

   Notes for GIJSBERT TUMENSEN:
   VG1981p187: ??? ouders Tijmen Gijsberts en Aeltje Maasen

   ii. MAARTHE TUMENSEN, b. 11-2-1731, Lunteren.

   Notes for MAARTHE TUMENSEN:
   VG1981p187.

7. LEENDERT⁴ GIJSBERTSEN *(GIJSBERT³ JANSEN, JAN TONIS² GIJSBERTSEN, TONIS¹)* was born 8-10-1699 in Lunteren, and died 24-1-1781 in Otterlo. He married WILMIJNTJE FERDINANDS 15-3-1724 in Otterlo.

Notes for LEENDERT GIJSBERTSEN:
VG1981p187: Van Barneveld hier ten doop gebracht, Leendert wordt in 1768 door de ambtsjonkers van Ede onder handen genomen, reden hiervan was dat

hij "Sig had onderwonden om ten nadeele van Gerrit Pothoven, koster en schoolmeester te Otterloo, in dwe buyrt van Westeneng op eygene authoriteyt een bijschool op te rechten"
DL13: Leender zv Gijsbert Jansen en Fijtjen Willems

Notes for WILMUNTJE FERDINANDS:
VG1981p187

Marriage Notes for LEENDERT GIJSBERTSEN and WILMUNTJE FERDINANDS:
VG1981p187: Beide wonen bij huwelijk te Harskamp

Children of LEENDERT GIJSBERTSEN and WIL-MIJNTJE FERDINANDS are:

   i. RIJCKJE[5] LEENDERTSEN, b. 6-5-1725, Otterlo; m. BEEREND BEERENDSEN, 20-10-1784, Ede; b. Voorst.

   Notes for RUCKJE LEENDERTSEN:
   VG1981p187
   DO25: Rijckijen dv Leendert Gysbertsen en Wilmijn Fernandsen tot Harskamp

   Notes for BEEREND BEERENDSEN:
   VG1981p187: Wonende te Harskamp

   ii. CORNELIS LEENDERTSEN, b. 25-6-1727, Otterlo.

   Notes for CORNELIS LEENDERTSEN:
   VG1981p187
   D026: Cornelis zv Leendert Gijsbertsen en Wilmijn Ferdinads tot Hars-camp

   iii. WILLEMPJE LEENDERTSEN, b. 4-5-1730, Otterlo; m. GERRIT DRIESEN, 4-8-1751, Otterlo.

   Notes for WILLEMPJE LEENDERTSEN:
   VG1981p187
   D027: 7 mei Willempije dv Leenders Gijsbert en Willemyen Ferdenans tot Otterloo

   iv. VYTJEN LEENDERTSEN, b. 13-7-1732, Otterlo; m. HENDRIK MULDER, 24-11-1761, Arnhem.

   Notes for VYTJEN LEENDERTSEN:
   VG1981p187
   D028: Vytjen dv Lenerd Gisbertsen en Willemina Ferdinads van Eschoten

   Notes for HENDRIK MULDER:
   VG1981p187: jm van Arnhem

   v. JANTJE LEENDERTSEN, b. 13-1-1734, Otterlo.

   Notes for JANTJE LEENDERTSEN:
   VG1981p187

8. vi. FERDINANDUS LEENDERTSEN, b. 3-10-1734, Otterlo.

9. vii. TUMEN LEENDERTSEN, b. 10-6-1742, Otterlo; d. 26-11-1803, Otterlo.

   viii. JAN LEENDERTSEN, b. 5-6-1745, Otterlo.

   Notes for JAN LEENDERTSEN:
   VG1981p187.

Generation No. 5

8. FERDINANDUS[5] LEENDERTSEN *(LEENDERT[4] GIJSBERTSEN, GIJSBERT[3] JANSEN, JAN TONIS[2] GIJSBERTSEN, TONIS[1])* was born 3-10-1734 in Otterlo. He married HENDRIKJE JANS 22-10-1758 in Otterlo, daughter of JAN WOUTERS and EVERTJEN GIJSBERTS. She was born 22-3-1739 in Otterlo.

Notes for FERDINANDUS LEENDERTSEN:
VG1981p187
D029: Ferdinandus zv Leendert Gisberts en Willemma Ferdinats tot Otterloo

Notes for HENDRIKJE JANS:
VG1981p187
D033: Hindrikje dv Jan Wouters en Evertje Gijsberts van Westeneng

Children of FERDINANDUS LEENDERTSEN and HENDRIKJE JANS are:

   i. EVERTJE[6] FERDINANDUSSEN, b. 13-4-1760, Otterlo; m. (1) KLAAS JANSEN, 25-6-1780, Otterlo; m. (2) GERRIT FLIPSEN, 2-1-1785, Otterlo; b. Barneveld.

   Notes for EVERTJE FERDINANDUSSEN:
   VG1981p187
   D047: Evertje dv Ferdinadus Leenderts en Hendrikje Jans te Westenend

   Notes for GERRIT FLIPSEN:
   VG1981p187: wonende Lunteren

   ii. WILLEMIJNTJE FERDINANDUSSEN, b. 4-4-1762, Otterlo.

   Notes for WILLEMUNTJE FERDINANDUSSEN:
   VG1981p187
   D048: Willemijntje dv Ferdinandus Leendertse en Hensdrikje Jans te Westeneng

   iii. JAN FERDINANDUSSEN, b. 26-8-1764, Otterlo.

   Notes for JAN FERDINANDUSSEN:
   VG1981p187
   D050: Jan zv Ferdinadus Leendertse en Hendrikje Jans te Westeneng

Descendants of Tonis Gijsbertsen

iv. LENA FERDINANDUSSEN, b. 15-1-1768, Otterlo.

Notes for LENA FERDINANDUSSEN:
VG1981pl87
D053: 24jan Lena dv Ferdinadus Leendertse en Hendrikje Jansd te Westeneng.

9. TUMEN[5] LEENDERTSEN *(LEENDER[4] GIJSBERTSEN, GIJSBERT[3] JANSEN, JAN TONIS[2] GIJSBERTSEN, TONIS[1])* was born 10-6-1742 in Otterlo, and died 26-11-1803 in Otterlo. He married NIESJE AALBERTSEN 29-11-1771 in Otterlo, daughter of AALBERT SEVENHUYSE and LUTJE TOMESSE. She was born 23-4-1753 in Otterlo.

Notes for TUMEN LEENDERTSEN:
VG1981p187
D035: Timmen zoon van Leendert Giesbersen en van Willemina Ferdinants

Notes for NIESJE AALBERTSEN:
VG1981p187: van Zevenhuyzen
D041: Niesje dochter van Aalbert Teunisse en Lutje Tomesse tot Dele

Children of TUMEN LEENDERTSEN and NIESJE AALBERTSEN are:

i. AALBERT TUMENSEN[6] VAN DEELEN, b. 1-5-1772, Otterlo Deelen; d. 7-9-1822, Renswoude; m. HENDRIKJE KORNELISSEN KREMER; b. 6-1-1777, Voorthuizen.

Notes for AALBERT TUMENSEN VAN DEELEN:
VG1981p187: Neemt te Ede op op 3-11-1812 de naam van De(e)len aan, met uitzondering van Luut die zich Leenderts blijft noemen nemen alle broers en zusters deze achtemaam aan
D057: 3 met Aalbert zv Tiemen Leendertsen en Niesje Aalbertsen te Deelen

Notes for HENDRIKJE KORNELISSEN KREMER:
VG1981p187

ii. WILLEMIJNTJE TUMENSEN VAN DEELEN, b. 1-9-1775, Otterlo Eschoten; d. 31-5-1851, Ede; m. GIJSBERT JANSEN KLOK, 30-4-1797, Ede.

Notes for WILLEMIJNTJE TUMENSEN VAN DEELEN:
VG1981p187
D059: 3 sep Willemyntje dv Tiemen Leenderts & Niesje Aalbertsen te Eschoten

iii. HENDRIKJE TUMENSEN VAN DEELEN, b. 20-12-1778, Otterlo Eschoten.

Notes for HENDRIKJE TUMENSEN VAN DEELEN:
VG1981p187

D060: 26 dec Hendrikje dv Tiemen Leendertsen & Niesje Aalbersten te Eschoten

iv. LUUTJE TUMENSEN VAN DEELEN, b. 19-1-1782, Otterlo Eschoten.

Notes for LUUTJE TUMENSEN VAN DEELEN:
VG1981p187
D062: 27 jan Luutje dv Tiemen Leenderts en Niesje Aalberts te Eschoten

10. v. LEENDERT TUMESEN VAN DEELEN, b. 3-2-1784, Otterlo Eschoten; d. 8-1-1830, Bennekom.

vi. LUUT TUMENSEN LEENDERTS, b. 9-4-1787, Otterlo Oud-Reemst; d. 5-5-1875, Ede; m. (1) JACOBA EVERTSEN HAVERKAMP, 10-10-1818, Ede; b. 28-6-1800, Lunteren; d. 23-4-1830, Ede; m. (2) GERRITJE HENDRIKS REUSTERMAN, 29-1-1831, Ede; b. 1778, Lochem; m. (3) WEUMPJE VAN DER HOVEN, 26-4-1853, Ede; b. 29-4-1787, Lunteren; d. 10-4-1859, Ede; m. (4) ANNETJE BERENDSEN, 4-4-1863, Ede; b. 12-11-1797, Ede.

Notes for LUUT TUMENSEN LEENDERTS:
VG1981pl87: Dagloner, schaapherder
D065: 15 apr Luut zv Tiemen Leenderts & Niesje Aalberts bij Oud-Reemst

Notes for JACOBA EVERTSEN HAVERKAMP:
VG1981p187
DL85: Koba dv Evert Kobessen en Dirkje Aartse

Notes for GERRITJE HENDRIKS REUSTERMAN:
VG1981p187

Notes for WEIJMPJE VAN DER HOVEN:
VG1981p187

Notes for ANNETJE BERENDSEN:
VG1981p187.

Generation No. 6

10. LEENDERT TIJMESEN[6] VAN DEELEN *(TIJMEN[5] LEENDERTSEN, LEENDERT[4] GIJSBERTSEN, GIJSBERT[3] JANSEN, JAN TONIS[2] GIJSBERTSEN, TONIS[1])* was born 3-2-1784 in Otterlo Eschoten, and died 8-1-1830 in Bennekom. He married WILLEMPJE CORNELISSEN WILLEMS 25-4-1809 in Otterlo.

Notes for LEENDERT TUMESEN VAN DEELEN:
VG1981p187: Dagloner
D062: Gedoopt 8-2, Leendert zoon van Tiemen Leenderts & Niesje Aalberts te Eschoten

Child of LEENDERT VAN DEELEN and WILLEMPJE WILLEMS is:

11. i. AALBERT⁷ VAN DEELEN, b. Abt. 1823; d. 14-10-1887.

Generation No. 7

11. AALBERT⁷ VAN DEELEN *(LEENDERT TIJMESEN⁶, TIJMEN⁵ LEENDERTSEN, LEENDERT⁴ GIJSBERTSEN, GIJSBERT³ JANSEN, JAN TONIS² GIJSBERTSEN, TONIS¹)* was born Abt. 1823, and died 14-10-1887. He married DIENTJE FRERIKS 6-3-1852 in Ede, daughter of WILLEM FRERIKS and GERRITJE DERKSEN. She was born Abt. 1831.

Notes for AALBERT VAN DEELEN:
VG1991p250

Marriage Notes for AALBERT VAN DEELEN and DIENTJE FRERIKS:
Archieflocatie: Gelderiand
Toegangnr: 0207
Inventarisnr: 5295
Gemeente: Ede
Soort akte: Huwelijksakte
Nummer: 18
Datum: 06-03-1852
Wettiging 1 kind

Children of AALBERT VAN DEELEN and DIENTJE FRERDCS are:

i. GERRITJE⁸ VAN DEELEN.

ii. JANNETJE VAN DEELEN.

12. iii. HELENA VAN DEELEN, b. 11-10-1858, Ede.

iv. WILLEMINA VAN DEELEN.

13. v. WILLEM VAN DEELEN, b. Abt 1862, Ede.

vi. JAN VAN DEELEN.

vii. GERRIT VAN DEELEN.

Generation No. 8

12. HELENA⁸ VAN DEELEN *(AALBERT⁷, LEENDERT TIJMESEN⁶, TIJMEN⁵ LEENDERTSEN, LEENDERT⁴ GIJSBERTSEN, GIJSBERT³ JANSEN, JAN TONIS² GIJSBERTSEN, TONIS¹)* was born 11-10-1858 in Ede. She married CASPER VERMEER 26-4-1879 m Ede. He was born 6-3-1852 m Wageningen, and died 26-10-1916 in Ede.

Notes for HELENA VAN DEELEN:
VG1994p272

Notes for CASPER VERMEER:
VG1994p272: Arbeider

Children of HELENA VAN DEELEN and CASPER VERMEER are:

i. JAN⁹ VERMEER, b. 30-10-1879, Bennekom; d. 17-11-1879, Bennekom.

ii. JAN VERMEER.

iii. DIENTJE VERMEER.

iv. AALTJE VERMEER, b. 10-12-1887, Bennekom; d. 1-2-1937, Renkum; m. GERARDUS KOERTING, 25-7-1908, Ede; b. 24-4-1877, Ede.

v. GRADUS VERMEER.

vi. JANNA VERMEER.

vii. CATHARINA VERMEER, b. 23-2-1897, Bennekom; d. 9-4-1945, Ede; m. WILLEM VAN DE BUL, 4-1-1930, Ede; b. 2-6-1897, Kesteren.

viii. GERRITJE VERMEER.

13. WILLEM⁸ VAN DEELEN *(AALBERT⁷, LEENDERT TIJMESEN⁶, TIJMEN⁵ LEENDERTSEN, LEENDERT⁴ GIJSBERTSEN, GIJSBERT³ JANSEN, JAN TONIS² GIJSBERTSEN, TONIS¹)* was born Abt. 1862 in Ede. He married RIKJE ESSENSTAM 30-1-1886 in Apeldoorn, daughter of JACOB ESSENSTAM and WILLEMPJE VAN DE HOEF.

Marriage Notes for WILLEM VAN DEELEN and RKJE ESSENSTAM: Archieflocatie: Gelderland Toegangnr: 0207 Inventarisnr: 6587 Gemeente: Apeldoom Soort akte: HuweUjksakte Nummer: 10 Datum: 30-01-1886

Child of WiLLEM VAN DEELEN and RIKJE ESSENSTAM is:

i. WILLEMINA⁹ VAN DEELEN, b. Abt. 1888, Ede; m. JAN VAN ROEKEL, 9-9-1911, Ede; b. 24-8-1885, Ede.

Notes for JAN VAN ROEKEL:
GR41: Emigreerde naar US Dudley, bezocht Nederland met zijn vrouw in 1926

Marriage Notes for WILLEMINA VAN DEELEN and JAN VAN ROEKEL:
Archieflocatie: Gelderland
Toegangnr: 0207
Inventarisnr: 8253
Gemeente: Ede
Soort akte: Huwelijksakte
Nummer: 87

Page 1:

Dudley nc
Oct 14 - 1932

Waarde Broer & zuster 3 Kinder

uw sult wel niet denken dat wy al weer zoo wat 6 weken thuis zyn wy hadden nog even zullen komen maar het reisen van de eene plaats naar de andere was zoo moeilyk met twee kinderen dat wy hebben het niet kunnen doen toch byn wy bly dat wy u allen nog eens weer gesien hebben of eens gesien waart dit was de eerste keer dat ik u ook gesien had. ik vond het erg gesellig by uw thuis en bedank u nog vriendelyk voor u moeite aan ons gedaan. weet u ook hoe moeder het maakt.

Page 2:

Jan is er nog een paar keer heer geweest en was nog het zelfde. hoe gaat het jullie allen gesond hoop ik. hoe maak Otuna het. en de ander. schryf eens een lange brief terug want ik mag graag van Holland wat horen en vooral hoe Jans Moeder het maakt Tante ik ben bly dat. ik weer in Holland geweest en u allen eens gesien heb. want ik had eigenlyk van Jan zyn familij nog maar een paar gesien Jan zegt hoe is Bart. of weet u hem niet veel. als u zyn adres eens wil schryven zal ik hem ook eens een brief schryven. zoo Tante wacht niet lang met schryven

Five-page letter from Willemina van Roekel to her family in Holland, continued.

Page 3:

Toen wij Van u af gingen zijn
wij bij Jans aar geweest en
die konder Jan dadelijk en
daar zijn wij een poosje geweest
en toen is Jans mee gegaan
naar Hentje en daar zijn wij
nacht over gebleven en ik
geloof die maken het heel
goed die man van Hentje
is een hele aardige man
Toen zijn wij de volgende dag
weer met de trein naar
Hondeloo gegaan. en zoo wat
een week later is Jar nog naar
Jans geweest en daar heft.
bij Gijs ook nog gezien en ik
geloof Gijs maakt het ook goed.
Jar zegt hij heeft Ger's van de
Woest ook nog gezien die kwam
bij Jans om Jan te zien en zag
er nog heel flink uit.

Page 4:

want wij zijn ver weg maar
denken toch nog veel aan uw
hoe gezellig wij hebber zitten
praten en Jan boven met Gijs
en Jar is een halve dag ze ziek
geweest komen terug maar
de kinder en ik heelmaal
niet maar ben zich geweest.
toen ik zoo wat een week thuis
was toen was het hier zoo heet
het is nu wat kouder maar nog
geen nacht vorst zoo als in Holland
onze bloemen zijn nog mooi
de dahlias staan nog prachtig
in bloem. well nu zal ik maar
eindigen met allen Hartelijke
groet Van Jar & kinder aan
u allen ook Tina & Jan & vrouw & Gijs
Van Mina

Page 5:

Ons adres is
Mr J van Roekel
   Dudley
     N C.
America.

Photocopy of the Ship's Manifest of Alien Passengers for the U.S. Immigration Officer at Port of Arrival: Ellis Island, New York, showing arrival of Jan and Willemina van Roekel (left half). See pages 14-16 for story.

Right half of Ship's Manifest.

Letter regarding Jan van Roekel's military service with the Yellow Riders.

Landmachtstaf

Sectie Militaire Geschiedenis

MPC 58 A
Postbus 90701
2509 LS Den Haag

Telefoon 070 - 316 5838
Telefax 070 - 316 5851
MDTN *06 546 65838

Kleine Alexanderkazerne
Oude Waalsdorperweg 25-35
2597 AK Den Haag

Mr. J.H. van Roekel
2425 Highway #9
Black Mountain, N.C. 28711
United States

Date	Our Reference	Your Reference
29 May 2000	SMG/2000/14032	
Subject		Dealt with by
Information about grandfather		Ms. P.C.M. Oorschot

Dear Mr Van Roekel,

In reply to your letter which the Military History Section received on 4 May 2000, I can inform you that the Section, with a few exceptions, does not possess personal details about military personnel. In the period in which your grandfather fulfilled his military service in the Mobile Artillery Corps and 4 Field Artillery Regiment these regiments were not involved in war situations. We have found very little information about this period. Annex 1 contains a photocopy from *De Onderofficier* (The NCO) from 1983 and from *200 jaar Rijdende Artillerie 1793-1993* (200 years of Mobile Artillery 1793-1993) written by B. Schoenmaker and J.P.C.M. van Hoof, which gives general information about the Mobile Artillery Corps.
Annex 2 contains a number of photocopies in which the history of 4 Field Artillery Regiment is described. As you can read in these articles, the battalions belonging to this regiment were stationed in both Ede and 's-Hertogenbosch.

In the annex you enclosed with your letter you describe how your grandfather was assigned to the Mobile Artillery Corps on 7 March 1905 via the lot system in the municipality of Ede in 1905. Following the first exercise, he was given long-term leave on 28 September 1907. On 1 April 1911 he was assigned to 4 Field Artillery Regiment and he completed his military service on 31 July 1913.
In accordance with the Militia Act of 1901, the conscripts were subject to this act for a period of eight years. During that period, after the first exercise they were recalled three times for repeat exercises. The personnel of the mounted regiments remained under arms for eighteen months, if applicable extended by a maximum of six months.

I wish you every success in your research.

Yours sincerely,

Head, Military History Section
Royal Netherlands Army

Drs. P.H. Kamphuis

Letter regarding Jan van Roekel's military service with the Yellow Riders.

RIJKSARCHIEF

Mr. John H. van Roekel
2425 Highway # 9
Black Mountain N.C.
28711 USA

Your letter: 23/02/00 Our reference number: DVi/ 406 Den Haag, 11/04/00
Your reference number: Handled by: V. van den Bergh
Subject: Direct tel. no.: 070-3315441
Jan van Roekel

Dear Sir

I herewith send you the copies of the registration of Jan van Roekel in the regimental roll of the Korps Rijdende Artillerie (Gele Rijders / Yellow Riders) from march 1905 and –since april 1911- in the regimental roll of the 4th regiment Veldartillerie (Fieldartillery). He left the army on july 31th 1913.
The bill for the research (NLG 54,-) will be sent to you separately

Yours sincerely,
On behalf of the Head of the Service Department

(V. van den Bergh)

Bijl.: 4 copies A3 size

Prins Willem-Alexanderhof 20 ▼ Den Haag ▼ Postadres: Postbus 90520 ▼ 2509 LM Den Haag

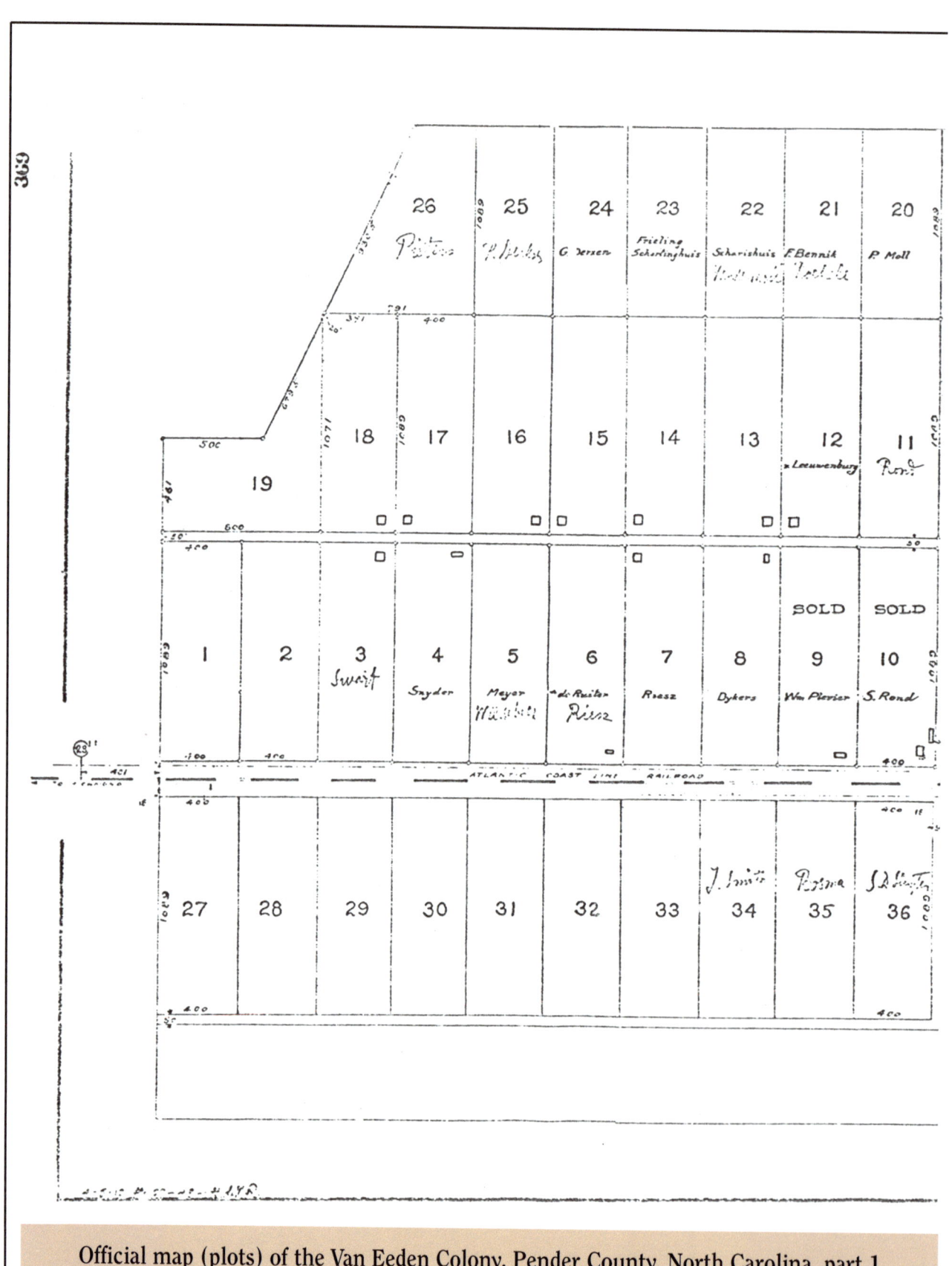

Official map (plots) of the Van Eeden Colony, Pender County, North Carolina, part 1.

Official map (plots) of the Van Eeden Colony, Pender County, North Carolina, part 2.

Where is Van Eeden, North Carolina ...

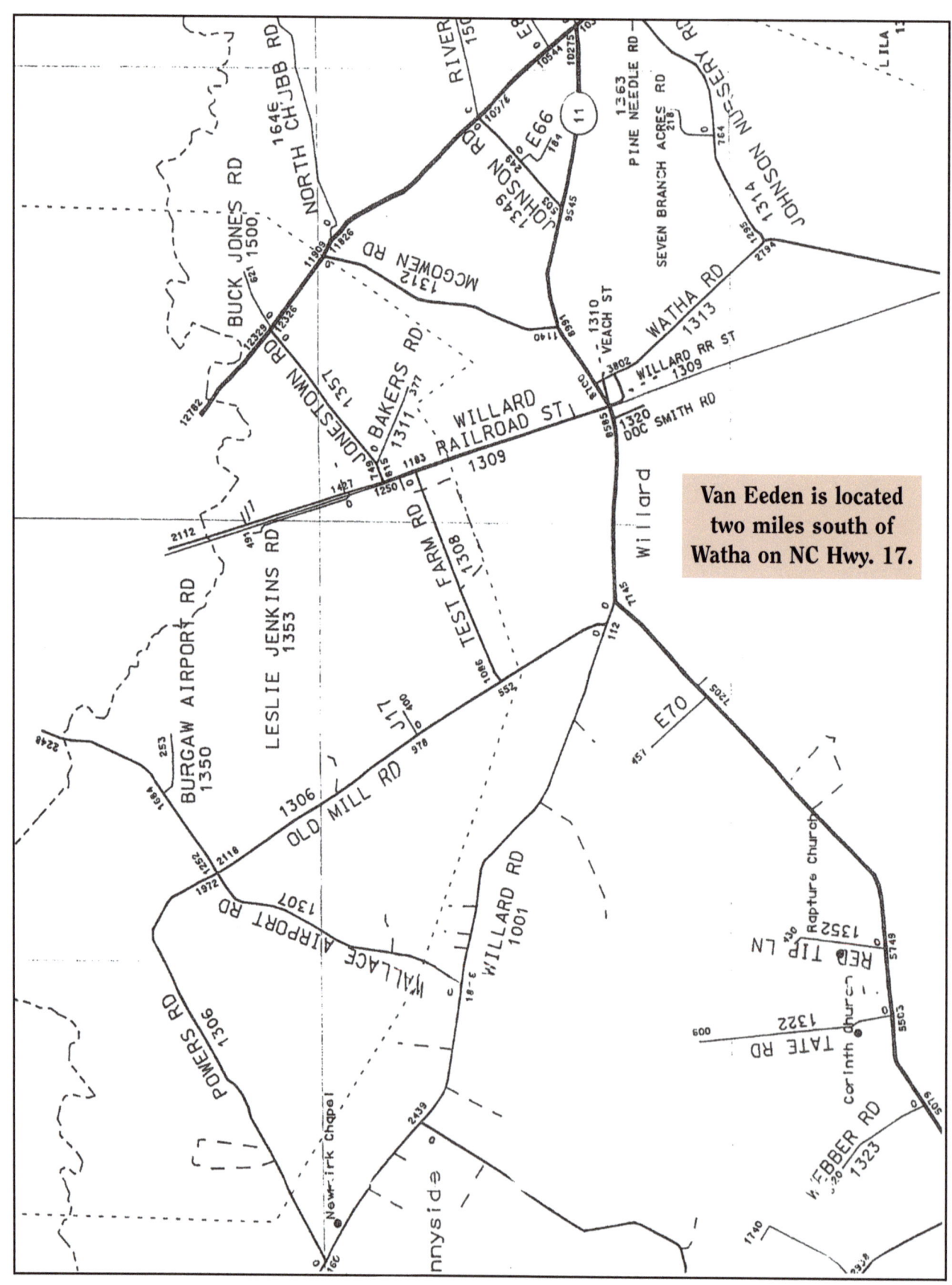

Van Eeden is located two miles south of Watha on NC Hwy. 17.

... and how do you get there?

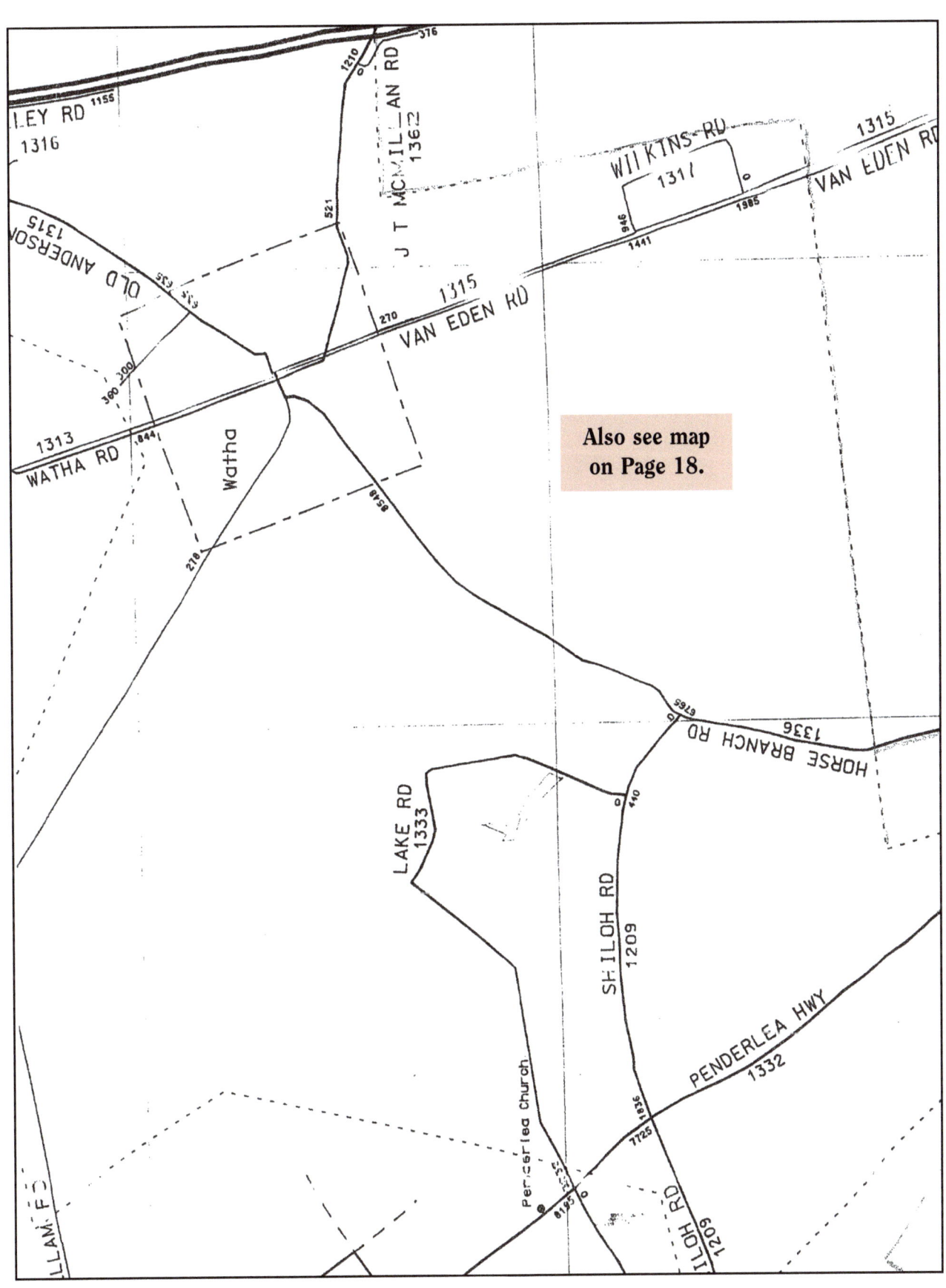

Also see map on Page 18.

Herman W.D.M. Vogels

Herman Vogel is identified in the immigration documents as the sponsor for Jan and Willemina van Roekel's move to America.

HERMAN WILHELMUS CORNELIS MARIE VOGELS was the son of Willem Pieter Vogels and Catharina Geertruida Dantz. He was born in The Hague on 16 August 1868 and died in Holland about 1930. He married Hendrika Johanna Eggink on 26 September 1895 in Utrecht.

Herman W.C.M. Vogels allegedly migrated to the United States around 1908 and sent for his family approximately two years later (1910), where they settled in Castle Hayne, North Carolina.

Herman and Hendrika divorced in the United States (probably the Castle Hayne area), and Herman eventually returned to Holland and allegedly remarried there, but had no other children from this union.

Hendrika remarried on 17 December 1920 in New York City to John W. Winders. He and Hendrika had met around 1916 or 1917 in Castle Hayne where he ran a General Store and Post Office. They went to New York to marry and then returned to Castle Hayne.

The following account of this family was accumulated from letters from Herman Gotfried Jan (Ben) Vogels. Most were written in 1973-1974.

"As I recall, we moved to a Villa in Barrendreght very near the Port of Rotterdam. This was shortly after Dad (Herman W.C.M. Vogels) gained employment in Rotterdam as a Commissioner for a huge produce exchange located there. He was a Horticulturist and Florist by trade. Each day he took the commuter train to and from work. Dad had graduated from a trade school and two universities, and he spoke Italian, English, French, German and Dutch. One of the universities was in Holland, and the other in Hiedelburg, Germany, I believe.

Dad took his father's inheritance (Willem Pieter Vogels, who died 1895) and went to the United States in about 1908 because he was fed up with the way things were in Holland and wanted a complete change. Mother and we children stayed in Holland until about two years later. After Dad's arrival in Castle Hayne, North Carolina, he boarded at the Holland Nursery, which was owned by Eiko Tinga and Hugo Van Ness. Later, he arranged for a house, which was owned by the Carolina Trucking & Development Company, namely Hugh MacCrae. It was built on the same rock where Hayne had built his castle. The castle had been destroyed during the Revolutionary War.

Oddly enough, this house had four rooms in the front, each equipped with a fireplace, and two smaller ones used by Mother as a laundry and the other by Dad as an office. The weatherboards were held by square nails rather than round ones, and the floor sills were pegged together by wooden pins. Much later, an annex of two rooms was built to the after part, which served as a kitchen and dining room. There was also a barn, a huge thing with iron bars across the windows. It was used as a prison during the seige. A railroad spur had been built on the site. It was used to transport phosphate from the back of the property.

Dad built a greenhouse and even put the glass in himself. He heated it with firewood. He might have used a steam coil, but I recall the energy being from firewood. He set out to plant Kiefer Pears on the remainder of his five acres of property. J.K. Cooper owned the other five acres. Before we arrived, he made a deal with Hugh McCrae for Tract No. 92 where the old phosphate mine was located, but after their divorce Mother learned that he had never completed the purchase on this tract and the Carolina Truck Grovers Association took possession of the land. She took an option on it and purchased about one half of the tract. Dad also bought a calf named "Butterboy." It had a pedigree.

Hugo Van Ness, a bachelor, came to Holland in about 1910 to visit his parents and to escort Mother and we children to the United States. We left Rotterdam on the Holland American Lines ship, "The New Amsterdam," and arrived in Hoboken, New York, in late summer or early fall. We stayed at the Grand Central Hotel across from the park of the same name while we waited for a steamer to come from Savannah, Georgia, to take us to Wilmington, North Carolina, the nearest port to Castle Hayne.

I believe that [Dad] spent some time in the horticulture and florist trade in Mississippi, Ohio, New York, and a few other states. He ultimately went back to his native country where he obtained a Dutch divorce as he did not trust an American divorce. I think it took him five years to do this. He was a traveling salesman in Germany, Holland, Belgium, and France, but I do not remember where he resided. He appraised antiques and diamonds, and he knew the flaw or purity of its value. He did remarry, but had no more children. I think he died in Holland in 1929 from parantinitus.

That's about all I know of him. Mother had a brother (Ben Eggink), the youngest of five, who lived in Coalinga, California, and came to see her after Dad left. In about 1917, we all went to California and stayed with the Egginks for a few months before they left for Texas. We remained there in the Eggink house. About this time, the influenza epidemic broke out, and Mother worked as a practical nurse. People died like flies. Mother finally finished paying for her farm in Castle Hayne with Gerrit's support, her own earnings, and an inheritance from her own mother (Mina Arends 'Eggink).

VAN EEDEN-KOLONIE

IN

N. Carolina U. S. A.

BY DR. FREDERIK VAN EEDEN

AMSTERDAM. — W. VERSLUYS. — 1912.

**THE FOLLOWING PAGES WERE TRANSLATED
FROM THE ORIGINAL DUTCH LANGUAGE**

Dr. Frederik van Eeden (1860-1932)

On the East-Coast of the United States on ± 35° North-latitude, that is on the same latitude as Gibraltar and Greece, lies the state of North Carolina.

In consequence of this southern situation and of the nearness of the Golfsn-eam, which comes near to the coast and which levels the extremities of temperature, the climate of this country is very mild. A true winter does nor exist and abnormal hot sommers are unknown.

The Carolina Trucking Development Co atWilmington, which brought already a great many of acres of this land into cultivation, gives the to 11 owing informations about climate and land.

— Here the rainfall is ample, well distributed the year round. Man does not have to contend with prolonged droughts, so frequent in arid section and localities of poorly distributed rainfall.

In our section cyclones and blizzards are unknown. Here you can work out-doors the year round. The climate is tempered by the nearby Golf Stream, so in summer it is always pleasant.

Especially should it prove a delight to those who have been subjected to the cold, severe, changeable weather, which is experienced in the states further North.

At the same time the colonies are far enough North to escape the excessively warm weather in summer.

A study of the Gov. Weather Bureau statistics at Wilmington, covering a period of 34 years as given below is interesting.

From this table you will be able to judge the climatic conditions around Wilmington. Think of it — the coldest average month in 34 years was 37 degrees above Zero, and the warmest av. month in the same period 80 degrees. Could you find a climate more ideal as a place of residence or better adapted to agricultural pursuits?

The rainfall is abundant and evenly distributed. We get the greatest moisture during the warm months, when it is most needed, yet the remaining months have ample rain for all agricultural purposes.

	Average coldest temperature for 34 years. Fahrenheit.	Average warmest temperature for 34 years. Fahrenheit.	Average Rain Precipitation for 34 years. Inches.
Jan.	39	57	3.62
Feb	37	58	3.35
Mar	48	61	3.59
Apr	56	66	2.72
May	64	74	3.93
June	74	81	5.55
July	77	84	6.71
Aug	76	82	6.97
Sep	70	79	5.42
Oct	60	69	3.86
Nov	49	60	2.40
Dec	39	56	3.09

The quality of the land is clearly shown by the descriptions from soil-experts, wherefrom we quote the following.

From the standpoint of available agricultural land the country is very fortunately situated indeed, embracing as it does a large area of the excellent soils: Portsmouth and Norfolk fine and very fine Sandy loam, which types on account of the nearness of good clay subsoil to the surface are capable of being brought to and maintained at a high state of productivity without an unreasonable outlay. Owing to the flat surface configuration of the land away from the drainage influence of the streams a considerable part of the soils are in need of drainage, which can be secured satisfactorily and upon a comparatively cheap basis by the opening of substantial main ditches to receive drainage from open-ditch latterals.

A great deal of this land has natural drainage. This combined with the additional work we have done, provides drainage conditions seldom equalled in small farm subdivisions.

In our inspection of colonies in other sections, we have found that drainage is usually lasting — an important point to the farmer.

De familie Dijkers te Van-Eeden.

The company has further opened up roads, caused stations and donated ground and money for churches and schools — erected cottages, sunk artesian wells for use of the community. Even horses and implements are at disposal at small cost.

It can be easily understood that the farmer, under such favorable circumstances of climate and soil and with such an amount of aid finds in North Carolina a good occasion to settle easily and come to prosperity.

In one year (1907) from carefully measured ground on her demonstration farm, the company received the following cash returns p. acre:

Lettuce	600 doll.	Cucumbers	275 doll.
Brawberries	200 doll.	Cantaloupes	200 doll.
Beets	200 doll.	Radishes	75 doll.
Cauliflower	500 doll.	Onions	125 doll.
Beans	250 doll.	Peppers	150 doll.
Egg plant	750 doll.	Tomatoes	125 doll
Carrots	75 doll.	Asparagus	750 doll.
Cabbage	150 doll.	English peas	150 doll.
Spinage	150 doll.	Irish potatoes	175 doll.
Turnips	150 doll.		

While these are better than average results they show what is possible here with right methods.

The greater part of our acreage round Wilmington is occupied by "fine sandy loam" and "sandy loam" of the Wilmington and Southport types, being underlain by a clay sub-soil at an average depth of 20 inches.

The diversity of crops to which they are suited, their capacity for retaining fertilizers and their high capillary powers (guarding against droughts) make them ideal for any kind of truck.

The land, offered by the Car. Truck Company is not badly situated. As shows the map, the colonies are situated in the coastal plain section around Wilmington.

Wilmington is a beautiful and hospitable city, with a good municipal water system, paid fire department, fine public buildings, handsome residences, many miles of fine streets, etc.

It ranks as the fourth seaport in the United States in Cotton exports.

It is the headquarters of the Atlantic Coast Line Railroad system, which gives employment to about 800 people in the city. It is also an important terminal and seaport for the seaboard Airline Railroad. It has seven banks with aggregate resources of about 14.500.000 doll. It is a terminus for six railroad lines and has ample water facilities, the channel of the Cape Fear river being of sufficient depth to admit large draft Ocean vessels.

The distance from the great cities of the U.S.:

Washington	340	miles	22	hours
Baltimore	380	„	24	„
Philadelphia	476	„	27	„
New York	566	„	33	„
Boston	721	„	47	„
Pittsburg	709	„	43	„
Buffalo	776	„	47	„
Cincinnati	835	„	47	„
Cleveland	849	„	51	„
Chicago	1139	„	65	„

Hints and Warnings for the Workers in Van Eeden-Colony N. Carolina U.S.A.

As I was asked to be godfather to your dwelling-place, you will perhaps acknowledge my right to demand that you will not expose that name to ridicule and shame, but make it sound honorably in the world.

For that purpose I beg you to listen to a few remarks, leaving it entirely to your free judgment whether you will follow them or not.

Your aim is prosperity, getting rich, and as quickly as possible.

I have no objection to that. Prosperity includes most things desirable for mankind. Health, culture, above all liberty, meaning leisure to develop, to read, to think, to admire, to learn.

Let it be well understood, however, between you and me, that it is not a matter of indifference how prosperity is reached, nor how liberty is acquired. Prosperity may be got by making others lose. The straight term for that method is robbery. Liberty is sometimes sought for by oppressing others. The straight word for that is slavery.

In our time both these methods are still practised, though not openly. The verdict of public opinion condemns them, the laws of civilised nations seem to prohibit them.

Yet they are practised, openly in some out of the way corners, and still more in a clandestine way, under false pretence of fair transactions.

I take for granted that none of you approves of these methods under any form, however apparently legitimate and harmless. So I will warn you and explain how robbery and slavery are still existant notwithstanding general disapproval, how corruption and misery ensue, and in what way these evils can alone be prevented.

Wherever we find human misery, we may be certain to find also these open or clandestine forms of robbery and slavery. Those who take part in them tell us they are inevitable, and doubt that human misery can ever be alleviated.

Yet I can clearly show you that these abuses are not at all inevitable, — and that you yourself are able to prevent them. And though it might be true that human misery will never disappear entirely so long as we are but human — yet before we have all tried to take away its principal cause, nobody can foretell how far that misery may be diminished.

That has never been tried in such a thorough way as you may try it now. We know more and we have greater power than any former generation — and you have an opportunity to do what nobody did before.

Therefore you need not be exceptionally good or strong people. You need not be martyrs or heroes. You only have to be honest, healthy people of average ability. The only thing you want is cautious good sense and careful foresight.

How people can rob and keep slaves in our time, under the laws of civilised nations, may be explained in few words.

It is done by the abuse of so-called rights of property, or titles. It is possible to claim a right on things that other people want. On houses, soil, implements, machinery, etc. When other people are absolutely in want of these things, not being able to live without them, and you by your title can keep these people off, then it is clear that they are entirely in your power. You can compel them to work for you, or to give you so much from their earnings that they keep only their bare subsistence. They may be called as "free" as you, yet they are your slaves, for you keep the keys of Life for them. They have to submit to your conditions, although it is called free choice, for their life is at stake. Though it is said to be a fair transaction, you practically rob them of their earnings — and if your titles of property are only large enough, you may despoil thousands of people to the skin, and make them toil and drudge for you all their life, you yourself in the meanwhile growing richer and richer without moving a hand.

The principal condition being, of course, that the things on which you claim your rights of property are indispensable to others. Formerly, when the earth was less populated, it was not so easy to have property that was entirely indispensable to others, so much so as a spring is in a desert. For everybody had a chance to get at a piece of free soil, on which no one claimed any dominion.

Those days are past. Every little spot of valuable soil has an owner. Somebody is the possessor, and he who staid back in the run and got no possession, is dependent in life and body on those who got ahead of him, he is a slave and has to surrender on any condition.

The abuse of this advantage, these rights of property, gotten in any way whatever, is now quite common and fashionable. It is legitimate robbery and slavery, practised under protection of the law.

From this we may not draw the conclusion that rights of property are unjust, and that possession is against the human sense of equity.

By no means! — possession and rights of property can be in perfect harmony with the noblest human feelings, but only then, when these rights are defined by something else and limited accordingly.

The right of property of what one actually uses, is not offensive to the keenest sense of justice. The evil begins when there is abuse or non-use. When somebody claims rights on a thing that he is not able to use himself, and hinders others by those rights to make use of it, then he is doing what any normal modern human being feels as an injustice. *Because it is a wrong done to society.*

When I am proprietor of a hundred dwellings I can only live in one. Leaving all the others unused, while there are hundreds of people perishing from cold and wanting a home, and then forbidding the people to make use of what you can not use yourself, is injustice. Every good human being is aware of this. And what is a title, a right of property, but the right to forbid others the use of any object? That right is nowadays generally applied to take advantage of the need of others. With those rights and titles people compel others to submit to agreements, as advantageous as possible to the owner. And as these rights of property in our society are unlimited, so one man may keep thousands of others in his power and may rob them of everything. This is robbery and slavery and against the human sense of justice, even leaving aside Christian virtues like generosity or self-denial.

The value of property lies in its use. The owner of a hundred thousand acres is a poor man when there is nobody to use them. His right of property must include men, otherwise it is valueless. Here slavery comes in.

Righteous ownership can only extend to those goods that we can make valuable by our own use, own labour.

This does not imply equality of possessions, nor does it exclude paid service. The man of science wants a library and a laboratory, the farmer wants cattle and soil, to use his power most efficiently and to the best advantage for society. Both may want servants.

You will ask: who shall decide what each of us may call his property? Who determines whether one uses his property rightly or not? And what is the difference between slavery and justly paid service?

Now I want to point out to you that it is exactly for the answer to these questions that the world is waiting, and that it can only be given by practice, by action, and not by books and theories. And this practice and this action, that alone will bring the solution, I expect from you, because you, of all people, have the necessary opportunities.

Mind, I can take for granted that you are all aware of the terrible abuses of the rights of property. They are staring you in the face in every big town, with its mad luxury and horrid poverty, in every nation, with its declining rural population, its criminals, its prisons and poorhouses.

Thus far, none of you have taken part to any extent in these abuses. Some of you possess capital, but not so much as to allow any important abuse of it. You are all workers, and when you seek for prosperity, you seek it by means of honest, useful labour.

When you mean to try this each for himself, single-handed, one honest man against the whole of corrupted society, there is no chance for you. Society will be all-powerful against you. Society, as a whole, produces things that you want. Even if you have exactly the amount of property that is wanted for your special activity, and no more, society can compel you nevertheless to take part in those great general abuses from which results the social misery. For you want things that you can not make for yourself. You must enter into trade with society, you must buy and sell. You must make money for your produce and buy necessities for that money. And as soon as you enter into trade with society, you will have to pay your taxes to the great proprietors, to the big parasites, the powerful owners, who levy their taxes on everything that is paid with money, and who increase their rights constantly to exorbitant and monstrous figures.

The only way to get free from this terrible grip of the possessors would be: to subsist entirely on the produce of your own hands on your own bit of land.

One man tried it, D. H. Thoreau by name — but he had to give it up after two years, however frugal and strong he was.

Certainly it would not represent the "prosperity" that you have in view.

Yet what no man can do alone, a group of people can achieve very well. They can associate for common production on common soil.

A group of people subsisting on the products of their common labour on their own soil would be independent. Nobody could rob them, unless by force. The tricks of modern business could not harm them. It would not even be necessary for them to live in a cluster together in some out of the way place. They might be dispersed all over the country, according to their wants and inclinations, and yet be associated and produce and consume in common, on their own soil with their own implements.

You must form the first nucleus of such a group, if you sincerely intend to get prosperous in a honest way, by means of useful labour.

You must, I say, because it is utterly impossible in any other way.

If you do not form such a group, society will force you to take part in its unfair dealings. It will force you to share its abuses, or keep you in poverty. In order to become prosperous in present society you have to rob those that are weaker than you. When you try to follow the road of strict fairness and honesty in our society, you will remain poor, and those who are less scrupulous will fleece you.

When, on the other hand, you assist each other cooperating as a group, with firm decision not to suffer any abuse from property-rights or titles, then and only then you may grow prosperous, yea! more so in every respect than the members of ordinary society.

You will have to meet, of course, many difficulties, you will have to solve all sorts of small problems — yet these are all of them only to be overcome by practice.

Let us consider what will have to be the guiding principles of your activity.

In the first place your work must be useful. That is to say, you must produce, as far as possible, only those things that are wanted by nearly every man, things of real necessity.

For this is the ruling condition for your independence, that you produce together, with your associates, on your own soil, all those things that you want. Only then you will be free, in a social sense, only then nobody can force you, because you want nobody outside your own group.

I said: as far as possible, meaning to express that it will be impossible to keep this principle strictly from the very beginning. At first you will have to produce any thing that will bring you money in the market because you will want money first of all. This is all right, if you only make it a rule, in the extension of your business, or in the undertaking of new branches of production or industry, not to choose those things that are useless and superfluous, but those that can be used by you yourself and associates. This will further your independence and create a fixed market in your own group.

In the second place you will have to determine, mutually, the rights of property, in such a way that no abuses can take place.

You will have to distinguish *private property from common property.*

Common property is well-known in different forms. As state-property, municipal property, and as property of groups, companies, trusts, associations and the like.

Your aim must be to form a Company with common property, wherein better care is taken than in ordinary society, that all what really ought to be common property of the Company, practically remains so — and that *private property of the associates never becomes an instrument in the hands of the stronger to rob the weaker.*

If this principle had been strictly established by the founders of the Great Republic of the United States, it would have become a real Common-wealth, of which it has now only the name.

Perhaps you are scared by the thought of the tremendous difficulty of determining exactly what may be called use and what abuse, and where the limits as to private property are to be drawn.

Let me remind you that all laws of all civilized people have to deal with such difficulties. They all have to distinguish by terms of similar uncertainty and to draw limits of similar preciseness. Yet such laws are constantly made and work practically.

It is not necessary to control the private life of every individual, this can be left to the individual conscience. The only thing wanted is to prevent gross abuse, and it is possible to point out quite precisely where that comes in.

When a man owns, as private property, house and farm, working on it, managing it well, living in his house, paying his servants well, and bringing his economies to the Bank, nobody can have an objection. Nobody will contest his rights, nor oppose his leaving this property to his heirs, provided they use it in the same way.

As soon, however, as the man leaves his farm, letting it to somebody else, drawing from it a yearly revenue which he spends somewhere in a city, without rendering any real service in return, living in that way from a kind of tax levied on the labour of others, then a child may see that there is abuse.

The distinction is just as easy in money-matters. When a man makes a pile, by industrious labour, enabling himself to confront old age or invalidity without fear, and to give his children a fair lift to start with — nobody can have an objection.

On the other hand when a man acquires a big sum, by legacy, by speculation or in any accidental way, and he draws interest from it all his life, without any obligation for himself to give labour in return, without loosing one cent from his capital — then there is abuse, most evidently.

Even if he prefers to continue to work, the abuse and injustice remains. May his activity be ever so useful and good — the way in which he uses his property to force poorer people to pay him that form of private tax which is called interest, is unjust, against the sense of justice of a normal, modern human being.

This does *not* imply that capital and interest are wrong and ought to be abolished. It all depends whether they are used against the well-being of society, whether they are a wrong done to the common-wealth.

Most undoubtedly it is a wrong done to the common-wealth when matters stand like in ordinary society, where every enterprise, every mine, every railway, every factory, yea! every state is burdened with a host of private creditors, share-holders who have the right to levy taxes on the revenues of those bodies, in the form of interest and dividends, without the slightest obligation on their part to render something in return.

That such a state of affairs creates idlers and parasites, furthers poverty and pauperism, encourages senseless waste and luxury, exhausts production, paralyses the normal, natural inclination to work and increases criminality and vice in all forms — that must be clear to every unsophisticated mind.

When on the other hand a group of industrious people, who each according to his ability contribute to the common wealth, possess shares in their common enterprise and in such a way partake of the profits acquired by common effort, — there is nothing to object to that. It will in fact stimulate the inclination to work, heighten production, increase the common prosperity.

In a just and well-organised community the conditions are exactly the reverse of what they are now. At present the state is a debtor and the individuals are creditors. The state is obliged to pay taxes to individuals, in the form of interest, without any obligation on the side of those individuals.

In a well-organised society the community is the creditor and the individuals are debtors. The community ought to have the rights of ownership on capital and means of production, and the surplus of the common production, in the form of profits or interest, is due to the community, which will let each individual partake in them according to his labour or his merits.

This condition of things can be gradually approached in a group of people as you may form, a community or Company, which limits the rights of private ownership under a general control, which transfers its capital gradually into the hands of its members exclusively and strives to acquire full independence by the production of its own means of subsistance.

In the rules for your Company — called the Co-productive Company — as proposed by Mr. Hoggson and me, arrangements are made that will lead to such a condition in a gradual way. Practice will perhaps show the necessity of small alterations, yet according to men of great business experience, there can be no doubt of the possibility of their practical realisation, even as they stand.

Mind, that each of you begins, with the best of intentions, on a soil that is practically your own. As yet there is no questions of abuses. It depends on you now to take careful measures to avoid them when prosperity comes — for it is prosperity that will bring the danger.

And if you succeed you will set an example for the world.

To get rich in a honest way, by useful labour — there is your task.

Not only in a *lawful* way, mind, — for the law allows all sorts of dishonesty — but in a fair and just way. That is what I expect from you, and that is, in fact what you all desire, and every good human being desires. For that aim you have to form your company, and that has to be the only commandment of your creed. Every man who agrees to that can be welcome in your midst. No other common confession is wanted. When that is agreed to, you can leave all religious and political and philosophical questions to the individual conscience.

Many will say that getting rich is not the highest aim of humanity.

Perfectly true. Yet it is the *nearest* aim. When we have once an honestly prosperous, justly organised commonwealth — without waste, without pauperism, without idle luxury and starving drudgers, without the worst crimes, without robbing and cheating and stealing — then we will see and ask: what next?

At present the principal sore of our society is poverty. Not wealth but poverty, want. And that poverty is, indirectly, the result of the existing abuses, the general dishonesty and greed.

What makes wealth, and its representative gold, appear as the greatest evil of mankind? The greed it excites, and the abuse, that is made of its possession.

Do you not see, however, that this greed and this abuse are only the consequences of prevalent want? The fear of poverty is still haunting the whole of humanity. Hence the frantic rush, the mad excess.

If gold were as plentiful as air or water, would there be such shameful and ignoble fight for it? If abundance was a universal and common thing, would people cheat and steal and kill to get their share?

Where every man has enough, greed and excess vanish equally.

Getting rich honestly though perhaps somewhat more slowly, there is your motto, and I foretell you that this wealth will prove to be a pure blessing and no evil.

The greatest and noblest efforts to reform human society — and as such I consider first of all the tremendous movement called Christianity — have failed because wealth was considered the prime evil and Mammon the real Devil. Yet Mammon and Ploutos are in fact not only harmless but very benevolent deities, when they are only served in justice and wisdom.

Wealth can only be gotten by common labour. No honest man can suppress the feeling that every little thing he wants is due to the combined efforts of a multitude. When the farmer makes a better crop by the use of a new plough, he knows that he owes his increased profit to the mental and manual labour of thousands of men of science, inventors, engineers, labourers, who all contributed to the making of that new plough. We may say that we use hardly any object that is not in a way a product of the whole of mankind.

So the honest human being feels his obligation to society, and wants to give his share of usefulness and a part of his profits in return.

The principal feature, however, of a well-organised society is a fair exchange of services and goods. And for a fair exchange are required, besides equality of rights before the law, not only honesty but also openness. That is to say that the members of a society ought not to cheat each other, not only by intentional deceit, by lying, but also by dissimulating, by keeping silence. At present the amount of cheating and deceit practised in civilised society is enormous — not only by actual lying, but principally by keeping silence, by not telling the material facts. This is the rule in all trade and commerce. All business is done more or less secretly, clandestinely, and every businessman takes advantage on the ignorance of the others. The merchant, as a middleman, is careful not to betray his secrets about what he pays, where he buys and sells. His great profits spring exactly from that form of deceit.

This method is just as dishonest and unfair as actual lying. All secrets in business and industry are harmful to society. Yet our present laws protect them. And this does not increase wealth but poverty. The profits gotten by dissimulating the truth must come from somewhere. Either producer or consumer must be cheated, generally both. There is no fair cooperation, but a constant effort to run the other man down, to impede, to obstruct, to annihilate the work of others. The result is a tremendous waste, waste of energy and waste of goods, at the cost of the weak and the ignorant, who are carefully kept so on purpose.

In a society of honest men, such as you can form, there ought to be openness and mutual cooperation among all the associates. The middleman ought to be paid according to his services, controllable by all who are interested. Middlemen are indispensable in commerce, but it is not at all indispensable that they take advantage of the ignorance of producer and consumer. On the contrary this is one of the principal causes of existing waste, poverty and crime.

Now keep in mind that you have to form a *transition*. You can not make a perfect community at once. You will have to take part in the general struggle of our present society for the immediate time to come. You will have to fight, in order to resist and to form a beginning of something better. Many efforts failed because people had no notion of gradual transitions and wanted to jump at the ideal at once.

According to the plan outlined by Mr. Hoggson and me, nobody needs to submit to difficult conditions. Every one can keep his perfect independence and not associate before he is aware, by his own free insight, that it means an advantage to him.

The farmer can get his own piece of land, build his house on it and live on it as an owner, with a right on all the profits, with a right also to leave the property to his heirs. In joining the Company he will only agree not to neglect his property, nor let it be used by others drawing the profits to himself. In giving up these rights he acquires the right ro become share-holder of the company, and to partake in all advantages of cooperation, cooperative selling, buying and industrial enterprises. The company keeps the right to buy his land back in case of neglect or departure. Every associate may get shares in the common stock, up to a certain maximum, which shall yield dividends only so long as he is a member.

In the interest of a safe extension it must be understood that no industrial enterprises ought to be started unless they serve to work the products of the associates themselves, and produce articles that will find consumers among them. Such industries are e. g. a dairy farm, a canning factory, or a bakery. No risky undertakings that require a large market outside, and materials that are not drawn from the property of the associates themselves, ought to be started. This will mean a relatively slow extension but a safe one, and a surely growing independence. When the company is rich enough to buy mines and woods and large plantations, or when it can cooperate with other similar enterprises, it is time to start other industries.

There is no objection to engage wage-earning labourers, either in immediate service of the company, or in that of the associates. These wage-earners may become associates in time. Wage-paid service is no slavery, provided the agreement is concluded on fair terms and does not take advantage of the weaker position of the labourer. The company can provide for that by general rules, allowing higher pay for higher services, and forbidding any unfair exploitation.

The common property of the company, in real estate, factories, mines, etc., must be constantly increased — in such a way that every associate, besides his private property, knows himself to be rich and safe by the power of a great common property, in which he shares, to which he has contributed according his ability, and on which he may count, in times of need, in old age or invalidity.

This is indeed a condition of things that every human being will call desirable. It is no deadening equality, but a just distribution according to service rendered. It excludes humiliation by philanthropy and charity. It does not weaken the incitement to work but heightens it. It gives support to the weak but is inexorable to the parasite. It extends personal liberty to the widest practical limits. It prevents waste and excess, and gives opportunity to the best to come to the front. The malcontents in such an organisation can only blame themselves.

And this condition is not at all, as many contend, beyond practical realisation in our time. You can realise it, when you suck to your principle of "getting rich honestly." You will want however for further development of your organisation men of organising talent. You will have to find them out, to remunerate them liberally and to give them full opportunity.

So long as you cooperate as a group of farmers you may prosper rather easily. Introducing industry, handling money, doing business on a larger scale with growing wealth and number, will demand leaders of great ability and special gifts — for then the fight with the outside society will begin in full earnest.

Such leaders exist and you can make them join you when you allow them ample freedom to develop their powers, when you let them find satisfaction in their task; and when you do not worry them by distrust and narrowness.

Be on your guard against fanatics and zealots, they have always spoiled the best schemes. Allow access to your community in a large, broad-minded way. Your strength will increase with your number and your principle is universal and invincible. In fact, to work for each other, workers for workers, and to get rich in a honest way, are devices that no sane human being can oppose. Nothing more is wanted as the binding idea of your community. In all other respects you may allow full freedom of opinion.

Increasing numbers will mean in your community that more and more producers will be consumers of your products. Then most things of real necessity will be made by your associates. Things that can only be produced economically for a very large market are not of material importance, their production will not be necessary for your economic independence. Let those things that you use principally be made under fair conditions. Then you will have a fixed market and will need no waste in advertisement, which is only necessary in the present production at random. Instead of wasteful and harmful competition there will be economic emulation. Growing prosperity of your associates will mean growing wants and a greater market. And the increasing profits will benefit all your members who are share holders. This will form exactly the reverse of the vicious circle that, under present conditions, is the cause of periodical crises and panics. There will be no secrets among your associates, for every one is interested in the prosperity of his neighbour. It would be folly to hide from another those improvements that benefitted yourself.

There will be no unemployed among your associates. In the first place because there is always a demand for the things they produce. In the second place because they all belong to one concern, and care may be taken to shift the workers in different occupation according to season and opportunity.

And is it not clear that only in this direction, in the clever mutual organisation of production and consumption, lies the true and natural solution of the great problem of the unemployed, and also of the still greater problem of war and peace ?

What is the use of all endeavours for pacification, so long as great industries who produce at random, want constantly new and larger markets for their products, only in order to exist?

This blind way of producing will always want a reserve of poor, unemployed, half-starved workers, and armies and navies to force weaker people to buy.

They who call themselves socialists will tell you that it is only by making better laws that society can be reformed.

Yet I may ask what laws, in what country, even in Russia, *forbid* to form a community like I proposed! And if no law forbids it, is it then reasonable to wait until a law *commands* it?

Does that appear to you a free and rational method of development?

Let those who call themselves socialists try to live like socialists, they will not find any laws in their way.

Of course you will have to respect the laws of the state where in you are living. And not only that, but you will have to take care, by political action, that no laws are made, by your enemies, to hamper your free development. You will have public opinion on your side, and no legislator could venture to oppose openly to a work so beneficial as yours would be.

It is not the so called sinfulness of human nature that is in the way, it is only short-sightedness. A just relation between individuals, and a fair commerce is more advantageous to all concerned, rich and poor alike, and in every respect, moral and physical, than deceit and robbery. A community, based on such principals is desirable for every man, and the only fit surrounding for the complete development of the human race.

The great question is to keep awake that spirit of fairness and honesty, which can be developed in every normal human being, out of a true sense of self-interest and wise foresight.

To that spirit belong the following general rules:

Not to try to make money without giving an equivalent in useful labour

Not to try to acquire private property with another aim than for real personal use

to contribute to the common property each according to his ability, as prescribed by the bylaws of the group to which you belong

to maintain not only honesty but also openness in all commercial transactions

not to take advantage in business agreements of the other man's ignorance, helplessness or weakness

not to take part, directly or indirectly, in unfair and dishonest practices, and not to suffer that they are done by proxy, on our responsibility, by others

to strive that all the necessities of our life are made and acquired under fair conditions

to work and economise so long as we are able and so long as there is need to alleviate within our reach.

Are these rules not in accordance with the natural sense of justice of every normal human being? Are they opposed to the laws of any civilised state or the prescriptions of any religion?

On the contrary, they are so essential to human nature that we can trace them back to the oldest laws and find them more or less clearly expressed in the Old Testament.

And yet after two thousand years of Christianity we do not find one single state based on those simple principles, no single nation whose morals are in accordance with them.

You may find in all centuries good people who acknowledged and taught these rules, — and when you go through our present world you will find that the best individuals of every race, be they Japanese or Chinese, Arabs or Hindoo, will agree to their justice and value.

And when we must state that rules so simple and so just, which all mankind must acknowledge, are not yet put into practice by any human community, can we then wonder at the amount of poverty and misery, of crime and war that is still infesting humanity?

And it is only shortsightedness and frantic greed that is in the way, not the inner corruption of human nature, as some contend.

For selfishness, if it is not blind, would see that every individual is benefited by a fair trade and a just organisation.

Mankind need not be kinder or stronger than it is now, only a little less greedy and blind, only a little less *childish*, that is all.

The formation of such a community as I propose is not impossible. If you do not realise it, others will. If not, there would be no hope for humanity. You may do it, however, and show it to be a blessing for yourself and for our race.

FREDERIK VAN EEDEN

> *Dr. Frederik van Eeden often spoke and wrote about his utopic Socialist and Communist ideals. It is interesting to note that, in his later life, he became a Christian and a member of the Catholic Church.*

www.ingramcontent.com/pod-product-compliance
Lightning Source LLC
Chambersburg PA
CBHW040911020526

44116CB00026B/24